Mastering Ansible

Second Edition

Master the ins and outs of advanced operations with Ansible

Jesse Keating

BIRMINGHAM - MUMBAI

Mastering Ansible

Second Edition

First published: November 2015

Second edition: March 2017

Production reference: 1270317

Published by Packt Publishing Ltd.
Livery Place
35 Livery Street
Birmingham
B3 2PB, UK.
ISBN 978-1-78712-568-1

www.packtpub.com

Credits

Author

Jesse Keating

Reviewer

Sreenivas Makam

Acquisition Editor
Prachi Bisht

Content Development Editor
Trusha Shriyan

Technical Editor
Varsha Shivhare

Copy Editor

Safis Editing

Project Coordinator

Kinjal Bari

Proofreader

Safis Editing

Indexer

Pratik Shirodkar

Production Coordinator
Nilesh Mohite

Graphics
Kirk D'Penha

About the Author

Jesse Keating is an accomplished Ansible user, contributor, and presenter. He has been an active member of the Linux and open source community for over fifteen years. He has first-hand experience with a variety of IT activities, software development, and large-scale system administration. He has presented at numerous conferences and meet-ups, and has written many articles on a variety of topics.

About the Reviewer

Sreenivas Makam is a senior engineering manager at Cisco Systems, Bangalore. He has a master's in electrical engineering and has around 18 years' experience in the networking industry. He has worked in both startups and big, established companies. His interests include Containers, SDN, network automation, devops, and cloud technologies, and he likes to try out and follow open source projects in these areas. His blog can be found at `https://sreeninet.wordpress.com/`, he has presentations at `http://www.slideshare.net/SreenivasMakam`, and his hacky code is at `https://github.com/smakam`. Sreenivas is a Docker Captain, (`https://www.docker.com/community/docker-captains`) and his blog articles have been published in Docker weekly newsletters. He can be reached on Twitter at `@srmakam`.

He has written *Mastering CoreOS*, also reviewed *Mastering Ansible*, *CoreOS Cookbook*, all by Packt Publishing.

> *It was extra special that my second daughter, Masha, was born while reviewing this book. Thanks to my daughters, Sasha and Masha, for keeping me energetic.*

www.PacktPub.com

For support files and downloads related to your book, please visit www.PacktPub.com.

Did you know that Packt offers eBook versions of every book published, with PDF and ePub files available? You can upgrade to the eBook version at www.PacktPub.com and as a print book customer, you are entitled to a discount on the eBook copy. Get in touch with us at service@packtpub.com for more details.

At www.PacktPub.com, you can also read a collection of free technical articles, sign up for a range of free newsletters and receive exclusive discounts and offers on Packt books and eBooks.

https://www.packtpub.com/mapt

Get the most in-demand software skills with Mapt. Mapt gives you full access to all Packt books and video courses, as well as industry-leading tools to help you plan your personal development and advance your career.

Why subscribe?

- Fully searchable across every book published by Packt
- Copy and paste, print, and bookmark content
- On demand and accessible via a web browser

Customer Feedback

Thanks for purchasing this Packt book. At Packt, quality is at the heart of our editorial process. To help us improve, please leave us an honest review on this book's Amazon page at https://www.amazon.com/dp/1787282589.

If you'd like to join our team of regular reviewers, you can e-mail us at customerreviews@packtpub.com. We award our regular reviewers with free eBooks and videos in exchange for their valuable feedback. Help us be relentless in improving our products!

Table of Contents

Preface   1

Chapter 1: System Architecture and Design of Ansible   7

  Ansible version and configuration   8
  Inventory parsing and data sources   9
    Static inventory   9
    Inventory variable data   11
    Dynamic inventories   14
    Runtime inventory additions   16
    Inventory limiting   16
  Playbook parsing   20
    Order of operations   20
    Relative path assumptions   22
    Play behavior directives   25
    Execution strategies   26
    Host selection for plays and tasks   27
    Play and task names   28
  Module transport and execution   31
    Module reference   31
    Module arguments   32
    Module transport and execution   33
      Task performance   34
  Variable types and location   35
    Variable types   35
  Accessing external data   37
  Variable precedence   37
    Precedence order   37
    Merging hashes   38
  Summary   39

Chapter 2: Protecting Your Secrets with Ansible   41

  Encrypting data at rest   41
    Things Vault can encrypt   42
    Creating new encrypted files   43
      Password prompt   44
      Password file   45

Password script	46
Encrypting existing files	46
Editing encrypted files	48
Password rotation on encrypted files	49
Decrypting encrypted files	50
Executing Ansible-playbook with encrypted files	51
Protecting secrets while operating	53
Secrets transmitted to remote hosts	54
Secrets logged to remote or local files	54
Summary	56
Chapter 3: Unlocking the Power of Jinja2 Templates	57
Control structures	57
Conditionals	58
Inline conditionals	60
Loops	62
Filtering loop items	64
Loop indexing	65
Macros	68
Macro variables	69
name	70
arguments	71
defaults	72
catch_kwargs	73
catch_varargs	74
caller	75
Data manipulation	78
Syntax	78
Useful built-in filters	79
default	80
count	80
random	80
round	81
Useful Ansible provided custom filters	81
Filters related to task status	81
shuffle	82
Filters dealing with path names	83
basename	84
dirname	85
expanduser	85
Base64 encoding	86
Searching for content	88
Omitting undefined arguments	89
Python object methods	90

String methods	90
List methods	91
int and float methods	92
Comparing values	92
Comparisons	92
Logic	93
Tests	93
Summary	94
Chapter 4: Controlling Task Conditions	95
Defining a failure	95
Ignoring errors	95
Defining an error condition	97
Defining a change	103
Special handling of the command family	105
Suppressing a change	108
Error recovery	109
Rescue	110
Always	112
Summary	115
Chapter 5: Composing Reusable Ansible Content with Roles	117
Task, handler, variable, and playbook include concepts	118
Including tasks	118
Passing variable values to included tasks	121
Passing complex data to included tasks	123
Conditional task includes	125
Tagging included tasks	127
Task includes with loops	129
Including handlers	133
Including variables	135
vars_files	135
Dynamic vars_files inclusion	137
include_vars	138
extra-vars	141
Including playbooks	142
Roles	142
Role structure	142
Tasks	143
Handlers	143
Variables	143
Modules and plugins	144
Dependencies	144

Files and templates	144
Putting it all together	145
Role dependencies	146
Role dependency variables	146
Tags	147
Role dependency conditionals	148
Role application	148
Mixing roles and tasks	151
Role includes	154
Role sharing	154
Ansible Galaxy	154
Summary	159
Chapter 6: Minimizing Downtime with Rolling Deployments	161
In-place upgrades	161
Expanding and contracting	164
Failing fast	167
The any_errors_fatal option	168
The max_fail_percentage option	169
Forcing handlers	172
Minimizing disruptions	175
Delaying a disruption	175
Running destructive tasks only once	180
Serializing single tasks	181
Summary	184
Chapter 7: Troubleshooting Ansible	185
Playbook logging and verbosity	185
Verbosity	186
Logging	186
Variable introspection	187
Variable sub elements	190
Subelement versus Python object method	193
Debugging code execution	195
Playbook debugging	195
Debugging local code	198
Debugging inventory code	199
Debugging playbook code	204
Debugging executor code	205
Debugging remote code	209
Debugging the action plugins	213
Summary	214
Chapter 8: Extending Ansible	215

Developing modules   215
     The basic module construct   215
     Custom modules   216
     Simple module   217
       Module documentation   220
       Providing fact data   225
       The check mode   227
         Supporting the check mode   227
         Handling check mode   227
Developing plugins   229
     Connection type plugins   229
     Shell plugins   229
     Lookup plugins   229
     Vars plugins   230
     The fact caching plugins   230
     Filter plugins   230
     Callback plugins   232
     Action plugins   235
     Distributing plugins   235
Developing dynamic inventory plugins   236
     Listing hosts   237
     Listing host variables   237
     Simple inventory plugin   238
       Optimizing script performance   243
Contributing to the Ansible project   245
     Contribution submissions   245
       The ansible repository   246
       Executing tests   246
         Unit tests   247
         Integration tests   248
         Code style tests   250
       Making a pull request   251
Summary   251
Chapter 9: Infrastructure Provisioning   253
Managing cloud infrastructure   253
     Creating servers   254
       Booting virtual servers   255
       Adding to runtime inventory   258
     Using OpenStack inventory source   261
Interacting with Docker containers   267
     Building images   268

Building containers without a Dockerfile   271
Docker inventory   275
Previewing of Ansible container   279
Init   281
Build   284
Run   286
Summary   289
Index   291

Preface

Welcome to Mastering Ansible, your guide to a variety of advanced features and functionalities provided by Ansible, the automation and orchestration tool. This book will provide readers with the knowledge and skills to truly understand how Ansible functions at a fundamental level. This will allow readers to master the advanced capabilities needed to tackle complex automation challenges of today and the future. Readers will gain knowledge of Ansible workflows, explore use cases for advanced features, troubleshoot unexpected behavior, and extend Ansible through customization.

What this book covers

Chapter 1, *System Architecture and Design of Ansible*, looks at the ins and outs of how Ansible goes about performing tasks on behalf of an engineer, how it is designed, and how to work with inventory and variables.

Chapter 2, *Protecting Your Secrets with Ansible*, explores the tools available to encrypt data at rest and prevent secrets from being revealed at runtime.

Chapter 3, *Unlocking the Power of Jinja2 Templates*, states the varied uses of the Jinja2 templating engine within Ansible and discusses ways to make the most out of its capabilities.

Chapter 4, *Controlling Task Conditions*, describes the changing of the default behavior of Ansible to customize task error and change conditions.

Chapter 5, *Composing Reusable Ansible Content with Roles*, covers the approach to move beyond executing loosely-organized tasks on hosts to encapsulating clean and reusable abstractions to apply a specific functionality of a target set of hosts.

Chapter 6, *Minimizing Downtime with Rolling Deployments*, explains the common deployment and upgrade strategies to showcase relevant Ansible features.

Chapter 7, *Troubleshooting Ansible*, takes you through the various methods that can be employed to examine, introspect, modify, and debug the operations of Ansible.

Chapter 8, *Extending Ansible*, discovers the various ways in which new capabilities can be added to Ansible via modules, plugins, and inventory sources.

Chapter 9, *Infrastructure Provisioning,* will be working with cloud infrastructure providers and container systems to create an infrastructure to manage.

What you need for this book

To follow the examples provided in this book, you will need access to a computer platform capable of running Ansible. Currently, Ansible can be run on any machine with Python 2.6 or 2.7 installed (Windows isn't supported for the control machine). This includes Red Hat, Debian, CentOS, OS X, any of the BSDs, and so on.

This book uses the Ansible 2.2.x.x series release.

Ansible installation instructions can be found at `http://docs.ansible.com/ansible/intr o_installation.html`.

Some examples use Docker, version 1.12.6. Docker installation instructions can be found at: `http://www.d ocker.com/community-edition`.

Who this book is for

This book is for Ansible developers and operators who have an understanding of the core elements and applications but are now looking to enhance their skills in applying automation using Ansible.

Conventions

In this book, you will find a number of text styles that distinguish between different kinds of information. Here are some examples of these styles and an explanation of their meaning.

Code words in text, database table names, folder names, filenames, file extensions, pathnames, dummy URLs, user input, and Twitter handles are shown as follows: "We'll make use of this in a `failed_when` statement."

A block of code is set as follows:

```
 - name: query sessions
   command: /sbin/iscsiadm -m session
   register: sessions
   failed_when: sessions.rc not in (0, 21)
```

Any command-line input or output is written as follows:

```
$ source ./hacking/env-setup
```

Warnings or important notes appear in a box like this.

Tips and tricks appear like this.

Reader feedback

Feedback from our readers is always welcome. Let us know what you think about this book-what you liked or disliked. Reader feedback is important for us as it helps us develop titles that you will really get the most out of. To send us general feedback, simply e-mail feedback@packtpub.com, and mention the book's title in the subject of your message. If there is a topic that you have expertise in and you are interested in either writing or contributing to a book, see our author guide at www.packtpub.com/authors.

Customer support

Now that you are the proud owner of a Packt book, we have a number of things to help you to get the most from your purchase.

Downloading the example code

You can download the example code files for this book from your account at http://www.packtpub.com. If you purchased this book elsewhere, you can visit http://www.packtpub.com/support and register to have the files e-mailed directly to you.

You can download the code files by following these steps:

1. Log in or register to our website using your e-mail address and password.
2. Hover the mouse pointer on the **SUPPORT** tab at the top.
3. Click on **Code Downloads & Errata**.
4. Enter the name of the book in the **Search** box.

5. Select the book for which you're looking to download the code files.
6. Choose from the drop-down menu where you purchased this book from.
7. Click on **Code Download**.

Once the file is downloaded, please make sure that you unzip or extract the folder using the latest version of:

- WinRAR / 7-Zip for Windows
- Zipeg / iZip / UnRarX for Mac
- 7-Zip / PeaZip for Linux

The code bundle for the book is also hosted on GitHub at `https://github.com/PacktPubl ishing/Mastering-Ansible-Second-Edition`. We also have other code bundles from our rich catalog of books and videos available at `https://github.com/PacktPublishing/`. Check them out!

Downloading the color images of this book

We also provide you with a PDF file that has color images of the screenshots/diagrams used in this book. The color images will help you better understand the changes in the output. You can download this file from `https://www.packtpub.com/sites/default/files/down loads/MasteringAnsibleSecondEdition_ColorImages.pdf`.

Errata

Although we have taken every care to ensure the accuracy of our content, mistakes do happen. If you find a mistake in one of our books-maybe a mistake in the text or the code-we would be grateful if you could report this to us. By doing so, you can save other readers from frustration and help us improve subsequent versions of this book. If you find any errata, please report them by visiting `http://www.packtpub.com/submit-errata`, selecting your book, clicking on the **Errata Submission Form** link, and entering the details of your errata. Once your errata are verified, your submission will be accepted and the errata will be uploaded to our website or added to any list of existing errata under the Errata section of that title.

To view the previously submitted errata, go to `https://www.packtpub.com/books/conten t/support` and enter the name of the book in the search field. The required information will appear under the **Errata** section.

Piracy

Piracy of copyrighted material on the Internet is an ongoing problem across all media. At Packt, we take the protection of our copyright and licenses very seriously. If you come across any illegal copies of our works in any form on the Internet, please provide us with the location address or website name immediately so that we can pursue a remedy.

Please contact us at `copyright@packtpub.com` with a link to the suspected pirated material.

We appreciate your help in protecting our authors and our ability to bring you valuable content.

Questions

If you have a problem with any aspect of this book, you can contact us at `questions@packtpub.com`, and we will do our best to address the problem.

1

System Architecture and Design of Ansible

This chapter provides a detailed exploration of the architecture and design of how **Ansible** goes about performing tasks on your behalf. We will cover the basic concepts of inventory parsing and how the data is discovered, and then dive into playbook parsing. We will take a walk through module preparation, transportation, and execution. Lastly, we will detail variable types and find out where variables can be located, the scope they can be used in, and how precedence is determined when variables are defined in more than one location. All these things will be covered in order to lay the foundation for mastering Ansible!

In this chapter, we will cover the following topics:

- Ansible version and configuration
- Inventory parsing and data sources
- Playbook parsing
- Execution strategies
- Module transport and execution
- Variable types and locations
- Variable precedence

Ansible version and configuration

It is assumed that you have Ansible installed on your system. There are many documents out there that cover installing Ansible in a way that is appropriate for the operating system and version that you might be using. This book will assume the use of the Ansible 2.2.x.x version. To discover the version in use on a system with Ansible already installed, make use of the version argument, that is, either `ansible` or `ansible-playbook`:

```
2. jkeating@serenity: ~/src/mastery (zsh)
~/src/mastery> ansible-playbook --version
ansible-playbook 2.2.0.0
  config file =
  configured module search path = Default w/o overrides
~/src/mastery> _
```

Note that `ansible` is the executable for doing adhoc one-task executions and `ansible-playbook` is the executable that will process playbooks for orchestrating many tasks.

The configuration for Ansible can exist in a few different locations, where the first file found will be used. The search order changed slightly in version 1.5, with the new order being:

- `ANSIBLE_CFG`: This is an environment variable
- `~/ansible.cfg`: This is in the current directory
- `ansible.cfg`: This is in the user's home directory
- `./etc/ansible/ansible.cfg`

Some installation methods may include placing a `config` file in one of these locations. Look around to check whether such a file exists and see what settings are in the file to get an idea of how Ansible operation may be affected. This book will assume no settings in the `ansible.cfg` file that would affect the default operation of Ansible.

Inventory parsing and data sources

In Ansible, nothing happens without an inventory. Even ad hoc actions performed on localhost require an inventory, even if that inventory consists just of the localhost. The inventory is the most basic building block of Ansible architecture. When executing `ansible` or `ansible-playbook`, an inventory must be referenced. Inventories are either files or directories that exist on the same system that runs `ansible` or `ansible-playbook`. The location of the inventory can be referenced at runtime with the `--inventory-file` (`-i`) argument, or by defining the path in an Ansible `config` file.

Inventories can be static or dynamic, or even a combination of both, and Ansible is not limited to a single inventory. The standard practice is to split inventories across logical boundaries, such as staging and production, allowing an engineer to run a set of plays against their staging environment for validation, and then follow with the same exact plays run against the production inventory set.

Variable data, such as specific details on how to connect to a particular host in your inventory, can be included along with an inventory in a variety of ways as well, and we'll explore the options available to you.

Static inventory

The static inventory is the most basic of all the inventory options. Typically, a static inventory will consist of a single file in the `ini` format. Here is an example of a static inventory file describing a single host, `mastery.example.name`:

```
mastery.example.name
```

That is all there is to it. Simply list the names of the systems in your inventory. Of course, this does not take full advantage of all that an inventory has to offer. If every name were listed like this, all plays would have to reference specific hostname, or the special `all` group. This can be quite tedious when developing a playbook that operates across different sets of your infrastructure. At the very least, hosts should be arranged into groups. A design pattern that works well is to arrange your systems into groups based on expected functionality. At first, this may seem difficult if you have an environment where single systems can play many different roles, but that is perfectly fine. Systems in an inventory can exist in more than one group, and groups can even consist of other groups! Additionally, when listing groups and hosts, it's possible to list hosts without a group. These would have to be listed first, before any other group is defined. Let's build on our previous example and expand our inventory with a few more hosts and some groupings:

```
[web]
mastery.example.name

[dns]
backend.example.name

[database]
backend.example.name

[frontend:children]
web

[backend:children]
dns
database
```

What we have created here is a set of three groups with one system in each, and then two more groups, which logically group all three together. Yes, that's right; you can have groups of groups. The syntax used here is `[groupname:children]`, which indicates to Ansible's inventory parser that this group by the name of `groupname` is nothing more than a grouping of other groups. The children in this case are the names of the other groups. This inventory now allows writing plays against specific hosts, low-level role-specific groups, or high-level logical groupings, or any combination.

By utilizing generic group names, such as `dns` and `database`, Ansible plays can reference these generic groups rather than the explicit hosts within. An engineer can create one inventory file that fills in these groups with hosts from a preproduction staging environment and another inventory file with the production versions of these groupings. The playbook content does not need to change when executing on either staging or production environment because it refers to the generic group names that exist in both inventories. Simply refer to the right inventory to execute it in the desired environment.

Inventory variable data

Inventories provide more than just system names and groupings. Data about the systems can be passed along as well. This can include:

- Host-specific data to use in templates
- Group-specific data to use in task arguments or conditionals
- Behavioral parameters to tune how Ansible interacts with a system

Variables are a powerful construct within Ansible and can be used in a variety of ways, not just the ways described here. Nearly every single thing done in Ansible can include a variable reference. While Ansible can discover data about a system during the setup phase, not all data can be discovered. Defining data with the inventory is how to expand the dataset. Note that variable data can come from many different sources, and one source may override another source. Variable precedence order is covered later in this chapter.

Let's improve upon our existing example inventory and add to it some variable data. We will add some host-specific data as well as group-specific data:

```
[web]
mastery.example.name ansible_host=192.168.10.25

[dns]
backend.example.name

[database]
backend.example.name

[frontend:children]
web

[backend:children]
dns
database

[web:vars]
http_port=88
proxy_timeout=5

[backend:vars]
ansible_port=314

[all:vars]
ansible_ssh_user=otto
```

In this example, we defined `ansible_host` for `mastery.example.name` to be the IP address of `192.168.10.25`. The `ansible_host` variable is a **behavioral inventory variable**, which is intended to alter the way Ansible behaves when operating with this host. In this case, the variable instructs Ansible to connect to the system using the provided IP address rather than performing a DNS lookup on the name `mastery.example.name`. There are a number of other behavioral inventory variables, which are listed at the end of this section along with their intended use.

> As of version 2.0, the longer form of some behavioral inventory parameters has been deprecated. The `ssh` part of `ansible_ssh_host`, `ansible_ssh_user`, and `ansible_ssh_port` is no longer required. A future release may ignore the longer form of these variables.

Our new inventory data also provides group-level variables for the web and backend groups. The web group defines `http_port`, which may be used in an **nginx** configuration file, and `proxy_timeout`, which might be used to determine **HAProxy** behavior. The `backend` group makes use of another behavioral inventory parameter to instruct Ansible to connect to the hosts in this group using port `314` for SSH, rather than the default of `22`.

Finally, a construct is introduced that provides variable data across all the hosts in the inventory by utilizing a built-in `all` group. Variables defined within this group will apply to every host in the inventory. In this particular example, we instruct Ansible to log in as the `otto` user when connecting to the systems. This is also a behavioral change, as the Ansible default behavior is to log in as a user with the same name as the user executing `ansible` or `ansible-playbook` on the control host.

Here is a table of behavior inventory variables and the behavior they intend to modify:

Inventory parameters	Behaviour
`ansible_host`	This is the DNS name or IP address used to connect to the host, if different from the inventory name, or the name of the Docker container to connect to.
`ansible_port`	This is the SSH port number, if not `22`.
`ansible_user`	This is the default SSH username or user inside a Docker container to use.
`ansible_ssh_pass`	This is the SSH password to use (this is insecure; we strongly recommend using `--ask-pass` or the SSH keys).

`ansible_ssh_private_key_file`	This is the private key file used by SSH. This is useful if you use multiple keys and you don't want to use SSH agent.
`ansible_ssh_common_args`	This defines SSH arguments to append to the default arguments for `ssh`, `sftp`, and `scp`.
`ansible_sftp_extra_args`	This setting is always appended to the default `sftp` command-line arguments.
`ansible_scp_extra_args`	This setting is always appended to the default `scp` command-line arguments.
`ansible_ssh_extra_args`	This setting is always appended to the default `ssh` command-line arguments.
`ansible_ssh_pipelining`	This setting uses a Boolean to define whether or not SSH pipelining should be used for this host.
`ansible_ssh_executable`	This setting overrides the path to the SSH executable for this host.
`ansible_become`	This defines whether privilege escalation (`sudo` or otherwise) should be used with this host.
`ansible_become_method`	The method to use for privilege escalation. One of `sudo`, `su`, `pbrun`, `pfexec`, `doas`, `dzdo`, or `ksu`.
`ansible_become_user`	This is the user to become through privilege escalation.
`ansible_become_pass`	This is the password to use for privilege escalation.
`ansible_sudo_pass`	This is the sudo password to use (this is insecure; we strongly recommend using `--ask-sudo-pass`).
`ansible_connection`	This is the connection type of the host. Candidates are `local`, `smart`, `ssh`, `paramiko`, or `docker`. The default is `paramiko` before Ansible 1.2, and `smart` afterwards, which detects whether the usage of ssh will be feasible based on whether the SSH feature `ControlPersist` is supported.
`ansible_docker_extra_args`	This is a string of any extra arguments that can be passed to Docker. This is mainly used to define a remote Docker daemon to use.

`ansible_shell_type`	This is the shell type of the target system. By default, commands are formatted using the `sh-style` syntax. Setting this to `csh` or `fish` will cause commands to be executed on target systems to follow the syntax of `csh` or `fish` instead.
`ansible_shell_executable`	This sets the shell tool that will be used on the target system. This should only be used if the default of `/bin/sh` is not possible to use.
`ansible_python_interpreter`	This is the target host Python path. This is useful for systems with more than one Python, systems that are not located at `/usr/bin/python` (such as *BSD), or for systems where `/usr/bin/python` is not a 2.X series Python. We do not use the `/usr/bin/env` mechanism as it requires the remote user's path to be set right and also assumes that the Python executable is named Python, where the executable might be named something like `python26`.
`ansible_*_interpreter`	This works for anything such as Ruby or Perl and works just like `ansible_python_interpreter`. This replaces the shebang of modules which run on that host.

Dynamic inventories

A static inventory is great and enough for many situations. But there are times when a statically written set of hosts is just too unwieldy to manage. Consider situations where inventory data already exists in a different system, such as **LDAP**, a cloud computing provider, or an in-house **CMDB** (inventory, asset tracking, and data warehousing) system. It would be a waste of time and energy to duplicate that data, and in the modern world of on-demand infrastructure, that data would quickly grow stale or disastrously incorrect.

Another example of when a dynamic inventory source might be desired is when your site grows beyond a single set of playbooks. Multiple playbook repositories can fall into the trap of holding multiple copies of the same inventory data, or complicated processes have to be created to reference a single copy of the data. An external inventory can easily be leveraged to access the common inventory data stored outside of the playbook repository to simplify the setup. Thankfully, Ansible is not limited to static inventory files.

A dynamic inventory source (or plugin) is an executable script that Ansible will call at runtime to discover real-time inventory data. This script may reach out into external data sources and return data, or it can just parse local data that already exists but may not be in the Ansible inventory `ini` format. While it is possible and easy to develop your own dynamic inventory source, which we will cover this in a later chapter, Ansible provides a number of example inventory plugins, including but not limited to:

- OpenStack Nova
- Rackspace Public Cloud
- DigitalOcean
- Linode
- Amazon EC2
- Google Compute Engine
- Microsoft Azure
- Docker
- Vagrant

Many of these plugins require some level of configuration, such as user credentials for EC2 or authentication endpoint for OpenStack Nova. Since it is not possible to configure additional arguments for Ansible to pass along to the inventory script, the configuration for the script must either be managed via an `ini config` file read from a known location or environment variables read from the shell environment used to execute `ansible` or `ansible-playbook`.

When `ansible` or `ansible-playbook` is directed at an executable file for an inventory source, Ansible will execute that script with a single argument, `--list`. This is so that Ansible can get a listing of the entire inventory in order to build up its internal objects to represent the data. Once that data is built up, Ansible will then execute the script with a different argument for every host in the data to discover variable data. The argument used in this execution is `--host <hostname>`, which will return any variable data specific to that host.

In `Chapter 8`, *Extending Ansible,* we will develop our own custom inventory plugin to demonstrate how they operate.

Runtime inventory additions

Just like static inventory files, it is important to remember that Ansible will parse this data once, and only once, per `ansible` or `ansible-playbook` execution. This is a fairly common stumbling point for users of cloud dynamic sources, where frequently a playbook will create a new cloud resource and then attempt to use it as if it were part of the inventory. This will fail, as the resource was not part of the inventory when the playbook launched. All is not lost though! A special module is provided that allows a playbook to temporarily add inventory to the in-memory inventory object, the `add_host` module.

The `add_host` module takes two options, `name` and `groups`. The name should be obvious, it defines the hostname that Ansible will use when connecting to this particular system. The `groups` option is a comma-separated list of groups to add this new system to. Any other option passed to this module will become the host variable data for this host. For example, if we want to add a new system, name it `newmastery.example.name`, add it to the `web` group, and instruct Ansible to connect to it by way of IP address `192.168.10.30`, we will create a task same as this:

```
- name: add new node into runtime inventory
  add_host:
    name: newmastery.example.name
    groups: web
    ansible_host: 192.168.10.30
```

This new host will be available to use, by way of the name provided, or by way of the web group, for the rest of the `ansible-playbook` execution. However, once the execution has completed, this host will not be available unless it has been added to the inventory source itself. Of course, if this were a new cloud resource created, the next `ansible` or `ansible-playbook` execution that sourced inventory from that cloud would pick up the new member.

Inventory limiting

As mentioned earlier, every execution of `ansible` or `ansible-playbook` will parse the entire inventory it has been directed at. This is even true when a limit has been applied. A limit is applied at runtime by making use of the `--limit` runtime argument to `ansible` or `ansible-playbook`. This argument accepts a pattern, which is basically a mask to apply to the inventory. The entire inventory is parsed, and at each play the supplied limit mask further limits the host pattern listed for the play.

Let's take our previous inventory example and demonstrate the behavior of Ansible with and without a limit. If you recall, we have the special group `all` that we can use to reference all the hosts within an inventory. Let's assume that our inventory is written out in the current working directory in a file named `mastery-hosts`, and we will construct a playbook to demonstrate the host on which Ansible is operating. Let's write this playbook out as `mastery.yaml`:

```
---
- name: limit example play
  hosts: all
  gather_facts: false

  tasks:
    - name: tell us which host we are on
      debug:
        var: inventory_hostname
```

The debug module is used to print out text, or values of variables. We'll use this module a lot in this book to simulate actual work being done on a host.

Now, let's execute this simple playbook without supplying a limit. For simplicity's sake, we will instruct Ansible to utilize a local connection method, which will execute locally rather than attempting to SSH to these nonexistent hosts. Let's take a look at the following screenshot:

As we can see, both hosts, `backend.example.name` and `mastery.example.name`, were operated on. Let's see what happens if we supply a limit, specifically to limit our run to only frontend systems:

```
2. jkeating@serenity: ~/src/mastery (zsh)
~/src/mastery> ansible-playbook -i mastery-hosts -c local -v --limit frontend ma
stery.yaml
No config file found; using defaults

PLAY [limit example play] ****************************************************

TASK [tell us which host we are on] ******************************************
ok: [mastery.example.name] => {
    "inventory_hostname": "mastery.example.name"
}

PLAY RECAP *******************************************************************
mastery.example.name       : ok=1    changed=0    unreachable=0    failed=0

~/src/mastery> _
```

We can see that only `mastery.example.name` was operated in this time. While there are no visual clues that the entire inventory was parsed, if we dive into the Ansible code and examine the inventory object, we will indeed find all the hosts within, and see how the limit is applied every time the object is queried for items.

It is important to remember that regardless of the host's pattern used in a play, or the limit supplied at runtime, Ansible will still parse the entire inventory set during each run. In fact, we can prove this by attempting to the access host variable data for a system that would otherwise be masked by our limit. Let's expand our playbook slightly and attempt to access the `ansible_port` variable from `backend.example.name`:

```
---
- name: limit example play
  hosts: all
  gather_facts: false

  tasks:
    - name: tell us which host we are on
      debug:
        var: inventory_hostname

    - name: grab variable data from backend
```

```
debug:
    var: hostvars['backend.example.name']['ansible_port']
```

We will still apply our limit, which will restrict our operations to just
`mastery.example.name`:

```
2. jkeating@serenity: ~/src/mastery (zsh)

~/src/mastery> ansible-playbook -i mastery-hosts -c local -v --limit frontend ma
stery.yaml
No config file found; using defaults

PLAY [limit example play] ******************************************************

TASK [tell us which host we are on] ********************************************
ok: [mastery.example.name] => {
    "inventory_hostname": "mastery.example.name"
}

TASK [grab variable data from backend] *****************************************
ok: [mastery.example.name] => {
    "hostvars['backend.example.name']['ansible_port']": "314"
}

PLAY RECAP *********************************************************************
mastery.example.name         : ok=2    changed=0    unreachable=0    failed=0

~/src/mastery>
```

We have successfully accessed the host variable data (by way of group variables) for a
system that was otherwise limited out. This is a key skill to understand, as it allows for
more advanced scenarios, such as directing a task at a host that is otherwise limited out.
Delegation can be used to manipulate a load balancer to put a system into maintenance
mode while being upgraded without having to include the load balancer system in your
limit mask.

Playbook parsing

The whole purpose of an inventory source is to have systems to manipulate. The manipulation comes from playbooks (or in the case of `ansible` ad hoc execution, simple single-task plays). You should already have a base understanding of playbook construction so we won't spend a lot of time covering that; however, we will delve into some specifics of how a playbook is parsed. Specifically, we will cover the following:

- Order of operations
- Relative path assumptions
- Play behavior keys
- Host selection for plays and tasks
- Play and task names

Order of operations

Ansible is designed to be as easy as possible for a human to understand. The developers strive to strike the best balance of human comprehension and machine efficiency. To that end, nearly everything in Ansible can be assumed to be executed in a top to bottom order; that is, the operation listed at the top of a file will be accomplished before the operation listed at the bottom of a file. Having said that, there are a few caveats and even a few ways to influence the order of operations.

A playbook has only two main operations it can accomplish. It can either run a play, or it can include another playbook from somewhere on the filesystem. The order in which these are accomplished is simply the order in which they appear in the playbook file, from top to bottom. It is important to note that while the operations are executed in order, the entire playbook and any included playbooks are completely parsed before any executions. This means that any included playbook file has to exist at the time of the playbook parsing. They cannot be generated in an earlier operation. This is specific to playbook includes, not necessarily to task includes that may appear within a play, which will be covered in a later chapter.

Within a play, there are a few more operations. While a playbook is strictly ordered from top to bottom, a play has a more nuanced order of operations. Here is a list of the possible operations and the order in which they will happen:

- Variable loading
- Fact gathering
- The `pre_tasks` execution

- Handlers notified from the `pre_tasks` execution
- Roles execution
- Tasks execution
- Handlers notified from roles or tasks execution
- The `post_tasks` execution
- Handlers notified from `post_tasks` execution

Here is an example play with most of these operations shown:

```
---
- hosts: localhost
  gather_facts: false

  vars:
    - a_var: derp

  pre_tasks:
    - name: pretask
      debug:
        msg: "a pre task"
      changed_when: true
      notify: say hi

  roles:
    - role: simple
      derp: newval

  tasks:
    - name: task
      debug:
        msg: "a task"
      changed_when: true
      notify: say hi

  post_tasks:
    - name: posttask
      debug:
        msg: "a post task"
      changed_when: true
      notify: say hi
```

Regardless of the order in which these blocks are listed in a play, the order detailed above is the order in which they will be processed. Handlers (the tasks that can be triggered by other tasks that result in a change) are a special case. There is a utility module, `meta`, which can be used to trigger handler processing at a specific point:

```
- meta: flush_handlers
```

This will instruct Ansible to process any pending handlers at that point before continuing on with the next task or next block of actions within a play. Understanding the order and being able to influence the order with `flush_handlers` is another key skill to have when there is a need for orchestrate complicated actions, where things such as service restarts are very sensitive to order. Consider the initial rollout of a service. The play will have tasks that modify `config` files and indicate that the service should be restarted when these files change. The play will also indicate that the service should be running. The first time this play happens, the `config` file will change and the service will change from not running to running. Then, the handlers will trigger, which will cause the service to restart immediately. This can be disruptive to any consumers of the service. It would be better to flush the handlers before a final task to ensure the service is running. This way, the restart will happen before the initial start, and thus, the service will start up once and stay up.

Relative path assumptions

When Ansible parses a playbook, there are certain assumptions that can be made about the relative paths of items referenced by the statements in a playbook. In most cases, paths for things such as variable files to include, task files to include, playbook files to include, files to copy, templates to render, scripts to execute, and so on, are all relative to the directory where the file referencing them lives. Let's explore this with an example playbook and directory listing to show where the things are:

- Directory structure:

```
.
├── a_vars_file.yaml
├── mastery-hosts
├── relative.yaml
└── tasks
    ├── a.yaml
    └── b.yaml
```

- Contents of `_vars_file.yaml`:

```
---
something: "better than nothing"
```

- Contents of `relative.yaml`:

```
---
- name: relative path play
  hosts: localhost
  gather_facts: false
  vars_files:
    - a_vars_file.yaml
  tasks:
    - name: who am I
      debug:
        msg: "I am mastery task"
    - name: var from file
      debug:
        var: something

    - include: tasks/a.yaml
```

- Contents of `tasks/a.yaml`:

```
---
- name: where am I
  debug:
    msg: "I am task a"

- include: b.yaml
```

- Contents of `tasks/b.yaml`:

```
---
- name: who am I
  debug:
    msg: "I am task b"
```

Execution of the playbook is shown as follows:

```
2. jkeating@serenity: ~/src/mastery (zsh)

~/src/mastery> ansible-playbook -i mastery-hosts -c local -v relative.yaml
No config file found; using defaults

PLAY [relative path play] ***********************************************

TASK [who am I] *********************************************************
ok: [localhost] => {
    "msg": "I am mastery task"
}

TASK [var from file] ****************************************************
ok: [localhost] => {
    "something": "better than nothing"
}

TASK [where am I] *******************************************************
ok: [localhost] => {
    "msg": "I am task a"
}

TASK [who am I] *********************************************************
ok: [localhost] => {
    "msg": "I am task b"
}

PLAY RECAP **************************************************************
localhost                  : ok=4   changed=0   unreachable=0   failed=0

~/src/mastery> _
```

We can clearly see the relative reference to paths and how they are relative to the file referencing them. When using roles, there are some additional relative path assumptions; however, we'll cover that in detail in a later chapter.

Play behavior directives

When Ansible parses a play, there are a few directives it looks for to define various behaviors for a play. These directives are written at the same level as the `hosts:` directive. Here are subset of the keys that can be used is described:

- `any_errors_fatal`: This Boolean directive is used to instruct Ansible to treat any failure as a fatal error to prevent any further tasks from being attempted. This changes the default where Ansible will continue until all the tasks are complete or all the hosts have failed.
- `connection`: This string directive defines which connection system to use for a given play. A common choice to make here is local, which instructs Ansible to do all the operations locally, but with the context of the system from the inventory.
- `gather_facts`: This Boolean directive controls whether or not Ansible will perform the fact gathering phase of operation, where a special task will run on a host to discover various facts about the system. Skipping fact gathering, when you are sure that you do not need any of the discovered data, can be a significant time-saver in a larger environment.
- `max_fail_percentage`: This number directive is similar to `any_errors_fatal`, but is more fine-grained. This allows you to define just what percentage of your hosts can fail before the whole operation is halted.
- `no_log`: This is a Boolean directive to control whether or not Ansible will log (to the screen and/or a configured `log` file) the command given or the results received from a task. This is important if your task or return deals with secrets. This key can also be applied to a task directly.
- `port`: This is a number directive to define what port SSH (or other remote connection plugin) should use to connect unless otherwise configured in inventory data.
- `remote_user`: This is a string directive that defines which user to log in with on the remote system. The default is to connect as the same user that `ansible-playbook` was started with.
- `serial`: This directive takes a number and controls how many systems Ansible will execute a task on before moving to the next task in a play. This is a drastic change from the normal order of operation where a task is executed across every system in a play before moving to the next. This is very useful in rolling update scenarios, which will be detailed in later chapters.

- `become`: This is a Boolean directive used to configure whether privilege escalation (sudo or otherwise) should be used on the remote host to execute tasks. This key can also be defined at a task level. Related directives include `become_user`, `become_method`, and `become_flags`. These can be used to configure how the escalation will occur.
- `strategy`: This directive sets the execution strategy to be used for the play.

Many of these keys will be used in example playbooks through this book.

For a full list of available play directives, see the online documentation at: `https://docs.ansible.com/ansible/playbooks_directives.html#play`.

Execution strategies

With the release of Ansible 2.0, a new way to control play execution behavior was introduced, strategy. A strategy defines how Ansible coordinates each task across the set of hosts. Each strategy is a plugin, and two come with Ansible, linear and free. The linear strategy, which is the default strategy, is how Ansible has always behaved. As a play is executed, all the hosts for a given play execute the first task. Once all are complete, Ansible moves to the next task. The serial directive can create batches of hosts to operate in this way, but the base strategy remains the same. All the targets for a given batch must complete a task before the next task is executed. The free strategy breaks from this traditional behavior. When using the free strategy, as soon as a host completes a task, Ansible will execute the next task for that host, without waiting for any other hosts to complete. This will happen for every host in the set, for every task in the play. The hosts will complete the tasks as fast as each are able to, minimizing the execution time of each specific host. While most playbooks will use the default linear strategy, there are situations where the free strategy would be advantageous. For example, upgrading a service across a large set of hosts. If the play has numerous tasks to perform the upgrade, which starts with shutting down the service, then it would be more important for each host to suffer as little downtime as possible. Allowing each host to independently move through the play as fast as it is able too will ensure that each host is down only for as long as necessary. Without using free, the entire fleet will be down for as long as the slowest host in the fleet takes to complete the tasks.

As the free strategy does not coordinate task completion across hosts, it is not possible to depend on the data that is generated during a task on one host to be available for use in a later task on a different host. There is no guarantee that the first host will have completed the task that generates the data.

Execution strategies are implemented as a plugin, and as such, custom strategies can be developed to extend Ansible behavior. Development of such plugins is beyond the scope of this book.

Host selection for plays and tasks

The first thing most plays define (after a name, of course) is a host pattern for the play. This is the pattern used to select hosts out of the inventory object to run the tasks on. Generally, this is straightforward; a host pattern contains one or more blocks indicating a host, group, wildcard pattern, or regex to use for the selection. Blocks are separated by a colon, wildcards are just an asterisk, and regex patterns start with a tilde:

```
hostname:groupname:*.example:~(web|db)\.example\.com
```

Advanced usage can include group index selection or even ranges within a group:

```
Webservers[0]:webservers[2:4]
```

Each block is treated as an inclusion block, that is, all the hosts found in the first pattern are added to all the hosts found in the next pattern, and so on. However, this can be manipulated with control characters to change their behavior. The use of an ampersand allows an inclusion selection (all the hosts that exist in both patterns). The use of an exclamation point allows exclusion selection (all the hosts that exist in the previous patterns that are NOT in the exclusion pattern):

```
Webservers:&dbservers
Webservers:!dbservers
```

Once Ansible parses the patterns, it will then apply restrictions, if any. Restrictions come in the form of limits or failed hosts. This result is stored for the duration of the play, and it is accessible via the `play_hosts` variable. As each task is executed, this data is consulted and an additional restriction may be placed upon it to handle serial operations. As failures are encountered, either failure to connect or a failure in execute tasks, the failed host is placed in a restriction list so that the host will be bypassed in the next task. If, at any time, a host selection routine gets restricted down to zero hosts, the play execution will stop with an error. A caveat here is that if the play is configured to have a `max_fail_precentage` or `any_errors_fatal` parameter, then the playbook execution stops immediately after the task where this condition is met.

Play and task names

While not strictly necessary, it is a good practice to label your plays and tasks with names. These names will show up in the command-line output of `ansible-playbook`, and will show up in the log file if `ansible-playbook` is directed to log to a file. Task names also come in handy to direct `ansible-playbook` to start at a specific task and to reference handlers.

There are two main points to consider when naming plays and tasks:

- Names of plays and tasks should be unique
- Beware of what kind of variables can be used in play and task names

Naming plays and tasks uniquely is a best practice in general that will help to quickly identify where a problematic task may reside in your hierarchy of playbooks, roles, task files, handlers, and so on. Uniqueness is more important when notifying a handler or when starting at a specific task. When task names have duplicates, the behavior of Ansible may be nondeterministic or at least nonobvious.

With uniqueness as a goal, many playbook authors will look to variables to satisfy this constraint. This strategy may work well but authors need to take care as to the source of the variable data they are referencing. Variable data can come from a variety of locations (which we will cover later in this chapter), and the values assigned to variables can be defined at a variety of times. For the sake of play and task names, it is important to remember that only variables for which the values can be determined at playbook parse time will parse and render correctly. If the data of a referenced variable is discovered via a task or other operation, the variable string will be displayed unparsed in the output. Let's look at an example playbook that utilizes variables for play and task names:

```
---
- name: play with a {{ var_name }}
  hosts: localhost
  gather_facts: false

  vars:
  - var_name: not-mastery

  tasks:
  - name: set a variable
    set_fact:
    task_var_name: "defined variable"

  - name: task with a {{ task_var_name }}
    debug:
    msg: "I am mastery task"

  - name: second play with a {{ task_var_name }}
    hosts: localhost
    gather_facts: false

  tasks:
  - name: task with a {{ runtime_var_name }}
    debug:
    msg: "I am another mastery task"
```

At first glance, one might expect at least `var_name` and `task_var_name` to render correctly. We can clearly see `task_var_name` being defined before its use. However, armed with our knowledge that playbooks are parsed in their entirety before execution, we know better:

```
2. jkeating@serenity: ~/src/mastery (zsh)

~/src/mastery> ansible-playbook -i mastery-hosts -c local names.yaml -vv
No config file found; using defaults

PLAYBOOK: names.yaml ********************************************************
2 plays in names.yaml

PLAY [play with a not-mastery] *********************************************

TASK [set a variable] ******************************************************
task path: /Users/jkeating/src/mastery/names.yaml:10
ok: [localhost] => {"ansible_facts": {"task_var_name": "defined variable"}, "cha
nged": false}

TASK [task with a defined variable] ****************************************
task path: /Users/jkeating/src/mastery/names.yaml:14
ok: [localhost] => {
    "msg": "I am mastery task"
}

PLAY [second play with a {{ task_var_name }}] ******************************

TASK [task with a {{ runtime_var_name }}] **********************************
task path: /Users/jkeating/src/mastery/names.yaml:23
ok: [localhost] => {
    "msg": "I am another mastery task"
}

PLAY RECAP *****************************************************************
localhost                  : ok=3    changed=0    unreachable=0    failed=0

~/src/mastery> _
```

As we can see, the only variable name that is properly rendered is `var_name`, as it was defined as a static play variable.

Module transport and execution

Once a playbook is parsed and the hosts are determined, Ansible is ready to execute a task. Tasks are made up of a name (optional, but please don't skip it), a module reference, module arguments, and task control directives. A later chapter will cover task control directives in detail, so we will only concern ourselves with the module reference and arguments.

Module reference

Every task has a module reference. This tells Ansible which bit of work to do. Ansible is designed to easily allow for custom modules to live alongside a playbook. These custom modules can be a wholly new functionality, or it can replace modules shipped with Ansible itself. When Ansible parses a task and discovers the name of the module to use for a task, it looks into a series of locations in order to find the module requested. Where it looks also depends on where the task lives, whether in a role or not.

If a task is in a role, Ansible will first look for the module within a directory tree named `library` within the role the task resides in. If the module is not found there, Ansible looks for a directory named `library` at the same level as the main playbook (the one referenced by the `ansible-playbook` execution). If the module is not found there, Ansible will finally look in the configured library path, which defaults to `/usr/share/ansible/`. This library path can be configured in an Ansible `config` file, or by way of the `ANSIBLE_LIBRARY` environment variable.

This design, allowing modules to be bundled with roles and playbooks, allows for adding functionality, or quickly repairing problems very easily.

Module arguments

Arguments to a module are not always required; the help output of a module will indicate which models are required and which are not. Module documentation can be accessed with the `ansible-doc` command:

```
2. jkeating@serenity: ~/src/mastery (zsh)
~/src/mastery> ansible-doc debug | cat -
> DEBUG

    This module prints statements during execution and can be useful for
    debugging variables or expressions without necessarily halting the
    playbook. Useful for debugging together with the 'when:' directive.

    * note: This module has a corresponding action plugin.

Options (= is mandatory):

- msg
        The customized message that is printed. If omitted, prints a
        generic message.
        [Default: Hello world!]
- var
        A variable name to debug.  Mutually exclusive with the 'msg'
        option.
        [Default: (null)]
- verbosity
        A number that controls when the debug is run, if you set to 3
        it will only run debug when -vvv or above
        [Default: 0]
EXAMPLES:
# Example that prints the loopback address and gateway for each host
- debug: msg="System {{ inventory_hostname }} has uuid {{ ansible_product_uuid }
}"

- debug: msg="System {{ inventory_hostname }} has gateway {{ ansible_default_ipv
4.gateway }}"
  when: ansible_default_ipv4.gateway is defined

- shell: /usr/bin/uptime
  register: result

- debug: var=result verbosity=2

- name: Display all variables/facts known for a host
  debug: var=hostvars[inventory_hostname] verbosity=4


MAINTAINERS: Michael DeHaan, Dag Wieers (@dagwieers)
~/src/mastery> _
```

This command was piped into `cat` to prevent shell paging from being used.

Arguments can be templated with **Jinja2**, which will be parsed at module execution time, allowing for data discovered in a previous task to be used in later tasks; this is a very powerful design element.

Arguments can be supplied in a `key=value` format, or in a complex format that is more native to YAML. Here are two examples of arguments being passed to a module showcasing the two formats:

```
- name: add a keypair to nova
  os_keypair: cloud={{ cloud_name }} name=admin-key wait=yes

- name: add a keypair to nova
  os_keypair:
  cloud: "{{ cloud_name }}"
  name: admin-key
  wait: yes
```

Both formats will lead to the same result in this example; however, the complex format is required if you wish to pass complex arguments into a module. Some modules expect a list object or a hash of data to be passed in; the complex format allows for this. While both formats are acceptable for many tasks, the complex format is the format used for the majority of examples in this book.

Module transport and execution

Once a module is found, Ansible has to execute it in some way. How the module is transported and executed depends on a few factors; however, the common process is to locate the module file on the local filesystem and read it into memory, and then add in the arguments passed to the module. Then the boilerplate module code from core Ansible is added to the file object in memory. This collection is zip compressed and base64 encoded, and then wrapped in a script. What happens next really depends on the connection method and runtime options (such as leaving the module code on the remote system for review).

The default connection method is `smart`, which most often resolves to the `ssh` connection method. With a default configuration, Ansible will open an SSH connection to the remote host, create a temporary directory, and close the connection. Ansible will then open another SSH connection in order to write out the wrapped ZIP file from memory (the result of local module file, task module arguments, and Ansible boilerplate code) into a file within the temporary directory that we just created and close the connection.

Finally, Ansible will open a third connection in order to execute the script and delete the temporary directory and all its contents. The module results are captured from stdout in the JSON format, which Ansible will parse and handle appropriately. If a task has an `async` control, Ansible will close the third connection before the module is complete, and SSH back in to the host to check the status of the task after a prescribed period until the module is complete or a prescribed timeout has been reached.

Task performance

The above description of how Ansible connects to hosts results in three connections to the host for every task. In a small fleet with a small number of tasks, this may not be a concern; however, as the task set grows and the fleet size grows, the time required to create and tear down SSH connections increases. Thankfully, there are a couple ways to mitigate this.

The first is an SSH feature, `ControlPersist`, which provides a mechanism to create persistent sockets when first connecting to a remote host that can be reused in subsequent connections to bypass some of the handshaking required when creating a connection. This can drastically reduce the amount of time Ansible spends on opening new connections. Ansible automatically utilizes this feature if the host platform where Ansible is run from supports it. To check whether your platform supports this feature, check the SSH main page for `ControlPersist`.

The second performance enhancement that can be utilized is an Ansible feature called pipelining. Pipelining is available to SSH-based connection methods and is configured in the Ansible configuration file within the `ssh_connection` section:

```
[ssh_connection]
pipelining=true
```

This setting changes how modules are transported. Instead of opening an SSH connection to create a directory, another to write out the composed module, and a third to execute and clean up, Ansible will instead open an SSH connection on the remote host. Then, over that live connection, Ansible will pipe in the zipped composed module code and script for execution. This reduces the connections from three to one, which can really add up. By default, pipelining is disabled.

Utilizing the combination of these two performance tweaks can keep your playbooks nice and fast even as you scale your fleet. However, keep in mind that Ansible will only address as many hosts at once as the number of forks Ansible is configured to run. Forks are the number of processes Ansible will split off as a worker to communicate with remote hosts. The default is five forks, which will address up to five hosts at once. Raise this number to address more hosts as your fleet grows by adjusting the `forks=` parameter in an Ansible configuration file, or by using the `--forks` (`-f`) argument with `ansible` or `ansible-playbook`.

Variable types and location

Variables are a key component to the Ansible design. Variables allow for dynamic play content and reusable plays across different sets of an inventory. Anything beyond the very basic of Ansible use will utilize variables. Understanding the different variable types and where they can be located, as well as learning how to access external data or prompt users to populate variable data, is the key to mastering Ansible.

Variable types

Before diving into the precedence of variables, we must first understand the various types and subtypes of variables available to Ansible, their location, and where they are valid for use.

The first major variable type is **inventory variables**. These are the variables that Ansible gets by way of the inventory. These can be defined as variables that are specific to `host_vars` to individual hosts or applicable to entire groups as `group_vars`. These variables can be written directly into the inventory file, delivered by the dynamic inventory plugin, or loaded from the `host_vars/<host>` or `group_vars/<group>` directories.

These types of variables might be used to define Ansible behavior when dealing with these hosts or site-specific data related to the applications that these hosts run. Whether a variable comes from `host_vars` or `group_vars`, it will be assigned to a host's `hostvars`, and it can be accessible from the playbooks and template files. Accessing a host's own variables can be done just by referencing the name, such as `{{ foobar }}`, and accessing another host's variables can be accomplished by accessing `hostvars`. For example, to access the `foobar` variable for `examplehost`: `{{ hostvars['examplehost']['foobar'] }}`. These variables have global scope.

The second major variable type is **role variables**. These are variables specific to a role and are utilized by the role tasks and have scope only within the role that they are defined in, which is to say that they can only be used within the role. These variables are often supplied as a **role default**, which are meant to provide a default value for the variable but can easily be overridden when applying the role. When roles are referenced, it is possible to supply variable data at the same time, either by overriding role defaults or creating wholly new data. We'll cover roles in depth in a later chapter. These variables apply to all hosts within the role and can be accessed directly much like a host's own `hostvars`.

The third major variable type is **play variables**. These variables are defined in the control keys of a play, either directly by the `vars` key or sourced from external files via the `vars_files` key. Additionally, the play can interactively prompt the user for variable data using `vars_prompt`. These variables are to be used within the scope of the play and in any tasks or included tasks of the play. The variables apply to all hosts within the play and can be referenced as if they are `hostvars`.

The fourth variable type is **task variables**. Task variables are made from data discovered while executing tasks or in the facts gathering phase of a play. These variables are host-specific and are added to the host's `hostvars` and can be used as such, which also means they have global scope *after* the point in which they were discovered or defined. Variables of this type can be discovered via `gather_facts` and **fact modules** (modules that do not alter state but rather return data), populated from task return data via the `register` task key, or defined directly by a task making use of the `set_fact` or `add_host` modules. Data can also be interactively obtained from the operator using the `prompt` argument to the `pause` module and registering the result:

```
 - name: get the operators name
   pause:
     prompt: "Please enter your name"
   register: opname
```

There is one last variable type, the **extra variables**, or `extra-vars` type. These are variables supplied on the command-line when executing `ansible-playbook` via `--extra-vars`. Variable data can be supplied as a list of `key=value` pairs, a quoted JSON data, or a reference to a YAML-formatted file with variable data defined within:

```
--extra-vars "foo=bar owner=fred"
--extra-vars '{"services":["nova-api","nova-conductor"]}'
--extra-vars @/path/to/data.yaml
```

Extra variables are considered global variables. They apply to every host and have scope throughout the entire playbook.

Accessing external data

Data for role variables, play variables, and task variables can also come from external sources. Ansible provides a mechanism to access and evaluate data from the **control machine** (the machine running `ansible-playbook`). The mechanism is called a **lookup plugin**, and a number of them come with Ansible. These plugins can be used to lookup or access data by reading files, generate and locally store passwords on the Ansible host for later reuse, evaluate environment variables, pipe data in from executables, access data in the `Redis` or `etcd` systems, render data from template files, query `dnstxt` records, and more. The syntax is as follows:

```
lookup('<plugin_name>', 'plugin_argument')
```

For example, to use the `mastery` value from `etcd` in a debug task:

```
- name: show data from etcd
  debug:
    msg: "{{ lookup('etcd', 'mastery') }}"
```

Lookups are evaluated when the task referencing them is executed, which allows for dynamic data discovery. To reuse a particular lookup in multiple tasks and reevaluate it each time, a playbook variable can be defined with a lookup value. Each time the playbook variable is referenced, the lookup will be executed, potentially providing different values over time.

Variable precedence

As you learned in the previous section, there are a few major types of variables that can be defined in a myriad of locations. This leads to a very important question: what happens when the same variable name is used in multiple locations? Ansible has a precedence for loading variable data, and thus it has an order and a definition to decide which variable will *win*. Variable value overriding is an advanced usage of Ansible, so it is important to fully understand the semantics before attempting such a scenario.

Precedence order

Ansible defines the precedence order as follows:

1. Extra `vars` (from command-line) always win.
2. Task `vars` (only for the specific task).

3. Block `vars` (only for the tasks within the block).

4. Role and include `vars`.

5. Vars created with `set_fact`.

6. Vars created with the `register` task directive.

7. Play `vars_files`.

8. Play `vars_prompt`.

9. Play `vars`.

10. Host facts.

11. Playbook `host_vars`.

12. Playbook `group_vars`.

13. Inventory `host_vars`.

14. Inventory `group_vars`.

15. Inventory `vars`.

16. Role defaults.

Merging hashes

In the previous section, we focused on the precedence in which variables will override each other. The default behavior of Ansible is that any overriding definition for a variable name will completely mask the previous definition of that variable. However, that behavior can be altered for one type of variable, the hash. A hash variable (a *dictionary* in Python terms) is a dataset of keys and values. Values can be of different types for each key, and can even be hashes themselves for complex data structures.

In some advanced scenarios, it is desirable to replace just one bit of a hash or add to an existing hash rather than replacing the hash altogether. To unlock this ability, a configuration change is necessary in an Ansible `config` file. The config entry is `hash_behavior`, which takes one of **replace**, or **merge**. A setting of merge will instruct Ansible to merge or blend the values of two hashes when presented with an override scenario rather than the default of replace, which will completely replace the old variable data with the new data.

Let's walk through an example of the two behaviors. We will start with a hash loaded with data and simulate a scenario where a different value for the hash is provided as a higher priority variable.

Starting data:

```
hash_var:
  fred:
    home: Seattle
    transport: Bicycle
```

New data loaded via `include_vars`:

```
hash_var:
  fred:
    transport: Bus
```

With the default behavior, the new value for `hash_var` will be as follows:

```
hash_var:
  fred:
    transport: Bus
```

However, if we enable the merge behavior, we will get the following result:

```
hash_var:
  fred:
    home: Seattle
    transport: Bus
```

There are even more nuances and undefined behaviors when using merge, and as such, it is strongly recommended to only use this setting if absolutely needed.

Summary

While the design of Ansible focuses on simplicity and ease of use, the architecture itself is very powerful. In this chapter, we covered key design and architecture concepts of Ansible, such as version and configuration, playbook parsing, module transport and execution, variable types and locations, and variable precedence.

You learned that playbooks contain variables and tasks. Tasks link bits of code called modules with arguments, which can be populated by variable data. These combinations are transported to selected hosts from provided inventory sources. The fundamental understanding of these building blocks is the platform on which you can build a mastery of all things Ansible!

In the next chapter, you will learn how to secure secret data while operating Ansible.

2

Protecting Your Secrets with Ansible

Secrets are meant to stay secret. Whether they are login credentials to a cloud service or passwords to database resources, they are secret for a reason. Should they fall into the wrong hands, they can be used to discover trade secrets, customers' private data, create infrastructure for nefarious purposes, or worse. All of which could cost you or your organization a lot of time, money, and headache! In this chapter, we cover how to keep your secrets safe with Ansible:

- Encrypting data at rest
- Protecting secrets while operating

Encrypting data at rest

As a configuration management system or an orchestration engine, Ansible has great power. In order to wield that power, it is necessary to entrust secret data to Ansible. An automation system that prompts the operator for passwords each connection is not very efficient. To maximize the power of Ansible, secret data has to be written to a file that Ansible can read and utilize the data from within.

This creates a risk though! Your secrets are sitting there on your filesystem in plain text. This is a physical and digital risk. Physically, the computer could be taken from you and pawed through for secret data. Digitally, any malicious software that can break the boundaries set upon it could read any data your user account has access to. If you utilize a source control system, the infrastructure that houses the repository is just as much at risk.

Thankfully, Ansible provides a facility to protect your data at rest. That facility is Vault. This facility allows for encrypting text files so that they are stored at rest in an encrypted format. Without the key or a significant amount of computing power, the data is indecipherable.

The key lessons to learn when dealing with encrypting data at rest are:

- Valid encryption targets
- Creating new encrypted files
- Encrypting existing unencrypted files
- Editing encrypted files
- Changing the encryption password on files
- Decrypting encrypted files
- Running `ansible-playbook` referencing encrypted files

Things Vault can encrypt

The Vault feature can be used to encrypt any **structured data** file used by Ansible. This is essentially any YAML (or JSON) file that Ansible uses during its operation. This can include:

- `group_vars/` files
- `host_vars/` files
- `include_vars` targets
- `vars_files` targets
- `--extra-vars` targets
- role variables
- role defaults
- task files
- handler files
- source files for `copy` module

If the file can be expressed in YAML and read by Ansible, or if the file is to be transported with the `copy` module, it is a valid file to encrypt with Vault. Because the entire file will be unreadable at rest, care should be taken to not be overzealous in picking which files to encrypt. Any source control operations with the files will be done with the encrypted content, making it very difficult to peer review. As a best practice, the smallest amount of data possible should be encrypted, which may even mean moving some variables into a file all by themselves.

Creating new encrypted files

To create new files, Ansible provides a new program, `ansible-vault`. This program is used to create and interact with Vault encrypted files. The subroutine to create encrypted files is the `create` subroutine:

```
2. jkeating@serenity: ~/src/mastery (zsh)
~/src/mastery> ansible-vault create --help
Usage: ansible-vault create [options] file_name

Options:
    --ask-vault-pass        ask for vault password
  -h, --help                show this help message and exit
    --new-vault-password-file=NEW_VAULT_PASSWORD_FILE
                            new vault password file for rekey
    --output=OUTPUT_FILE    output file name for encrypt or decrypt; use - for
                            stdout
    --vault-password-file=VAULT_PASSWORD_FILE
                            vault password file
  -v, --verbose             verbose mode (-vvv for more, -vvvv to enable
                            connection debugging)
    --version               show program's version number and exit
~/src/mastery>
```

To create a new file, you'll need to know two things ahead of time. The first is the password `Vault` should use to encrypt the file, and the second is the file name itself. Once provided with this information, `ansible-vault` will launch a text editor, whichever editor is defined in the environment variable `EDITOR`. Once you save the file and exit the editor, `ansible-vault` will use the supplied password as a key to encrypt the file with `AES256 cypher`.

All Vault encrypted files referenced by a playbook need to be encrypted with the same key, otherwise `ansible-playbook` will be unable to read them.

The `ansible-vault` program will prompt for a `password`, unless the path to a file is provided as an argument. The `password` file can either be a plain text file with the password stored as a single line, or it can be an executable file that outputs the password as a single line to standard out.

Let's walk through a few examples of creating encrypted files. First, we'll create one and be prompted for a password, then we will provide a `password` file, and lastly we'll create an executable to deliver the password.

Password prompt

```
● ● ●                2. ansible-vault create secrets.yaml (python)
~/src/mastery> ansible-vault create secrets.yaml
Vault password: _
```

Once the passphrase is entered, our editor opens and we're able to put content into the file:

```
● ● ●                2. ansible-vault create secrets.yaml (vim)
---
my_secret: is_safe
~
~
~
~
:wq
```

On my system, the configured editor is vim. Your system may be different, and you may need to set your preferred editor as the value for the EDITOR environment variable.

Now, we save the file. If we try to read the contents, we'll see that they are in fact encrypted, with a small header hint for Ansible to use later:

```
2. jkeating@serenity: ~/src/mastery (zsh)
~/src/mastery> ansible-vault create secrets.yaml
Vault password:
~/src/mastery> cat secrets.yaml
$ANSIBLE_VAULT;1.1;AES256
383931356339346234636136393663306565396335333306230633863656565363665306132623661
636164653035366561353139303330336133613936566639350a38336634633835363030835533646233
65366262323064393734303962663663838326231303364306164616433613838303165333733366231
613163337343361383000a3961373130343262366626537386432643634323435623930623366633738
386465383962666161623837636461653539633316465616262656161386266326632643936
~/src/mastery> _
```

Password file

In order to use ansible-vault with a password file, we first need to create the password file. Simply echoing a password into a file can do this. Then, we can reference this file when calling ansible-vault to create another encrypted file:

```
2. jkeating@serenity: ~/src/mastery (zsh)
~/src/mastery> echo "my long password" > password_file
~/src/mastery> ansible-vault create --vault-password-file password_file more_sec
rets.yaml_
```

Just as with being prompted for a password, the editor will open and we can write out our data.

Password script

This last example uses a password script. This is useful for designing a system where a password can be stored in a central system for storing credentials and shared with contributors to the playbook tree. Each contributor could have his or her own password to the shared credentials store, where the Vault password would be retrieved from. Our example will be far more simple: just a simple output to standard out with a password. This file will be saved as password.sh. The file needs to be marked as an executable for Ansible to treat it as such:

```
2. jkeating@serenity: ~/src/mastery (zsh)
~/src/mastery> vim password.sh
~/src/mastery> cat password.sh
#!/bin/bash

echo "a long password"
~/src/mastery> chmod +x password.sh
~/src/mastery> ansible-vault create --vault-password-file password.sh even_more_
secrets.yaml
```

Encrypting existing files

The previous examples all dealt with creating new encrypted files using the create subroutine. But what if we want to take an established file and encrypt it? A subroutine exists for this as well. It is named encrypt:

```
~/src/mastery> ansible-vault encrypt --help
Usage: ansible-vault encrypt [options] file_name

Options:
  --ask-vault-pass          ask for vault password
  -h, --help                show this help message and exit
  --new-vault-password-file=NEW_VAULT_PASSWORD_FILE
                            new vault password file for rekey
  --output=OUTPUT_FILE      output file name for encrypt or decrypt; use - for
                            stdout
  --vault-password-file=VAULT_PASSWORD_FILE
                            vault password file
  -v, --verbose             verbose mode (-vvv for more, -vvvv to enable
                            connection debugging)
  --version                 show program's version number and exit
~/src/mastery>
```

As before our editor opens up, with our content in plain text visible to us. As with `create`, `encrypt` expects a `password` (or `password` file) and the path to a file. In this case, however, the file must already exist. Let's demonstrate this by encrypting an existing file we have from a previous Chapter 1, *System Architecture and Design of Ansible*, `a_vars_file.yaml`:

```
~/src/mastery> cat a_vars_file.yaml
---
something: "better than nothing"
~/src/mastery> ansible-vault encrypt --vault-password-file password.sh a_vars_fi
le.yaml
Encryption successful
~/src/mastery> cat a_vars_file.yaml
$ANSIBLE_VAULT;1.1;AES256
3263316232231386335356138336261663864363535323735323034663530616338326262626436453 3
3562353266653938386665616533386161386465363363340a3439626439316662663533623233562
3831366438356663663333353232366236353356136626237356364333238383461623030163656646133
3966636664663961380a626434646462393865353864343433633386661636164393665346636393338
3139323662633739633664313562393336635363532646236656466366553732346330336533326137
6631316530383731646432356562383834333356633337346233064
~/src/mastery>
```

We can see the file contents before and after the call to `encrypt`, whereafter the contents are indeed encrypted. Unlike the `create` subroutine, `encrypt` can operate on multiple files, making it easy to protect all the important data in one action. Simply list all the files to be encrypted, separated by spaces.

 Attempting to encrypt already encrypted files will result in an error.

Editing encrypted files

Once a file has been encrypted with `ansible-vault`, it cannot be directly edited. Opening the file in an editor would result in the encrypted data being shown. Making any changes to the file would damage the file and Ansible would be unable to read the contents correctly. We need a subroutine that will first decrypt the contents of the file, allow us to edit those contents, and then encrypt the new contents, before saving it back to the file. Such a subroutine exists, called edit:

```
2. jkeating@serenity: ~/src/mastery (zsh)
~/src/mastery> ansible-vault edit --help
Usage: ansible-vault edit [options] file_name

Options:
  --ask-vault-pass      ask for vault password
  -h, --help            show this help message and exit
  --new-vault-password-file=NEW_VAULT_PASSWORD_FILE
                        new vault password file for rekey
  --output=OUTPUT_FILE  output file name for encrypt or decrypt; use - for
                        stdout
  --vault-password-file=VAULT_PASSWORD_FILE
                        vault password file
  -v, --verbose         verbose mode (-vvv for more, -vvvv to enable
                        connection debugging)
  --version             show program's version number and exit
~/src/mastery>
```

As previously our editor opens up, with our content in plain text visible to us. All our familiar options are back, an optional `password` file/script and the file to edit. If we edit the file we just encrypted, we'll notice that `ansible-vault` opens our editor with a temporary file as the file path. The editor will save this and then `ansible-vault` will encrypt it and move it to replace the original file:

```
2. jkeating@serenity: ~/src/mastery (zsh)
~/src/mastery> ansible-vault edit --vault-password-file password.sh a_vars_file.
yaml_
```

```
2. ansible-vault edit --vault-password-file password.sh a_vars_file.yaml (python)

something: "better than nothing"
~
~
~
~
~
<zzsqj2j4hdghh6z93z1rhgw0000gn/T/tmpAOuOxf" 2L, 37C                1,1          All
```

Password rotation on encrypted files

Over time, as contributors come and go, it is a good idea to rotate the password used to
encrypt your secrets. Encryption is only as good as the protection of the password.
`ansible-vault` provides a subroutine that allows us to change the password, named
`rekey`:

```
2. jkeating@serenity: ~/src/mastery (zsh)
~/src/mastery> ansible-vault rekey --help
Usage: ansible-vault rekey [options] file_name

Options:
  --ask-vault-pass          ask for vault password
  -h, --help                show this help message and exit
  --new-vault-password-file=NEW_VAULT_PASSWORD_FILE
                            new vault password file for rekey
  --output=OUTPUT_FILE      output file name for encrypt or decrypt; use - for
                            stdout
  --vault-password-file=VAULT_PASSWORD_FILE
                            vault password file
  -v, --verbose             verbose mode (-vvv for more, -vvvv to enable
                            connection debugging)
  --version                 show program's version number and exit
~/src/mastery> _
```

The `rekey` subroutine operates much like the `edit` subroutine. It takes in an optional `password` file/script and one or more files to `rekey`. Note that, while you can supply a file/script for decryption of the existing files, you cannot supply one for the new passphrase. You will be prompted to input the new passphrase. Let's `rekey` our `even_more_secrets.yaml` file:

```
2. jkeating@serenity: ~/src/mastery (zsh)
~/src/mastery> ansible-vault rekey --vault-password-file password.sh even_more_s
ecrets.yaml
New Vault password:
Confirm New Vault password:
Rekey successful
~/src/mastery>
```

Remember that all the encrypted files need to have a matching key. Be sure to `rekey` all the files at the same time.

Decrypting encrypted files

If, at some point, the need to encrypt data files goes away, `ansible-vault` provides a subroutine that can be used to remove encryption for one or more encrypted files. This subroutine is (surprisingly) named `decrypt`:

```
~/src/mastery> ansible-vault decrypt --help
Usage: ansible-vault decrypt [options] file_name

Options:
  --ask-vault-pass        ask for vault password
  -h, --help              show this help message and exit
  --new-vault-password-file=NEW_VAULT_PASSWORD_FILE
                          new vault password file for rekey
  --output=OUTPUT_FILE    output file name for encrypt or decrypt; use - for
                          stdout
  --vault-password-file=VAULT_PASSWORD_FILE
                          vault password file
  -v, --verbose           verbose mode (-vvv for more, -vvvv to enable
                          connection debugging)
  --version               show program's version number and exit
~/src/mastery>
```

Once again, we have an optional argument for a `password` file/script and then one or more file paths to decrypt. Let's decrypt the file we created earlier, using our `password` file:

```
~/src/mastery> cat more_secrets.yaml
$ANSIBLE_VAULT;1.1;AES256
6161653537353732663138376538323965353436653062343233353361363137316632626630636 2
3837613934313962356134346536383839386431383861300a3132306462306364333435383636363 0
6330353731383838313631656531346461366230646639313566326462306436663335306166303336 2
3737643235663764620a646134333393438343963383835666366303139366538653530376238656666437
30306239356231366165386632326663333383532353537613035373565343735363633261
~/src/mastery> ansible-vault decrypt --vault-password-file password_file more_se
crets.yaml
Decryption successful
~/src/mastery> cat more_secrets.yaml
---
more: secrets
~/src/mastery>
```

Executing Ansible-playbook with encrypted files

To make use of our encrypted content, we need to be able to inform `ansible-playbook` how to access any encrypted data it might encounter. Unlike `ansible-vault`, which exists solely to deal with file encryption/decryption, `ansible-playbook` is more general-purpose, and it will not assume it is dealing with encrypted data by default. There are two ways to indicate that encrypted data may be encountered. The first is the argument `--ask-vault-pass`, which will prompt at the very beginning of a playbook execution for the Vault password required to unlock any encountered encrypted files. Ansible will hold this provided password in memory for the duration of the playbook execution. The second method is to reference a `password` file or script via the familiar `--vault-password-file` argument.

Let's create a simple playbook named `show_me.yaml` that will print out the value of the variable inside of `a_vars_file.yaml`, which we encrypted in a previous example:

```
---
- name: show me an encrypted var
  hosts: localhost
  gather_facts: false

  vars_files:
    - a_vars_file.yaml

  tasks:
    - name: print the variable
      debug:
        var: something
```

```
2. jkeating@serenity: ~/src/mastery (zsh)
~/src/mastery> ansible-playbook -i mastery-hosts --vault-password-file password.
sh show_me.yaml -vv
No config file found; using defaults

PLAYBOOK: show_me.yaml **************************************************
1 plays in show_me.yaml

PLAY [show me an encrypted var] *****************************************

TASK [print the variable] **********************************************
task path: /Users/jkeating/src/mastery/show_me.yaml:10
ok: [localhost] => {
    "something": "better than nothing"
}

PLAY RECAP *************************************************************
localhost                  : ok=1    changed=0    unreachable=0    failed=0

~/src/mastery> _
```

Protecting secrets while operating

In the previous section of this chapter, we covered protecting your secrets at rest on the filesystem. However, that is not the only concern when operating Ansible with secrets. That secret data is going to be used in tasks as module arguments or loop inputs or any number of other things. This may cause the data to be transmitted to remote hosts, logged to local or remote log files, or displayed onscreen. This section of the chapter will discuss strategies for protecting your secrets during operation.

Secrets transmitted to remote hosts

As we learned in `Chapter 1`, *System Architecture and Design of Ansible*, Ansible will combine module code and arguments and write this out to a temporary directory on the `remote` host. This means your secret data is transferred over the wire **AND** written to the `remote` filesystem. Unless you are using a connection plugin other than ssh, the data over the wire is already encrypted preventing your secrets from being discovered by simple snooping. If you are using a connection plugin other than ssh, be aware of whether or not data is encrypted, while in transit. Using any connection method that is not encrypted is strongly discouraged.

Once the data is transmitted, Ansible may write this data out in clear form to the filesystem. This can happen if `pipelining` (which we learned about in `Chapter 1`, *System Architecture and Design of Ansible*) is not in use, **OR** if Ansible has been instructed to leave `remote` files in place via the `ANSIBLE_KEEP_REMOTE_FILES` environment variable. Without pipelining, Ansible will write out the module, code plus arguments, into a temporary directory that is to be deleted upon execution. Should there be a loss of connectivity between writing out the file and executing it, the file will be left on the `remote` filesystem until manually removed. If Ansible is explicitly instructed to keep `remote` files in place, then, even if pipelining is enabled, Ansible will write out and leave a `remote` file in place. Care should be taken with these options when dealing with highly sensitive secrets, even though, typically, only the user Ansible logs in as (or becomes via privilege escalation) on the `remote` host should have access to the leftover file. Simply deleting anything in the `~/.ansible/tmp/` path for the `remote` user will suffice to clean secrets.

Secrets logged to remote or local files

When Ansible operates on a host, it will attempt to log the action to `syslog` (if verbosity level three or more is used). If this action is being done with a user with appropriate rights, it will cause a message to appear in the `syslog` file of the host. This message includes the module name and the arguments passed along to that command, which could include your secrets. To prevent this from happening, a play and task key exists named `no_log`. Setting `no_log` to true will prevent Ansible from logging the action to `syslog`.

Locally, Ansible can be instructed to log its actions as well. An environment variable controls this, called ANSIBLE_LOG_PATH. Without this variable set, Ansible will only log to standard out. Setting this variable to a path that can be written to by the user running ansible-playbook will cause Ansible to log actions to this path. The verbosity of this logging matches that of the verbosity shown onscreen. By default, no variables or return details are displayed onscreen. With a verbosity level of one (-v), return data is displayed onscreen (and potentially in the local log file). With verbosity turned up to level 3 (-vvv), the input parameters may also be displayed. Since this can include secrets, the no_log setting applies to onscreen display as well. Let's take our previous example of displaying an encrypted secret and add a no_log key to the task to prevent showing its value:

```
---
- name: show me an encrypted var
  hosts: localhost
  gather_facts: false

  vars_files:
    - a_vars_file.yaml

  tasks:
    - name: print the variable
      debug:
        var: something
      no_log: true
```

If we execute this playbook, we should see that our secret data is protected:

Ansible censored itself to prevent showing sensitive data.

The no_log key can be used as a directive for a play, a role, a block, or a task.

Summary

Ansible can deal with sensitive data. It is important to understand how this data is stored at rest and how this data is treated when utilized. With a little care and attention, Ansible can keep your secrets secret. Encrypting secrets with `ansible-vault` can protect them while dormant on your filesystem or in a shared source control repository. Preventing Ansible from logging task data can protect against leaking data to `remote log` files or onscreen displays.

In our next chapter, we will explore the powers of the Jinja2 templating engine, as used by Ansible.

3

Unlocking the Power of Jinja2 Templates

Templating is the lifeblood of Ansible. From configuration file content to variable substitution in tasks, to conditional statements and beyond, templating comes into play with nearly every Ansible facet. The templating engine of Ansible is **Jinja2**, a modern and designer-friendly templating language for Python. This chapter will cover a few advanced features of Jinja2 templating:

- Control structures
- Data manipulation
- Comparisons

Control structures

In Jinja2, a control structure refers to things in a template that controls the flow of the engine parsing the template. These structures include, but are not limited to, conditionals, loops, and macros. Within Jinja2 (assuming the defaults are in use), a control structure will appear inside blocks of {% ... %}. These opening and closing blocks alert the Jinja2 parser that a control statement is provided instead of a normal string or variable name.

Conditionals

A conditional within a template creates a decision path. The engine will consider the conditional and choose from two or more potential blocks of code. There is always a minimum of two: a path if the conditional is met (evaluated as true) and an implied else path of an empty block.

The statement for conditionals is the `if` statement. This statement works much same as it does in Python. An `if` statement can be combined with one or more optional `elif` with an optional final `else`, and unlike Python, requires an explicit `endif`. The following example shows a `config` file template snippet combining both regular variable replacement and an `if else` structure:

```
setting = {{ setting }}
{% if feature.enabled %}
feature = True
{% else %}
feature = False
{% endif %}
another_setting = {{ another_setting }}
```

In this example, the variable `feature.enabled` is checked to see if it exists and is not set to `False`. If this is `True`, then the text `feature = True` is used; otherwise, the text `feature = False` is used. Outside of this control block, the parser does the normal variable substitution for the variables inside the mustache brackets. Multiple paths can be defined by using an `elif` statement, which presents the parser with another test to perform should the previous tests equate to `false`.

To demonstrate rendering the template, we'll save the example template as `demo.j2` and then make a playbook named `template-demo.yaml` that defines the variables in use and then uses a template lookup as part of a `pause` task to display the rendered template on screen:

```
---
- name: demo the template
  hosts: localhost
  gather_facts: false
  vars:
    setting: a_val
    feature:
      enabled: true
    another_setting: b_val
  tasks:
    - name: pause with render
      pause:
```

```
prompt: "{{ lookup('template', 'demo.j2') }}"
```

Executing this playbook will show the rendered template on screen while waiting for input. We can simply press *Enter* to complete the playbook:

```
                    2. jkeating@serenity-2: ~/src/mastery (zsh)
~/src/mastery> ansible-playbook -i mastery-hosts template-demo.yml -vv
No config file found; using defaults

PLAYBOOK: template-demo.yml ***************************************************
1 plays in template-demo.yml


PLAY [demo the template] *****************************************************

TASK [pause with render] *****************************************************
task path: /Users/jkeating/src/mastery/template-demo.yml:13
[pause with render]
setting = a_val
feature = True
another_setting = b_val
:
ok: [localhost] => {"changed": false, "delta": 1, "rc": 0, "start": "2016-12-29
12:13:15.286170", "stderr": "", "stdout": "Paused for 0.03 minutes", "stop": "20
16-12-29 12:13:17.107023", "user_input": ""}

PLAY RECAP *******************************************************************
localhost                  : ok=1    changed=0    unreachable=0    failed=0

~/src/mastery> _
```

If we were to change the value of `feature.enabled` to `False`, the output would be slightly different:

```
● ● ●                    2. jkeating@serenity-2: ~/src/mastery (zsh)
~/src/mastery> ansible-playbook -i mastery-hosts template-demo.yml -vv
No config file found; using defaults

PLAYBOOK: template-demo.yml ***********************************************
1 plays in template-demo.yml

PLAY [demo the template] **************************************************

TASK [pause with render] *************************************************
task path: /Users/jkeating/src/mastery/template-demo.yml:13
[pause with render]
setting = a_val
feature = False
another_setting = b_val
:
ok: [localhost] => {"changed": false, "delta": 1, "rc": 0, "start": "2016-12-29
12:14:25.599895", "stderr": "", "stdout": "Paused for 0.02 minutes", "stop": "20
16-12-29 12:14:26.880526", "user_input": ""}

PLAY RECAP ***************************************************************
localhost                  : ok=1    changed=0    unreachable=0    failed=0

~/src/mastery> _
```

Inline conditionals

The `If` statements can be used inside of inline expressions. This can be useful in some scenarios where additional newlines are not desired. Let's construct a scenario where we need to define an `API` as either `cinder` or `cinderv2`:

```
API = cinder{{ 'v2' if api.v2 else '' }}
```

This example assumes `api.v2` is defined as Boolean `True` or `False`. Inline `if` expressions follow the syntax of `<do something>` `if` `<conditional is true>` `else` `<do something else>`. In an inline `if` expression, there is an implied `else`; however, that implied `else` is meant to evaluate as an undefined object, which will normally create an error. We protect against this by defining an explicit `else`, which renders a zero length string.

Let's modify our playbook to demonstrate an inline conditional. This time, we'll use the `debug` module to render the simple template:

```
---
- name: demo the template
  hosts: localhost
  gather_facts: false
    vars:
    api:
      v2: true
  tasks:
    - name: pause with render
      debug:
        msg: "API = cinder{{ 'v2' if api.v2 else '' }}"
```

Execution of the playbook will show the template being rendered:

```
2. jkeating@serenity-2: ~/src/mastery (zsh)
~/src/mastery> ansible-playbook -i mastery-hosts template-demo.yml -vv
No config file found; using defaults

PLAYBOOK: template-demo.yml ********************************************************
1 plays in template-demo.yml

PLAY [demo the template] ***********************************************************

TASK [pause with render] ***********************************************************
task path: /Users/jkeating/src/mastery/template-demo.yml:11
ok: [localhost] => {
    "msg": "API = cinderv2"
}

PLAY RECAP *************************************************************************
localhost                  : ok=1    changed=0    unreachable=0    failed=0

~/src/mastery>
```

Changing the value of `api.v2` to `false` leads to a different result:

```
2. jkeating@serenity-2: ~/src/mastery (zsh)
~/src/mastery> ansible-playbook -i mastery-hosts template-demo.yml -vv
No config file found; using defaults

PLAYBOOK: template-demo.yml ***********************************************
1 plays in template-demo.yml

PLAY [demo the template] **************************************************

TASK [pause with render] *************************************************
task path: /Users/jkeating/src/mastery/template-demo.yml:11
ok: [localhost] => {
    "msg": "API = cinder"
}

PLAY RECAP ***************************************************************
localhost                  : ok=1    changed=0    unreachable=0    failed=0

~/src/mastery>
```

Loops

A loop allows you to create dynamically created sections in template files and is useful when you know you need to operate on an unknown number of items in the same way. To start a loop control structure, the `for` statement is used. Let's look at a simple way to loop over a list of directories where a fictional service might find data:

```
# data dirs
{% for dir in data_dirs %}
data_dir = {{ dir }}
{% endfor %}
```

In this example, we will get one `data_dir` = line per item within the `data_dirs` variable, assuming `data_dirs` is a list with at least one item in it. If the variable is not a list (or other iterable type) or is not defined, an error will be generated. If the variable is an iterable type but is empty, then no lines will be generated. Jinja2 allows for the reacting to this scenario and also allows substituting in a line when no items are found in the variable via an `else` statement. In this next example, assume that `data_dirs` is an empty list:

```
# data dirs
{% for dir in data_dirs %}
data_dir = {{ dir }}
{% else %}
# no data dirs found
{% endfor %}
```

We can test this by modifying our playbook and template file again. We'll update `demo.j2` with the earlier template content and make use of a `prompt` in our playbook again:

```
---
- name: demo the template
  hosts: localhost
  gather_facts: false
  vars:
    data_dirs: []
  tasks:
    - name: pause with render
      pause:
        prompt: "{{ lookup('template', 'demo.j2') }}"
```

Running our playbook will show the following result:

```
2. jkeating@serenity-2: ~/src/mastery (zsh)

~/src/mastery> ansible-playbook -i mastery-hosts template-demo.yml -vv
No config file found; using defaults

PLAYBOOK: template-demo.yml *********************************************
1 plays in template-demo.yml

PLAY [demo the template] ***********************************************

TASK [pause with render] ***********************************************
task path: /Users/jkeating/src/mastery/template-demo.yml:10
[pause with render]
# data dirs
# no data dirs found

:
ok: [localhost] => {"changed": false, "delta": 1, "rc": 0, "start": "2016-12-29
12:21:43.543140", "stderr": "", "stdout": "Paused for 0.02 minutes", "stop": "20
16-12-29 12:21:44.843838", "user_input": ""}

PLAY RECAP *************************************************************
localhost                  : ok=1    changed=0    unreachable=0    failed=0

~/src/mastery> _
```

Filtering loop items

Loops can be combined with conditionals, as well. Within the loop structure, an `if` statement can be used to check a condition using the current loop item as part of the conditional. Let's extend our example and protect against using (/) as a `data_dir`:

```
# data dirs
{% for dir in data_dirs %}
{% if dir != "/" %}
data_dir = {{ dir }}
{% endif %}
{% else %}
# no data dirs found
{% endfor %}
```

The preceding example successfully filters out any `data_dirs` item that is (/) but takes more typing than should be necessary. Jinja2 provides a convenience that allows you to filter loop items easily as part of the `for` statement. Let's repeat the previous example using this convenience:

```
# data dirs
{% for dir in data_dirs if dir != "/" %}
data_dir = {{ dir }}
{% else %}
# no data dirs found
{% endfor %}
```

Not only does this structure require less typing, but it also correctly counts the loops, which we'll learn about in the next section.

Loop indexing

Loop counting is provided for free, yielding an index of the current iteration of the loop. As variables, this can be accessed a few different ways. The following table outlines the ways they can be referenced:

Variable	Description
loop.index	The current iteration of the loop (1 indexed)
loop.index0	The current iteration of the loop (0 indexed)
loop.revindex	The number of iterations until the end of the loop (1 indexed)
loop.revindex0	The number of iterations until the end of the loop (0 indexed)
loop.first	Boolean True if the first iteration
loop.last	Boolean True if the last iteration
loop.length	The number of items in the sequence

Having information related to the position within the loop can help with logic around what content to render. Considering our previous examples, instead of rendering multiple lines of `data_dir` to express each data directory, we could instead provide a single line with comma-separated values. Without having access to loop iteration data, this would be difficult, but in using this data, it can be fairly easy. For the sake of simplicity, this example assumes a trailing comma after the last item is allowed and that white-space (newlines) between items are also allowed:

```
# data dirs
{% for dir in data_dirs if dir != "/" %}
{% if loop.first %}
data_dir = {{ dir }},
{% else %}
        {{ dir }},
{% endif %}
{% else %}
# no data dirs found
{% endfor %}
```

The preceding example made use of the `loop.first` variable in order to determine if it needed to render the `data_dir =` part or if it just needed to render the appropriately spaced padded directory. By using a filter in the `for` statement, we get a correct value for `loop.first`, even if the first item in `data_dirs` is the undesired (`/`). To test this, we'll once again modify `demo.j2` with the updated template and modify `template-demo.yaml` to define some `data_dirs`, including one of `/` that should be filtered out:

```
---
- name: demo the template
  hosts: localhost
  gather_facts: false
  vars:
    data_dirs: ['/', '/foo', '/bar']
  tasks:
    - name: pause with render
      pause:
        prompt: "{{ lookup('template', 'demo.j2') }}"
```

Now, we can execute the playbook and see our rendered content:

```
● ● ●                    2. jkeating@serenity-2: ~/src/mastery (zsh)
~/src/mastery> ansible-playbook -i mastery-hosts template-demo.yml -vv
No config file found; using defaults

PLAYBOOK: template-demo.yml *********************************************
1 plays in template-demo.yml

PLAY [demo the template] ***********************************************

TASK [pause with render] ***********************************************
task path: /Users/jkeating/src/mastery/template-demo.yml:10
[pause with render]
# data dirs
data_dir = /foo,
           /bar,
:
ok: [localhost] => {"changed": false, "delta": 1, "rc": 0, "start": "2016-12-29
12:25:58.276128", "stderr": "", "stdout": "Paused for 0.02 minutes", "stop": "20
16-12-29 12:25:59.753653", "user_input": ""}

PLAY RECAP *************************************************************
localhost                  : ok=1     changed=0    unreachable=0    failed=0

~/src/mastery> _
```

If in the preceding example trailing commas were not allowed, we could utilize inline `if` statements to determine if we're done with the loop and render commas correctly, as shown in the following example:

```
# data dirs.
{% for dir in data_dirs if dir != "/" %}
{% if loop.first %}
data_dir = {{ dir }}{{ ',' if not loop.last else '' }}
{% else %}
           {{ dir }}{{ ',' if not loop.last else '' }}
{% endif %}
{% else %}
# no data dirs found
{% endfor %}
```

Using inline `if` statements allows us to construct a template that will only render a comma if there are more items in the loop that passed our initial filter. Once more, we'll update `demo.j2` with the earlier content and execute the playbook:

```
 ● ● ●              2. jkeating@serenity-2: ~/src/mastery (zsh)
~/src/mastery> ansible-playbook -i mastery-hosts template-demo.yml -vv
No config file found; using defaults

PLAYBOOK: template-demo.yml *********************************************
1 plays in template-demo.yml

PLAY [demo the template] ***********************************************

TASK [pause with render] ***********************************************
task path: /Users/jkeating/src/mastery/template-demo.yml:10
[pause with render]
# data dirs
data_dir = /foo,
           /bar
:
ok: [localhost] => {"changed": false, "delta": 0, "rc": 0, "start": "2016-12-29
12:28:02.531782", "stderr": "", "stdout": "Paused for 0.02 minutes", "stop": "20
16-12-29 12:28:03.479376", "user_input": ""}

PLAY RECAP *************************************************************
localhost                  : ok=1    changed=0    unreachable=0    failed=0

~/src/mastery> _
```

Macros

The astute reader will have noticed that in the previous example, we had some repeated code. Repeating code is the enemy of any developer and thankfully, Jinja2 has a way to help! A macro is like a function in a regular programming language; it's a way to define a reusable idiom. A macro is defined inside a `{% macro ... %}` ... `{% endmacro %}` block and has a name and can take zero or more arguments. Code within a macro does not inherit the namespace of the block calling the macro, so all arguments must be explicitly passed in. Macros are called within mustache blocks by name and with zero or more arguments passed in via parentheses. Let's create a simple macro named `comma` to take the place of our repeating code:

```
{% macro comma(loop) %}
{{ ',' if not loop.last else '' }}
{%- endmacro -%}
# data dirs.
{% for dir in data_dirs if dir != "/" %}
{% if loop.first %}
data_dir = {{ dir }}{{ comma(loop) }}
{% else %}
          {{ dir }}{{ comma(loop) }}
{% endif %}
{% else %}
# no data dirs found
{% endfor %}
```

Calling `comma` and passing it in the `loop` object allows the macro to examine the loop and decide if a comma should be emitted or not. You may have noticed some special marks on the `endmacro` line. These marks, the (–) next to the (%), instructs Jinja2 to strip the whitespace before and right after the block. This allows us to have a newline between the macro and the start of the template for readability without actually rendering that newline when evaluating the template.

Macro variables

Macros have access inside them to any positional or keyword argument passed along when calling the macro. Positional arguments are arguments that are assigned to variables based on the order they are provided, while keyword arguments are unordered and explicitly assign data to variable names. Keyword arguments can also have a default value if they aren't defined when the macro is called. Three additional special variables are available:

- `varargs`
- `kwargs`
- `caller`

The `varargs` variable is a holding place for additional unexpected positional arguments passed along to the macro. These positional argument values will make up the `varargs` list.

The `kwargs` variable is same as `varargs`; however, instead of holding extra positional argument values, it will hold a hash of extra keyword arguments and their associated values.

The `caller` variable can be used to call back to a higher level macro that may have called this macro (yes, macros can call other macros).

In addition to these three special variables are a number of variables that expose internal details regarding the macro itself. These are a bit complicated, but we'll walk through their usage one by one. First, let's take a look at a short description of each variable:

- `name`: The name of the macro itself
- `arguments`: A tuple of the names of the arguments the macro accepts
- `defaults`: A tuple of the default values
- `catch_kwargs`: A Boolean that will be defined as true if the macro accesses (and thus accepts) the `kwargs` variable
- `catch_varargs`: A Boolean that will be defined as true if the macro accesses (and thus accepts) the `varargs` variable
- `caller`: A Boolean that will be defined as true if the macro accesses the `caller` variable (and thus may be called from another macro)

Similar to a class in Python, these variables need to be referenced via the name of the macro itself. Attempting to access these macros without prepending the name will result in undefined variables. Now, let's walk through and demonstrate the usage of each of them.

name

The `name` variable is actually very simple. It just provides a way to access the name of the macro as a variable, perhaps for further manipulation, or usage. The following template includes a macro that references the name of the macro in order to render it in the output:

```
{% macro test() %}
{{ test.name }}
{%- endmacro -%}
{{ test() }}
```

If we were to update `demo.j2` with this template and execute the `template-demo.yaml` playbook, the output would be:

```
● ● ●                    2. jkeating@serenity-2: ~/src/mastery (zsh)
~/src/mastery> ansible-playbook -i mastery-hosts template-demo.yml -vv
No config file found; using defaults

PLAYBOOK: template-demo.yml ********************************************
1 plays in template-demo.yml


PLAY [demo the template] **********************************************

TASK [pause with render] **********************************************
task path: /Users/jkeating/src/mastery/template-demo.yml:10
[pause with render]
test
:
ok: [localhost] => {"changed": false, "delta": 3, "rc": 0, "start": "2016-12-29
12:29:46.635609", "stderr": "", "stdout": "Paused for 0.06 minutes", "stop": "20
16-12-29 12:29:50.121284", "user_input": ""}


PLAY RECAP ***********************************************************
localhost                  : ok=1    changed=0    unreachable=0    failed=0

~/src/mastery>
```

arguments

The `arguments` variable is a tuple of the arguments the macro accepts. These are the explicitly defined arguments, not the special `kwargs` or `varargs`. Our previous example would have rendered an empty tuple `()`, so lets modify it to get something else:

```
{% macro test(var_a='a string') %}
{{ test.arguments }}
{%- endmacro -%}
{{ test() }}
```

Rendering this template will result in the following:

```
2. jkeating@serenity-2: ~/src/mastery (zsh)
~/src/mastery> ansible-playbook -i mastery-hosts template-demo.yml -vv
No config file found; using defaults

PLAYBOOK: template-demo.yml ***********************************************
1 plays in template-demo.yml

PLAY [demo the template] **************************************************

TASK [pause with render] *************************************************
task path: /Users/jkeating/src/mastery/template-demo.yml:10
[pause with render]
('var_a',)
:
ok: [localhost] => {"changed": false, "delta": 1, "rc": 0, "start": "2016-12-29
12:31:39.042984", "stderr": "", "stdout": "Paused for 0.02 minutes", "stop": "20
16-12-29 12:31:40.090304", "user_input": ""}

PLAY RECAP ***************************************************************
localhost                  : ok=1    changed=0    unreachable=0    failed=0

~/src/mastery> _
```

defaults

The `defaults` variable is a tuple of the default values for any keyword arguments the macro explicitly accepts. Let's change our macro to display the default values as well as the arguments:

```
{% macro test(var_a='a string') %}
{{ test.arguments }}
{{ test.defaults }}
{%- endmacro -%}
{{ test() }}
```

Rendering this version of the template will result in the following:

```
● ● ●                    2. jkeating@serenity-2: ~/src/mastery,(zsh)
~/src/mastery> ansible-playbook -i mastery-hosts template-demo.yml -vv
No config file found; using defaults

PLAYBOOK: template-demo.yml ***********************************************
1 plays in template-demo.yml

PLAY [demo the template] **************************************************

TASK [pause with render] *************************************************
task path: /Users/jkeating/src/mastery/template-demo.yml:10
[pause with render]
('var_a',)
('a string',)
:
ok: [localhost] => {"changed": false, "delta": 0, "rc": 0, "start": "2016-12-29
12:32:34.676897", "stderr": "", "stdout": "Paused for 0.01 minutes", "stop": "20
16-12-29 12:32:35.302267", "user_input": ""}

PLAY RECAP ***************************************************************
localhost                  : ok=1    changed=0    unreachable=0    failed=0

~/src/mastery> _
```

catch_kwargs

This variable is only defined if the macro itself accesses the `kwargs` variable in order to catch any extra keyword arguments that might have been passed along. Without accessing the `kwargs` variable, any extra keyword arguments in a call to the macro will result in an error when rendering the template. Likewise, accessing `catch_kwargs` without also accessing `kwargs` will result in an undefined error. Let's modify our example template again so that we can pass along extra `kwargs`:

```
{% macro test() %}
{{ kwargs }}
{{ test.catch_kwargs }}
{%- endmacro -%}
{{ test(unexpected='surprise') }}
```

The rendered version of this template will be:

```
                    2. jkeating@serenity-2: ~/src/mastery (zsh)
~/src/mastery> ansible-playbook -i mastery-hosts template-demo.yml -vv
No config file found; using defaults

PLAYBOOK: template-demo.yml ************************************************
1 plays in template-demo.yml

PLAY [demo the template] **************************************************

TASK [pause with render] *************************************************
task path: /Users/jkeating/src/mastery/template-demo.yml:10
[pause with render]
{'unexpected': 'surprise'}
True
:
ok: [localhost] => {"changed": false, "delta": 1, "rc": 0, "start": "2016-12-29
12:34:04.684260", "stderr": "", "stdout": "Paused for 0.02 minutes", "stop": "20
16-12-29 12:34:05.844906", "user_input": ""}

PLAY RECAP ***************************************************************
localhost                  : ok=1    changed=0    unreachable=0    failed=0

~/src/mastery> 
```

catch_varargs

Much like `catch_kwargs`, this variable exists if the macro accesses the `varargs` variable. Modifying our example once more, we can see this in action:

```
{% macro test() %}
{{ varargs }}
{{ test.catch_varargs }}
{%- endmacro -%}
{{ test('surprise') }}
```

The template's rendered result will be:

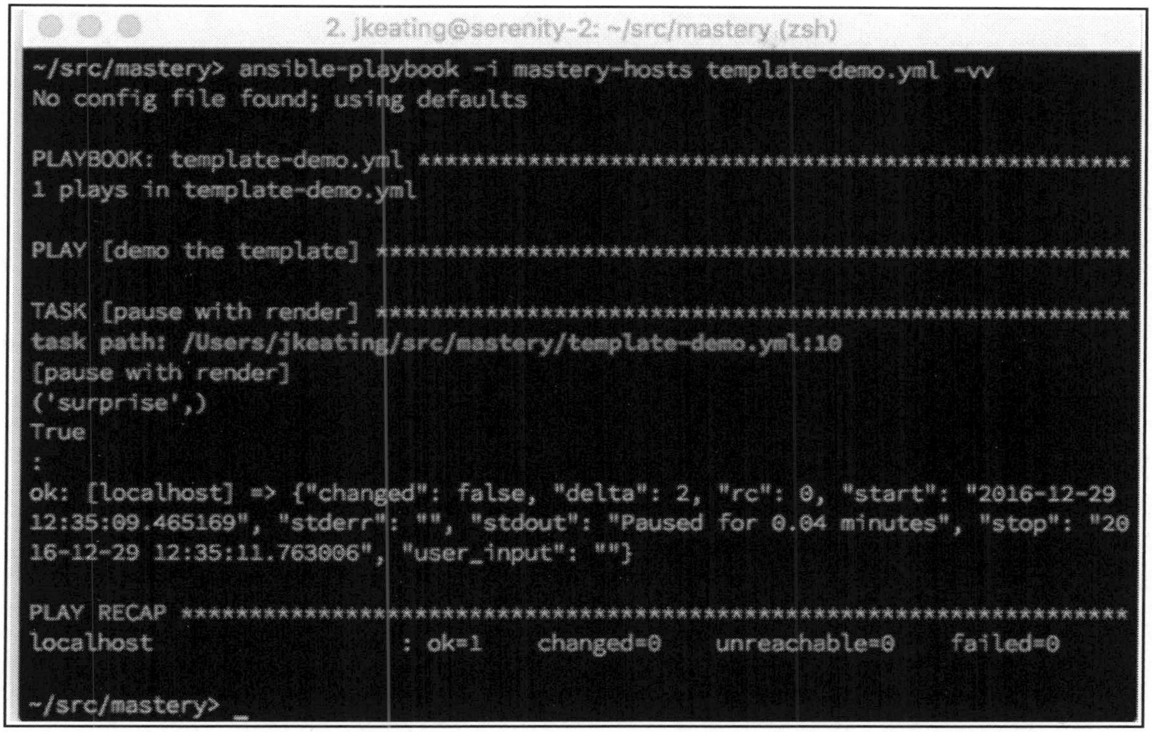
2. jkeating@serenity-2: ~/src/mastery (zsh)
~/src/mastery> ansible-playbook -i mastery-hosts template-demo.yml -vv
No config file found; using defaults
PLAYBOOK: template-demo.yml ***
1 plays in template-demo.yml
PLAY [demo the template] **
TASK [pause with render] **
task path: /Users/jkeating/src/mastery/template-demo.yml:10
[pause with render]
('surprise',)
True
:
ok: [localhost] => {"changed": false, "delta": 2, "rc": 0, "start": "2016-12-29 12:35:09.465169", "stderr": "", "stdout": "Paused for 0.04 minutes", "stop": "2016-12-29 12:35:11.763006", "user_input": ""}
PLAY RECAP **
localhost : ok=1 changed=0 unreachable=0 failed=0
~/src/mastery> _

caller

The `caller` variable takes a bit more explaining. A macro can call out to another macro. This can be useful if the same chunk of the template will be used multiple times, but part of the inside changes more than what could easily be passed as a macro parameter. The `Caller` variable isn't exactly a variable; it's more of a reference back to the call in order to get the contents of that calling macro. Let's update our template to demonstrate the usage:

```
{% macro test() %}
The text from the caller follows:
{{ caller() }}
{%- endmacro -%}
{% call test() %}
This is text inside the call
{% endcall %}
```

The rendered result will be:

```
● ● ●                    2. jkeating@serenity-2: ~/src/mastery (zsh)
~/src/mastery> ansible-playbook -i mastery-hosts template-demo.yml -vv
No config file found; using defaults

PLAYBOOK: template-demo.yml ***********************************************
1 plays in template-demo.yml

PLAY [demo the template] **************************************************

TASK [pause with render] *************************************************
task path: /Users/jkeating/src/mastery/template-demo.yml:10
[pause with render]
The text from caller follows:
This is text inside the call
:
ok: [localhost] => {"changed": false, "delta": 0, "rc": 0, "start": "2016-12-29
12:36:47.172805", "stderr": "", "stdout": "Paused for 0.01 minutes", "stop": "20
16-12-29 12:36:48.056495", "user_input": ""}

PLAY RECAP ***************************************************************
localhost                  : ok=1    changed=0    unreachable=0    failed=0

~/src/mastery> _
```

A call to a macro can still pass arguments to that macro; any combination of arguments or keyword arguments can be passed. If the macro utilizes `varargs` or `kwargs`, then extras of those can be passed along, as well. Additionally, a macro can pass arguments back to the caller, too! To demonstrate this, let's create a larger example. This time, our example will generate out a file suitable for an Ansible inventory:

```
{% macro test(group, hosts) %}
[{{ group }}]
{% for host in hosts %}
{{ host }} {{ caller(host) }}
{%- endfor %}
{%- endmacro -%}
{% call(host) test('web', ['host1', 'host2', 'host3']) %}
ssh_host_name={{ host }}.example.name ansible_sudo=true
{% endcall %}
{% call(host) test('db', ['db1', 'db2']) %}
ssh_host_name={{ host }}.example.name
{% endcall %}
```

Once rendered, the result will be:

```
● ● ●                    2. jkeating@serenity-2: ~/src/mastery (zsh)
~/src/mastery> ansible-playbook -i mastery-hosts template-demo.yml -vv
No config file found; using defaults

PLAYBOOK: template-demo.yml ********************************************************
1 plays in template-demo.yml

PLAY [demo the template] **********************************************************

TASK [pause with render] *********************************************************
task path: /Users/jkeating/src/mastery/template-demo.yml:10
[pause with render]
[web]
host1 ssh_host_name=host1.example.name ansible_sudo=true
host2 ssh_host_name=host2.example.name ansible_sudo=true
host3 ssh_host_name=host3.example.name ansible_sudo=true

[db]
db1 ssh_host_name=db1.example.name
db2 ssh_host_name=db2.example.name
:
ok: [localhost] => {"changed": false, "delta": 2, "rc": 0, "start": "2016-12-29
12:39:16.647766", "stderr": "", "stdout": "Paused for 0.04 minutes", "stop": "20
16-12-29 12:39:19.016156", "user_input": ""}

PLAY RECAP ************************************************************************
localhost                  : ok=1    changed=0    unreachable=0    failed=0

~/src/mastery> _
```

We called the `test` macro twice, once per each group we wanted to define. Each group had a subtly different set of host variables to apply, and those were defined in the call itself. We saved typing by having the macro call back to the caller, passing along the host from the current loop.

Control blocks provide programming power inside of templates, allowing template authors to make their templates efficient. The efficiency isn't necessarily in the initial draft of the template; instead, the efficiency really comes into play when a small change to a repeating value is needed.

Data manipulation

While control structures influence the flow of template processing, another tool exists to modify the contents of a variable. This tool is called a **filter**. Filters are same as small functions, or methods, that can be run on the variable. Some filters operate without arguments, some take optional arguments, and some require arguments. Filters can be chained together, as well, where the result of one filter action is fed into the next filter and the next. Jinja2 comes with many built-in filters, and Ansible extends these with many custom filters available to you when using Jinja2 within templates, tasks, or any other place Ansible allows templating.

Syntax

A filter is applied to a variable by way of the pipe symbol (|) followed by the name of the filter and then any arguments for the filter inside parentheses. There can be a space between the variable name and the pipe symbol as well as a space between the pipe symbol and the filter name. For example, if we wanted to apply the filter `lower` (which makes all the characters lowercase) to the variable `my_word`, we would use the following syntax:

```
{{ my_word | lower }}
```

Because the lower filter does not take any arguments, it is not necessary to attach an empty parentheses set to it. If we use a different filter, one that requires arguments, we can see how that looks. Let's use the `replace` filter, which allows us to replace all occurrences of a substring with another substring. In this example, we want to replace all occurrences of the substring `no` with `yes` in the variable `answers`:

```
{{ answers | replace('no', 'yes') }}
```

Applying multiple filters is accomplished by simply adding more pipe symbols and more filter names. Let's combine both `replace` and `lower` to demonstrate the syntax:

```
{{ answers | replace('no', 'yes') | lower }}
```

We can easily demonstrate this with a simple play that uses the `debug` command to render the line:

```
---
- name: demo the template
  hosts: localhost
  gather_facts: false
  tasks:
    - name: debug the template
```

```
debug:
    msg: "{{ answers | replace('no', 'yes') | lower }}"
```

Now, we can execute the playbook and provide a value for `answers` at run time:

```
2. jkeating@serenity-2: ~/src/mastery (zsh)
~/src/mastery> ansible-playbook -i mastery-hosts template-demo.yml -vv -e "answe
rs='no so yes no'"
No config file found; using defaults

PLAYBOOK: template-demo.yml ***********************************************
1 plays in template-demo.yml

PLAY [demo the template] **************************************************

TASK [debug the template] ************************************************
task path: /Users/jkeating/src/mastery/template-demo.yml:7
ok: [localhost] => {
    "msg": "yes so yes yes"
}

PLAY RECAP ***************************************************************
localhost                  : ok=1    changed=0    unreachable=0    failed=0

~/src/mastery>
```

Useful built-in filters

A full list of the filters built into Jinja2 can be found in the Jinja2 documentation. At the time of writing this book, there are over 45 built-in filters, too many to describe here. Instead, we'll take a look at some of the more commonly used filters.

default

The `default` filter is a way to provide a default value for an otherwise undefined variable, which will prevent Ansible from generating an error. It is shorthand for a complex `if` statement checking if a variable is defined before trying to use it, with an `else` clause to provide a different value. Let's look at two examples that render the same thing. One will use the `if/else` structure while the other uses the `default` filter:

```
{% if some_variable is defined %}
{{ some_variable }}
{% else %}
default_value
{% endif %}
{{ some_variable | default('default_value') }}
```

The rendered result of each of these examples is the same; however, the example using the `default` filter is much quicker to write and easier to read.

While `default` is very useful, proceed with caution if you are using the same variable in multiple locations. Changing a default value can become a hassle, and it may be more efficient to define the variable with a default at the play or role level.

count

The `count` filter will return the length of a sequence or hash. In fact, `length` is an alias of `count` to accomplish the same thing. This filter can be useful for performing any sort of math around the size of a set of hosts or any other case where the count of some set needs to be known. Let's create an example where we set a `max_threads` configuration entry to match the count of hosts in the play:

```
max_threads: {{ play_hosts | count }}
```

random

The `random` filter is used to make a random selection from a sequence. Let's use this filter to delegate a task to a random selection from the `db_servers` group:

```
- name: backup the database
  shell: mysqldump -u root nova > /data/nova.backup.sql
  delegate_to: "{{ groups['db_servers'] | random }}"
  run_once: true
```

round

The round filter exists to round a number. This can be useful if you need to perform floating-point math and then turn the result into a rounded integer. The round filter takes optional arguments to define a precision (default of 0) and a rounding method. The possible rounding methods are common (rounds up or down, the default), ceil (always round up), and floor (always round down). In this example, we'll chain two filters together to commonly round a math result to zero precision and then turn that into an int:

```
{{ math_result | round | int }}
```

Useful Ansible provided custom filters

While there are many provided filters with Jinja2, Ansible includes some additional filters that playbook authors may find particularly useful. We'll outline a few of them here.

Filters related to task status

Ansible tracks task data for each task. This data is used to determine if a task has failed, resulted in a change, or was skipped all together. Playbook authors can register the results of a task and then use filters to easily check the task status. These are most often used in conditionals with later tasks. The filters are aptly named failed, success, changed, and skipped. They each return a Boolean value. Here is a playbook that demonstrates the use of a couple of these:

```
---
- name: demo the filters
  hosts: localhost
  gather_facts: false
  tasks:
    - name: fail a task
      debug:
        msg: "I am not a change"
      register: derp
    - name: only do this on change
      debug:
        msg: "You had a change"
      when: derp | changed
    - name: only do this on success
      debug:
        msg: "You had a success"
      when: derp | success
```

The output is as shown in the following screenshot:

```
●  ●  ●                  2. jkeating@serenity-2: ~/src/mastery (zsh)
~/src/mastery> ansible-playbook -i mastery-hosts template-demo.yml -vv
No config file found; using defaults

PLAYBOOK: template-demo.yml ******************************************************
1 plays in template-demo.yml

PLAY [demo the filters] *********************************************************

TASK [fail a task] **************************************************************
task path: /Users/jkeating/src/mastery/template-demo.yml:7
ok: [localhost] => {
    "msg": "I am not a change"
}

TASK [only do this on change] ***************************************************
task path: /Users/jkeating/src/mastery/template-demo.yml:12
skipping: [localhost] => {"changed": false, "skip_reason": "Conditional check fa
iled", "skipped": true}

TASK [only do this on success] **************************************************
task path: /Users/jkeating/src/mastery/template-demo.yml:17
ok: [localhost] => {
    "msg": "You had a success"
}

PLAY RECAP **********************************************************************
localhost                  : ok=2    changed=0    unreachable=0    failed=0

~/src/mastery> _
```

shuffle

Similar to the `random` filter, the `shuffle` filter can be used to produce randomized results. Unlike the `random` filter, which selects one random choice from a list, the `shuffle` filter will shuffle the items in a sequence and return the full sequence back:

```
---
- name: demo the filters
  hosts: localhost
```

```
    gather_facts: false
    tasks:
      - name: shuffle the cards
        debug:
          msg: "{{ ['Ace', 'Queen', 'King', 'Deuce'] | shuffle }}"
```

The output is as shown in the following screenshot:

```
2. jkeating@serenity-2: ~/src/mastery (zsh)
~/src/mastery> ansible-playbook -i mastery-hosts template-demo.yml -vv
No config file found; using defaults

PLAYBOOK: template-demo.yml *************************************************
1 plays in template-demo.yml

PLAY [demo the filters] *****************************************************

TASK [shuffle the cards] ****************************************************
task path: /Users/jkeating/src/mastery/template-demo.yml:7
ok: [localhost] => {
    "msg": [
        "Ace",
        "Queen",
        "Deuce",
        "King"
    ]
}

PLAY RECAP ******************************************************************
localhost                  : ok=1    changed=0    unreachable=0    failed=0

~/src/mastery>
```

Filters dealing with path names

Configuration management and orchestration frequently refers to path names, but often only part of the path is desired. Ansible provides a few filters to help.

basename

To obtain the last part of a file path, use the `basename` filter. For example:

```
---
- name: demo the filters
  hosts: localhost
  gather_facts: false
  tasks:
    - name: demo basename
      debug:
        msg: "{{ '/var/log/nova/nova-api.log' | basename }}"
```

The output is as shown in the following screenshot:

```
2. jkeating@serenity-2: ~/src/mastery (zsh)
~/src/mastery> ansible-playbook -i mastery-hosts template-demo.yml -vv
No config file found; using defaults

PLAYBOOK: template-demo.yml ****************************************************
1 plays in template-demo.yml

PLAY [demo the filters] ********************************************************

TASK [demo basename] **********************************************************
task path: /Users/jkeating/src/mastery/template-demo.yml:7
ok: [localhost] => {
    "msg": "nova-api.log"
}

PLAY RECAP ********************************************************************
localhost                  : ok=1    changed=0    unreachable=0    failed=0

~/src/mastery> _
```

dirname

The inverse of `basename` is `dirname`. Instead of returning the final part of a path, `dirname` will return everything except the final part. Let's change our previous play to use `dirname` and run it again:

```
2. jkeating@serenity-2: ~/src/mastery (zsh)
~/src/mastery> ansible-playbook -i mastery-hosts template-demo.yml -vv
No config file found; using defaults

PLAYBOOK: template-demo.yml ********************************************************
1 plays in template-demo.yml

PLAY [demo the filters] ********************************************************

TASK [demo basename] ********************************************************
task path: /Users/jkeating/src/mastery/template-demo.yml:7
ok: [localhost] => {
    "msg": "/var/log/nova"
}

PLAY RECAP ********************************************************
localhost                  : ok=1    changed=0    unreachable=0    failed=0

~/src/mastery> _
```

expanduser

Often, paths to various things are supplied with a user shortcut, such as `~/.stackrc`. However some uses may require the full path to the file. Rather than the complicated `command` and `register` calls, the `expanduser` filter provides a way to expand the path to the full definition. In this example, the user name is `jkeating`:

```
---
- name: demo the filters
  hosts: localhost
  gather_facts: false
  tasks:
    - name: demo filter
      debug:
        msg: "{{ '~/.stackrc' | expanduser }}"
```

The output is as shown in the following screenshot:

```
2. jkeating@serenity-2: ~/src/mastery (zsh)
~/src/mastery> ansible-playbook -i mastery-hosts template-demo.yml -vv
No config file found; using defaults

PLAYBOOK: template-demo.yml **********************************************
1 plays in template-demo.yml

PLAY [demo the filters] **************************************************

TASK [demo filter] ******************************************************
task path: /Users/jkeating/src/mastery/template-demo.yml:7
ok: [localhost] => {
    "msg": "/Users/jkeating/.stackrc"
}

PLAY RECAP **************************************************************
localhost                  : ok=1    changed=0    unreachable=0    failed=0

~/src/mastery>
```

Base64 encoding

When reading content from remote hosts, same as with the `slurp` module (used to read file content from remote hosts into a variable), the content will be `Base64` encoded. To decode such content, Ansible provides a `b64decode` filter. Similarly, if running a task that requires `Base64` encoded input, regular strings can be encoded with the `b64encode` filter.

Let's read content from the file `derp`:

```
---
- name: demo the filters
  hosts: localhost
  gather_facts: false
  tasks:
    - name: read file
      slurp:
        src: derp
      register: derp
    - name: display file content (undecoded)
      debug:
```

```
    var: derp.content
  - name: display file content (decoded)
    debug:
      var: derp.content | b64decode
```

The output is as shown in the following screenshot:

```
● ● ●              2. jkeating@serenity-2: ~/src/mastery (zsh)
~/src/mastery> ansible-playbook -i mastery-hosts template-demo.yml -vv
No config file found; using defaults

PLAYBOOK: template-demo.yml *****************************************************
1 plays in template-demo.yml

PLAY [demo the filters] ********************************************************

TASK [read file] **************************************************************
task path: /Users/jkeating/src/mastery/template-demo.yml:7
ok: [localhost] => {"changed": false, "content": "SSBhbSBhIG1vZGVybiBtYWpvciBnZW
5lcmFsLgo=", "encoding": "base64", "source": "derp"}

TASK [display file content (undecoded)] ****************************************
task path: /Users/jkeating/src/mastery/template-demo.yml:12
ok: [localhost] => {
    "derp.content": "SSBhbSBhIG1vZGVybiBtYWpvciBnZW5lcmFsLgo="
}

TASK [display file content (decoded)] ******************************************
task path: /Users/jkeating/src/mastery/template-demo.yml:16
ok: [localhost] => {
    "derp.content | b64decode": "I am a modern major general.\n"
}

PLAY RECAP ********************************************************************
localhost                  : ok=3    changed=0    unreachable=0    failed=0

~/src/mastery>
```

Searching for content

It is fairly common in Ansible to search a string for a substring. In particular, the common administrator task of running a command and grepping the output for a particular key piece of data is a reoccurring construct in many playbooks. While it's possible to replicate this with a `shell` task to execute a command and pipe the output into `grep` and use careful handling of `failed_when` to catch `grep` exit codes, a far better strategy is to use a `command` task, `register` the output, and then utilize Ansible provided regex filters in later conditionals. Let's look at two examples, one using the `shell`, `pipe`, `grep` method and another using the `search` filter:

```
- name: check database version
  shell: neutron-manage current |grep juno
  register: neutron_db_ver
  failed_when: false
- name: upgrade db
  command: neutron-manage db_sync
  when: neutron_db_ver|failed
```

The preceding example works by forcing Ansible to always see the task as successful, but assumes that if the exit code from the shell is non-zero then the string `juno` was not found in the output of the `neutron-manage` command. This construct is functional, but a bit clunky, and could mask real errors from the command. Let's try again using the `search` filter:

```
- name: check database version
  command: neutron-manage current
  register: neutron_db_ver
- name: upgrade db
  command: neutron-manage db_sync
  when: not neutron_db_ver.stdout | search('juno')
```

This version is much cleaner to follow and does not mask errors from the first task.

The `search` filter searches a string and will return `True` if the substring is found anywhere within the input string. If an exact complete match is desired instead, the `match` filter can be used. Full Python regex syntax can be utilized inside the `search`/`match` string.

Omitting undefined arguments

The `omit` variable takes a bit of explaining. Sometimes, when iterating over a hash of data to construct task arguments, it may be necessary to only provide some arguments for some of the items in the hash. Even though Jinja2 supports in-line `if` statements to conditionally render parts of a line, this does not work well in an Ansible task. Traditionally, playbook authors would create multiple tasks, one for each set of potential arguments passed in, and use conditionals to sort the loop members between each task set. A recently added magic variable named `omit` solves this problem when used in conjunction with the `default` filter. The `omit` variable will remove the argument the variable was used with all together.

To illustrate how this works, let's consider a scenario where we need to install a set of Python packages with `pip`. Some of the packages have a specific version while others do not. These packages are in a list of hashes named `pips`. Each hash has a `name` key and potentially a `ver` key. Our first example utilizes two different tasks to complete the installs:

```
- name: install pips with versions
  pip: name={{ item.name }} version={{ item.ver }}
  with_items: pips
  when: item.ver is defined
- name: install pips without versions
  pip: name={{ item.name }}
  with_items: pips
  when: item.ver is undefined
```

This construct works, but the loop is iterated twice and some of the iterations will be skipped in each task. This next example collapses the two tasks into one and utilizes the `omit` variable:

```
- name: install pips
  pip: name={{ item.name }} version={{ item.ver | default(omit) }}
  with_items: pips
```

This example is shorter, cleaner, and doesn't generate extra skipped tasks.

Python object methods

Jinja2 is a Python-based template engine. Because of this, Python object methods are available within templates. Object methods are methods, or functions, that are directly accessible by the variable object (typically a `string`, `list`, `int`, or `float`). A good way to think about this is if you were writing Python code and could write the variable, then a period, then a method call, and then you would have access to do the same in Jinja2. Within Ansible, only methods that return modified content or a Boolean are typically used. Let's explore some common object methods that might be useful in Ansible.

String methods

String methods can be used to return new strings or a list of strings modified in some way, or to test the string for various conditions and return a Boolean. Some useful methods are as follows:

- `endswith`: Determines if the string ends with a substring
- `startswith`: Same as `endswith`, but from the start
- `split`: Splits the string on characters (default is space) into a list of substrings
- `rsplit`: The same as split, but starts from the end of the string and works backwards
- `splitlines`: Splits the string at newlines into a list of substrings
- `upper`: Returns a copy of the string all in uppercase
- `lower`: Returns a copy of the string all in lowercase
- `capitalize`: Returns a copy of the string with just the first character in uppercase

We can create a simple play that will utilize some of these methods in a single task:

```
---
- name: demo the filters
  hosts: localhost
  gather_facts: false
  tasks:
    - name: string methods
      debug:
        msg: "{{ 'foo bar baz'.upper().split() }}"
```

The output is as shown in the following screenshot:

```
●  ●  ●                    2. jkeating@serenity-2: ~/src/mastery (zsh)
~/src/mastery> ansible-playbook -i mastery-hosts template-demo.yml -vv
No config file found; using defaults

PLAYBOOK: template-demo.yml ************************************************
1 plays in template-demo.yml

PLAY [demo the filters] ****************************************************

TASK [string methods] *****************************************************
task path: /Users/jkeating/src/mastery/template-demo.yml:7
ok: [localhost] => {
    "msg": [
        "FOO",
        "BAR",
        "BAZ"
    ]
}

PLAY RECAP *****************************************************************
localhost                  : ok=1    changed=0    unreachable=0    failed=0

~/src/mastery> _
```

Because these are object methods, we need to access them with dot notation rather than as a filter via (|).

List methods

Only a couple methods do something other than modify the list in-place rather than returning a new list, and they are as follows:

- `Index`: Returns the first index position of a provided value
- `Count`: Counts the items in the list

int and float methods

Most `int` and `float` methods are not useful for Ansible.

Sometimes, our variables are not exactly in the format we want them in. However, instead of defining more and more variables that slightly modify the same content, we can make use of Jinja2 filters to do the manipulation for us in the various places that require that modification. This allows us to stay efficient with the definition of our data, preventing many duplicate variables and tasks that may have to be changed later.

Comparing values

Comparisons are used in many places with Ansible. Task conditionals are comparisons. Jinja2 control structures often use comparisons. Some filters use comparisons, as well. To master Ansible's usage of Jinja2, it is important to understand which comparisons are available.

Comparisons

Like most languages, Jinja2 comes equipped with the standard set of comparison expressions you would expect, which will render a Boolean `true` or `false`.

The expressions in Jinja2 are as follows:

Expression	Definition
==	Compares two objects for equality
!=	Compares two objects for inequality
>	True if the left-hand side is greater than the right-hand side
<	True if the left-hand side is less than the right- hand side
>=	True if the left-hand side is greater than or equal to the right-hand side
<=	True if the left-hand side is less than or equal to the right-hand side

Logic

Logic helps group two or more comparisons together. Each comparison is referred to as an operand:

- And: Returns `true` if the left and the right operand are true
- Or: Returns `true` if the left or the right operand is true
- Not: Negates an operand
- (): Wraps a set of operands together to form a larger operand

Tests

A test in Jinja2 is used to see if a value is something. In fact, the `is` operator is used to initiate a test. Tests are used any place a Boolean result is desired, such as with `if` expressions and task conditionals. There are many built-in tests, but we'll highlight a few of the particularly useful ones:

- Defined: Returns `true` if the variable is defined
- Undefined: The opposite of defined
- None: Returns `true` if the variable is defined, but the value is none
- Even: Returns `true` if the number is divisible by 2
- odd: Returns `true` if the number is not divisible by 2

To test if a value is not something, simply use `is not`.

We can create a playbook that will demonstrate some of these value comparisons:

```
---
- name: demo the logic
  hosts: localhost
  gather_facts: false
  vars:
    num1: 10
    num3: 10
  tasks:
    - name: logic and comparison
      debug:
        msg: "Can you read me?"
      when: num1 >= num3 and num1 is even and num2 is not defined
```

The output is as shown in the following screenshot:

```
                2. jkeating@serenity-2: ~/src/mastery (zsh)
~/src/mastery> ansible-playbook -i mastery-hosts template-demo.yml -vv
No config file found; using defaults

PLAYBOOK: template-demo.yml ***********************************************
1 plays in template-demo.yml

PLAY [demo the logic] *****************************************************

TASK [logic and comparison] ***********************************************
task path: /Users/jkeating/src/mastery/template-demo.yml:11
ok: [localhost] => {
    "msg": "Can you read me?"
}

PLAY RECAP ****************************************************************
localhost                  : ok=1     changed=0    unreachable=0    failed=0

~/src/mastery> _
```

Summary

Jinja2 is a powerful language that is used by Ansible. Not only is it used to generate file content, but it is also used to make portions of playbooks dynamic. Mastering Jinja2 is vital to creating and maintaining elegant and efficient playbooks and roles.

In the next chapter, we will explore more in depth Ansible's capability to define what constitutes a change or failure for tasks within a play.

4

Controlling Task Conditions

Ansible fundamentally operates on the concept of task statuses: **ok, changed, failed**, or **skipped**. These statuses determine whether any further tasks should be executed on a host and handlers should be notified due of any changes. Tasks can also make use of conditionals that check the status of previous tasks to control operation.

In this chapter, we'll explore ways to influence Ansible when determining the task status:

- Controlling what defines a failure
- Recovering gracefully from a failure
- Controlling what defines a change

Defining a failure

Most modules that ship with Ansible have an opinion on what constitutes an error. An error condition is highly dependent upon the module and what the module is attempting to accomplish. When a module returns an error, the host will be removed from the set of available hosts, preventing any further tasks or handlers from being executed on that host. Further, the `ansible-playbook` function or Ansible execution will exit with nonzero, indicating failure. However, we are not limited by a module's opinion of what an error is. We can ignore errors or redefine the error condition.

Ignoring errors

A task condition, named `ignore_errors`, is used to ignore errors. This condition is a Boolean, meaning that the value should be something Ansible understands to be `true`, such as `yes`, `on`, `true`, or `1` (string or integer).

To demonstrate how to use `ignore_errors`, let's create a playbook named `errors.yaml`, where we attempt to query a webserver that doesn't exist. Normally, this would be an error, and if we don't define `ignore_errors`, we get the default behavior, that is, the host will be marked as failed and no further tasks will be attempted on that host. Let's take a look at the following code snippet:

```
-name: broken website
   uri:
     url: http://notahost.nodomain
```

Running the task as is will give us an error:

```
● ● ●                    2. jkeating@serenity-2: ~/src/mastery (zsh)
~/src/mastery> ansible-playbook -i mastery-hosts errors.yaml -vv
No config file found; using defaults

PLAYBOOK: errors.yaml ************************************************************
1 plays in errors.yaml


PLAY [error handling] ***********************************************************

TASK [broken website] ***********************************************************
task path: /Users/jkeating/src/mastery/errors.yaml:7
fatal: [localhost]: FAILED! => {"changed": false, "content": "", "failed": true,
 "msg": "Status code was not [200]: Request failed: <urlopen error [Errno 8] nod
ename nor servname provided, or not known>", "redirected": false, "status": -1,
"url": "http://notahost.nodomain"}
        to retry, use: --limit @/Users/jkeating/src/mastery/errors.retry


PLAY RECAP **********************************************************************
localhost                  : ok=0    changed=0    unreachable=0    failed=1

exit 2
~/src/mastery>
```

Now, let's imagine that we didn't want Ansible to stop here, and instead we wanted it to continue. We can add the `ignore_errors` condition to our task like this:

```
 - name: broken website
   uri:
     url: http://notahost.nodomain
   ignore_errors: true
```

This time when we run the playbook, our error will be ignored, as we can see here:

```
● ● ●                    2. jkeating@serenity-2: ~/src/mastery (zsh)
~/src/mastery> ansible-playbook -i mastery-hosts errors.yaml -vv
No config file found; using defaults

PLAYBOOK: errors.yaml ******************************************************
1 plays in errors.yaml

PLAY [error handling] ******************************************************

TASK [broken website] ******************************************************
task path: /Users/jkeating/src/mastery/errors.yaml:7
fatal: [localhost]: FAILED! => {"changed": false, "content": "", "failed": true,
 "msg": "Status code was not [200]: Request failed: <urlopen error [Errno 8] nod
ename nor servname provided, or not known>", "redirected": false, "status": -1,
"url": "http://notahost.nodomain"}
...ignoring

PLAY RECAP *****************************************************************
localhost                  : ok=1    changed=0    unreachable=0    failed=0

~/src/mastery> _
```

Our task error is ignored. Any further tasks for that host will still be attempted and the playbook does not register any failed hosts.

Defining an error condition

The `ignore_errors` condition is a bit of a blunt hammer. Any error generated from the module used by the task will be ignored. Further, the output, at first glance, still appears like an error, and may be confusing to an operator attempting to discover a real failure. A more subtle tool is the `failed_when` condition. This condition is more like a fine scalpel, allowing a playbook author to be very specific as to what constitutes an error for a task. This condition performs a test to generate a Boolean result, much like the `when` condition. If the condition results in a Boolean is truth, the task will be considered a failure. Otherwise, the task will be considered successful.

The `failed_when` condition is quite useful when used in combination with the `command` or `shell` module and registering the result of the execution. Many programs that are executed can have detailed nonzero exit codes that mean different things, however, these modules all consider an exit code of anything other than zero to be a failure. Let's look at the `iscsiadm` utility. This utility can be used for many things related to iSCSI. For the sake of our demonstration we'll use it to discover any active `iscsi` sessions:

```
- name: query sessions
  command: /sbin/iscsiadm -m session
  register: sessions
```

If this were to be run on a system where there were no active sessions, we'd see output like this:

```
2. jkeating@serenity-2: ~/src/mastery (zsh)

~/src/mastery> ansible-playbook -i mastery-hosts errors.yaml -vv
No config file found; using defaults

PLAYBOOK: errors.yaml ********************************************************
1 plays in errors.yaml

PLAY [error handling] *******************************************************

TASK [query sessions] *******************************************************
task path: /Users/jkeating/src/mastery/errors.yaml:7
fatal: [scsihost]: FAILED! => {"changed": true, "cmd": ["/sbin/iscsiadm", "-m",
"session"], "delta": "0:00:00.002891", "end": "2016-12-30 00:11:21.769468", "fai
led": true, "rc": 21, "start": "2016-12-30 00:11:21.766577", "stderr": "iscsiadm
: No active sessions.", "stdout": "", "stdout_lines": [], "warnings": []}
        to retry, use: --limit @/Users/jkeating/src/mastery/errors.retry

PLAY RECAP ******************************************************************
scsihost                   : ok=0    changed=0    unreachable=0    failed=1

exit 2
~/src/mastery> _
```

We can just use the ignore_errors condition, but that would mask other problems with iscsi; so, instead of this, we want to instruct Ansible that an exit code of 21 is acceptable. To that end, we can make use of the registered variable to access the rc variable, which holds the return code. We'll make use of this in a failed_when statement:

```
- name: query sessions
  command: /sbin/iscsiadm -m session
  register: sessions
  failed_when: sessions.rc not in (0, 21)
```

We simply stated that any exit code other than 0 or 21 should be considered a failure. Let's see the new output after this modification:

```
2. jkeating@serenity-2: ~/src/mastery (zsh)
~/src/mastery> ansible-playbook -i mastery-hosts errors.yaml -vv
No config file found; using defaults

PLAYBOOK: errors.yaml *******************************************************
1 plays in errors.yaml

PLAY [error handling] *******************************************************

TASK [query sessions] *******************************************************
task path: /Users/jkeating/src/mastery/errors.yaml:7
changed: [scsihost] => {"changed": true, "cmd": ["/sbin/iscsiadm", "-m", "sessio
n"], "delta": "0:00:00.003154", "end": "2016-12-30 00:13:36.504164", "failed": f
alse, "failed_when_result": false, "rc": 21, "start": "2016-12-30 00:13:36.50101
0", "stderr": "iscsiadm: No active sessions.", "stdout": "", "stdout_lines": [],
 "warnings": []}

PLAY RECAP ******************************************************************
scsihost                   : ok=1    changed=1    unreachable=0    failed=0

~/src/mastery> _
```

The output now shows no error, and, in fact, we see a new data key in the results- failed_when_result. This shows whether our failed_when statement rendered true or false, which was false in this case.

Many command-line tools do not have detailed exit codes. In fact, most typically use zero for success and one other non-zero code for all failure types. Thankfully, the failed_when statement is not just limited to the exit code of the application; it is a free form Boolean statement that can access any sort of data required. Let's look at a different problem, one involving git. We'll imagine a scenario where we want to ensure that a particular branch does not exist in a git checkout. This task assumes a git repository checked out in the /srv/app directory. The command to delete a git branch is git branch -D. Let's have a look at the following code snippet:

```
- name: delete branch bad
  command: git branch -D badfeature
  args:
    chdir: /srv/app
```

 The command and shell modules use a different format for providing module arguments. The command itself is provided a free form, while module arguments go into a args hash.

If we start with just this command, we'll get an error, an exit code of 1 if the branch does not exist:

```
2. jkeating@serenity-2: ~/src/mastery (zsh)
~/src/mastery> ansible-playbook -i mastery-hosts errors.yaml -vv
No config file found; using defaults

PLAYBOOK: errors.yaml ****************************************************
1 plays in errors.yaml

PLAY [error handling] ***************************************************

TASK [delete branch bad] ************************************************
task path: /Users/jkeating/src/mastery/errors.yaml:7
fatal: [localhost]: FAILED! => {"changed": true, "cmd": ["git", "branch", "-D",
"badfeature"], "delta": "0:00:00.021737", "end": "2016-12-29 16:17:17.590875", "
failed": true, "rc": 1, "start": "2016-12-29 16:17:17.569138", "stderr": "error:
 branch 'badfeature' not found.", "stdout": "", "stdout_lines": [], "warnings":
[]}
        to retry, use: --limit @/Users/jkeating/src/mastery/errors.retry

PLAY RECAP ************************************************************
localhost                  : ok=0    changed=0    unreachable=0    failed=1

exit 2
~/src/mastery> _
```

We're using the command module to easily demonstrate our topic despite the existence of the git module. When dealing with git repositories the git module should be used instead.

Without the failed_when and changed_when conditions, we would have to create a two-step task combo to protect ourselves from errors:

```
- name: check if branch badfeature exists
  command: git branch
  args:
    chdir: /srv/app
  register: branches
- name: delete branch bad
  command: git branch -D badfeature
  args:
    chdir: /srv/app
  when: branches.stdout | search('badfeature')
```

In the scenario where the branch doesn't exist, running these tasks looks as follows:

```
~/src/mastery> ansible-playbook -i mastery-hosts errors.yaml -vv
No config file found; using defaults

PLAYBOOK: errors.yaml **************************************************
1 plays in errors.yaml

PLAY [error handling] *************************************************

TASK [check if branch badfeature exists] *****************************
task path: /Users/jkeating/src/mastery/errors.yaml:7
changed: [localhost] => {"changed": true, "cmd": ["git", "branch"], "delta": "0:
00:00.014943", "end": "2016-12-29 16:20:38.287924", "rc": 0, "start": "2016-12-2
9 16:20:38.272981", "stderr": "", "stdout": "* master", "stdout_lines": ["* mast
er"], "warnings": []}

TASK [delete branch bad] *********************************************
task path: /Users/jkeating/src/mastery/errors.yaml:13
skipping: [localhost] => {"changed": false, "skip_reason": "Conditional check fa
iled", "skipped": true}

PLAY RECAP ***********************************************************
localhost                  : ok=1    changed=1    unreachable=0    failed=0

~/src/mastery>
```

While the task set is functional, it is not efficient. Let's improve upon this and leverage the `failed_when` functionality to reduce the two tasks into one:

```
- name: delete branch bad
  command: git branch -D badfeature
  args:
    chdir: /srv/app
  register: gitout
  failed_when:
- gitout.rc != 0
- not gitout.stderr | search('branch.*not found')
```

 Multiple conditions that would normally be joined with an `and` can instead be expressed as list elements. This can make playbooks easier to read and logic issues easier to find.

We check the command return code for anything other than 0 and then use the search filter to search the `stderr` value with a regex `branch.*not found`. We use the Jinja2 logic to combine the two conditions, which will evaluate to an inclusive `true` or `false` option:

```
● ● ●              2. jkeating@serenity-2: ~/src/mastery (zsh)
~/src/mastery> ansible-playbook -i mastery-hosts errors.yaml -vv
No config file found; using defaults

PLAYBOOK: errors.yaml ***********************************************************
1 plays in errors.yaml

PLAY [error handling] **********************************************************

TASK [delete branch bad] *******************************************************
task path: /Users/jkeating/src/mastery/errors.yaml:7
changed: [localhost] => {"changed": true, "cmd": ["git", "branch", "-D", "badfea
ture"], "delta": "0:00:00.012246", "end": "2016-12-29 16:27:47.906103", "failed"
: false, "failed_when_result": false, "rc": 1, "start": "2016-12-29 16:27:47.893
857", "stderr": "error: branch 'badfeature' not found.", "stdout": "", "stdout_l
ines": [], "warnings": []}

PLAY RECAP *********************************************************************
localhost                  : ok=1    changed=1    unreachable=0    failed=0

~/src/mastery>
```

Defining a change

Similar to defining a task failure, it is also possible to define what constitutes a changed task result. This capability is particularly useful with the command family of modules (command, shell, raw, and script). Unlike most other modules, the modules of this family do not have an inherent idea of what a change may be. In fact, unless otherwise directed, these modules *only* result in **failed, changed,** or **skipped**. There is simply no way for these modules to assume a changed condition versus unchanged.

The changed_when condition allows a playbook author to instruct a module how to interpret a change. Just like failed_when, changed_when performs a test to generate a Boolean result. Frequently, the tasks used with changed_when are commands that will exit nonzero to indicate that no work is needed to be done, so often authors will combine changed_when and failed_when to fine-tune the task result evaluation. In our previous example, the failed_when condition caught the case where there was no work to be done but the task still showed a change. We want to register a change on the exit code 0, but not on any other exit code. Let's expand our example task to accomplish this:

```
- name: delete branch bad
  command: git branch -D badfeature
  args:
    chdir: /srv/app
  register: gitout
  failed_when:
- gitout.rc != 0
- not gitout.stderr | search('branch.*not found')
  changed_when: gitout.rc == 0
```

Now, if we run our task when the branch still does not exist, we'll see the following output:

```
● ● ●                    2. jkeating@serenity-2: ~/src/mastery (zsh)
~/src/mastery> ansible-playbook -i mastery-hosts errors.yaml -vv
No config file found; using defaults

PLAYBOOK: errors.yaml **************************************************************
1 plays in errors.yaml

PLAY [error handling] *************************************************************

TASK [delete branch bad] *********************************************************
task path: /Users/jkeating/src/mastery/errors.yaml:7
ok: [localhost] => {"changed": false, "cmd": ["git", "branch", "-D", "badfeature
"], "delta": "0:00:00.011735", "end": "2016-12-29 16:29:28.500735", "failed": fa
lse, "failed_when_result": false, "rc": 1, "start": "2016-12-29 16:29:28.489000"
, "stderr": "error: branch 'badfeature' not found.", "stdout": "", "stdout_lines
": [], "warnings": []}

PLAY RECAP ***********************************************************************
localhost                  : ok=1    changed=0    unreachable=0    failed=0

~/src/mastery> _
```

Note how the key `changed` now has the value `false`.

Just to be complete, we'll change the scenario so that the branch does exist and run it again. To create the branch, simply run `git branch badfeature` from the /srv/app directory. Now, we can execute our playbook once again to see the output, which is as follows:

```
● ● ●                    2. jkeating@serenity-2: ~/src/mastery (zsh)
~/src/mastery> ansible-playbook ~i mastery-hosts errors.yaml -vv
No config file found; using defaults

PLAYBOOK: errors.yaml ********************************************************
1 plays in errors.yaml


PLAY [error handling] *******************************************************


TASK [delete branch bad] ****************************************************
task path: /Users/jkeating/src/mastery/errors.yaml:7
changed: [localhost] => {"changed": true, "cmd": ["git", "branch", "-D", "badfea
ture"], "delta": "0:00:00.016050", "end": "2016-12-29 16:31:05.491502", "failed"
: false, "failed_when_result": false, "rc": 0, "start": "2016-12-29 16:31:05.475
452", "stderr": "", "stdout": "Deleted branch badfeature (was 08077d5).", "stdou
t_lines": ["Deleted branch badfeature (was 08077d5)."], "warnings": []}

PLAY RECAP ******************************************************************
localhost                  : ok=1    changed=1    unreachable=0    failed=0

~/src/mastery> _
```

This time, our output is different; it's registering a change, and the stdout data shows the branch being deleted.

Special handling of the command family

A subset of the command family of modules (command, shell, and script) has a pair of special arguments that will influence whether or not the task work has already been done, and thus, whether or not a task will result in a change. The options are creates and removes. These two arguments expect a file path as a value. When Ansible attempts to execute a task with the creates or removes arguments, it will first check whether the referenced file path exists. If the path exists and the creates argument was used, Ansible will consider that the work has already been completed and will return Ok. Conversely, if the path does not exist and the removes argument is used, then Ansible will again consider the work to be complete, and it will return ok. Any other combination will cause the work to actually happen. The expectation is that whatever work the task is doing will result in either the creation or removal of the file that is referenced.

The convenience of `creates` and `removes` saves developers from having to do a two-task combo. Let's create a scenario where we want to run the script `frobitz` from the files/ subdirectory of our project root. In our scenario, we know that the `frobitz` script will create a path `/srv/whiskey/tango`. In fact, the source of `frobitz` is the following:

```bash
#!/bin/bash
rm -rf /srv/whiskey/tango
mkdir /srv/whiskey/tango
```

We don't want this script to run twice as it can be destructive to any existing data. The two-task combo will look like this:

```
- name: discover tango directory
  stat: path=/srv/whiskey/tango
  register: tango
- name: run frobitz
  script: files/frobitz --initialize /srv/whiskey/tango
  when: not tango.stat.exists
```

Assuming that the file already exists, the output will be as follows:

```
                    2. jkeating@serenity-2: ~/src/mastery (zsh)
~/src/mastery> ansible-playbook -i mastery-hosts errors.yaml -vv
No config file found; using defaults

PLAYBOOK: errors.yaml ********************************************************
1 plays in errors.yaml

PLAY [error handling] *******************************************************

TASK [discover tango directory] *********************************************
task path: /Users/jkeating/src/mastery/errors.yaml:7
ok: [localhost] => {"changed": false, "stat": {"atime": 1444194872.0, "ctime": 1
444194872.0, "dev": 16777220, "executable": true, "exists": true, "gid": 0, "gr_
name": "wheel", "inode": 3181585, "isblk": false, "ischr": false, "isdir": true,
 "isfifo": false, "isgid": false, "islnk": false, "isreg": false, "issock": fals
e, "isuid": false, "mode": "0755", "mtime": 1444194872.0, "nlink": 2, "path": "/
srv/whiskey/tango", "pw_name": "root", "readable": true, "rgrp": true, "roth": t
rue, "rusr": true, "size": 68, "uid": 0, "wgrp": false, "woth": false, "writeabl
e": false, "wusr": true, "xgrp": true, "xoth": true, "xusr": true}}

TASK [run frobitz] **********************************************************
task path: /Users/jkeating/src/mastery/errors.yaml:11
skipping: [localhost] => {"changed": false, "skip_reason": "Conditional check fa
iled", "skipped": true}

PLAY RECAP ******************************************************************
localhost                  : ok=1    changed=0    unreachable=0    failed=0

~/src/mastery> _
```

If the `/srv/whiskey/tango` path did not exist, the stat module would have returned far less data, and the `exists` key would have a value of `false`. Thus, our `frobitz` script would have been run.

Now, we'll use `creates` to reduce this down to a single task:

```
- name: run frobitz
  script: files/frobitz creates=/srv/whiskey/tango
```

 The `script` module is actually an `action_plugin`, which will be discussed in `Chapter 8`, *Extending Ansible*. The script `action_plugin` only accepts arguments in the `key=value` format.

This time, our output will be slightly different:

```
● ● ●                2. jkeating@serenity-2: ~/src/mastery (zsh)
~/src/mastery> ansible-playbook -i mastery-hosts errors.yaml -vv
No config file found; using defaults

PLAYBOOK: errors.yaml ************************************************************
1 plays in errors.yaml

PLAY [error handling] ***********************************************************

TASK [run frobitz] **************************************************************
task path: /Users/jkeating/src/mastery/errors.yaml:7
skipping: [localhost] => {"changed": false, "msg": "skipped, since /srv/whiskey/
tango exists", "skipped": true}

PLAY RECAP **********************************************************************
localhost                  : ok=0    changed=0    unreachable=0    failed=0

~/src/mastery> _
```

Making good use of `creates` and `removes` will keep your playbooks concise and efficient.

Suppressing a change

Sometimes it can be desirable to completely suppress changes. This is often used when executing a command in order to gather data. The command execution isn't actually changing anything; instead, it's just gathering info, like the `setup` module. Suppressing changes on such tasks can be helpful for quickly determining whether a playbook run resulted in any actual change in the fleet.

To suppress change, simply use `false` as an argument to the `changed_when` task key. Let's extend one of our previous examples to discover the active `iscsi` sessions to suppress changes:

```
- name: discover iscsi sessions
  command: /sbin/iscsiadm -m session
  register: sessions
  failed_when:
- sessions.rc != 0
- not sessions.stderr |
  search('No active sessions')
  changed_when: false
```

Now, no matter what comes in the return data, Ansible will treat the task as `Ok` rather than changed:

```
●  ●  ●              2. jkeating@serenity-2: ~/src/mastery (zsh)
~/src/mastery> ansible-playbook -i mastery-hosts errors.yaml -vv
No config file found; using defaults

PLAYBOOK: errors.yaml ****************************************************
1 plays in errors.yaml

PLAY [error handling] ***************************************************

TASK [discover iscsi sessions] *******************************************
task path: /Users/jkeating/src/mastery/errors.yaml:7
ok: [scsihost] => {"changed": false, "cmd": ["/sbin/iscsiadm", "-m", "session"],
  "delta": "0:00:00.003290", "end": "2016-12-30 00:49:34.679361", "failed": false
, "failed_when_result": false, "rc": 21, "start": "2016-12-30 00:49:34.676071",
"stderr": "iscsiadm: No active sessions.", "stdout": "", "stdout_lines": [], "wa
rnings": []}

PLAY RECAP ***************************************************************
scsihost                    : ok=1    changed=0    unreachable=0    failed=0

~/src/mastery> _
```

Error recovery

While error conditions can be narrowly defined, there will be times when real errors happen. Ansible provides a method to react to true errors, a method that allows running additional tasks when an error occurs, defining specific tasks that always execute even if there was an error, or even both. This method is the **blocks** feature.

The blocks feature, introduced with Ansible version 2.0, provides some additional structure to play task listings. Blocks can group tasks together into a logical unit, which can have task controls applied to the unit as a whole. In addition, a Block of tasks can have optional rescue and always sections.

Rescue

The `rescue` section of a block defines a logical unit of tasks that will be executed should a true failure be encountered within a `block`. As Ansible performs the tasks within a `block`, from top to bottom, when a true failure is encountered execution will jump to the first task of the `rescue` section of the `block`, if it exists. Then tasks are performed from top to bottom until either the end of the section is reached, or another error is encountered. After the `rescue` section completes, task execution continues with whatever comes after the `block`, as if there were no errors. This provides a way to gracefully handle errors, allowing clean up tasks to be defined so that a system is not left in a completely broken state, and the rest of a play can continue. This is far cleaner than a complex set of task registered results and task conditionals based on error status.

To demonstrate this, lets create a new task set inside of a `block`. This task set will have an unhandled error in it that will cause execution to switch to the `rescue` section, where we'll perform a cleanup task. We'll also provide a task after the `block` to ensure execution continues. We'll re-use the `errors.yaml` playbook:

```yaml
---
- name: error handling
  hosts: localhost
  gather_facts: false

  tasks:
    - block:
        - name: delete branch bad
          command: git branch -D badfeature
          args:
            chdir: /srv/app

        - name: this task is lost
          debug:
            msg: "I do not get seen"

      rescue:
        - name: cleanup task
          debug:
            msg: "I am cleaning up"

        - name: cleanup task 2
          debug:
            msg: "I am also cleaning up"
    - name: task after block
      debug:
        msg: "Execution goes on"
```

When this play executes, first task will result in an error, and the second task will be passed over. Execution continues with the clean up tasks, as we can see in this screenshot:

```
● ● ●                    2. jkeating@serenity-2: ~/src/mastery (zsh)
~/src/mastery> ansible-playbook -i mastery-hosts errors.yaml -vv
No config file found; using defaults

PLAYBOOK: errors.yaml ********************************************************
1 plays in errors.yaml

PLAY [error handling] *******************************************************

TASK [delete branch bad] ****************************************************
task path: /Users/jkeating/src/mastery/errors.yaml:8
fatal: [localhost]: FAILED! => {"changed": true, "cmd": ["git", "branch", "-D",
"badfeature"], "delta": "0:00:00.007540", "end": "2016-12-29 17:49:37.876734", "
failed": true, "rc": 1, "start": "2016-12-29 17:49:37.869194", "stderr": "error:
 branch 'badfeature' not found.", "stdout": "", "stdout_lines": [], "warnings":
[]}

TASK [cleanup task] *********************************************************
task path: /Users/jkeating/src/mastery/errors.yaml:18
ok: [localhost] => {
    "msg": "I am cleaning up"
}

TASK [cleanup task 2] *******************************************************
task path: /Users/jkeating/src/mastery/errors.yaml:22
ok: [localhost] => {
    "msg": "I am also cleaning up"
}

TASK [task after block] *****************************************************
task path: /Users/jkeating/src/mastery/errors.yaml:26
ok: [localhost] => {
    "msg": "Execution goes on"
}

PLAY RECAP ******************************************************************
localhost                  : ok=3    changed=0    unreachable=0    failed=0

~/src/mastery>
```

Not only did the rescue section get executed, the rest of the play completed as well, and the whole ansible-playbook execution was considered successful.

Always

In addition to `rescue`, another section is available, named `always`. This section of a `block` will always be executed whether there were errors or not. This feature is handy to ensure the state of a system is always left functional, whether a `block` of tasks was successful or not. As some tasks of a `block` may be skipped due to an error, and a `rescue` section is only executed when there is an error, the `always` section provides the guarantee of task execution in every case.

Let's extend our previous example and add an `always` section to our `block`:

```
always:
  - name: most important task
    debug:
      msg: "Never going to let you down"
```

Re-running our playbook we see the additional task displayed:

To verify that the `always` section does indeed always execute, we can alter the play so that the git task is considered successful. The full playbook is shown here for convenience:

```
---
- name: error handling
  hosts: localhost
  gather_facts: false

  tasks:
    - block:
        - name: delete branch bad
          command: git branch -D badfeature
          args:
            chdir: /srv/app
          register: gitout
          failed_when:
            - gitout.rc != 0
            - not gitout.stderr | search('branch.*not found')

        - name: this task is lost
          debug:
            msg: "I do not get seen"

      rescue:
        - name: cleanup task
          debug:
            msg: "I am cleaning up"

        - name: cleanup task 2
          debug:
            msg: "I am also cleaning up"

      always:
        - name: most important task
          debug:
            msg: "Never going to let you down"

    - name: task after block
      debug:
        msg: "Execution goes on"
```

This time when we execute the playbook our `rescue` section is skipped over, our previously masked by error task is executed, and our `always` block is still executed:

```
● ● ●                  2. jkeating@serenity-2: ~/src/mastery (zsh)
~/src/mastery> ansible-playbook -i mastery-hosts errors.yaml -vv
No config file found; using defaults

PLAYBOOK: errors.yaml ************************************************************
1 plays in errors.yaml

PLAY [error handling] ***********************************************************

TASK [delete branch bad] ********************************************************
task path: /Users/jkeating/src/mastery/errors.yaml:8
changed: [localhost] => {"changed": true, "cmd": ["git", "branch", "-D", "badfea
ture"], "delta": "0:00:00.013764", "end": "2016-12-29 18:03:32.373085", "failed"
: false, "failed_when_result": false, "rc": 1, "start": "2016-12-29 18:03:32.359
321", "stderr": "error: branch 'badfeature' not found.", "stdout": "", "stdout_l
ines": [], "warnings": []}

TASK [this task is lost] ********************************************************
task path: /Users/jkeating/src/mastery/errors.yaml:17
ok: [localhost] => {
    "msg": "I do not get seen"
}

TASK [most important task] ******************************************************
task path: /Users/jkeating/src/mastery/errors.yaml:31
ok: [localhost] => {
    "msg": "Never going to let you down"
}

TASK [task after block] *********************************************************
task path: /Users/jkeating/src/mastery/errors.yaml:35
ok: [localhost] => {
    "msg": "Execution goes on"
}

PLAY RECAP **********************************************************************
localhost                  : ok=4    changed=1    unreachable=0    failed=0

~/src/mastery> _
```

Summary

In general, Ansible does a great job at determining when there are failures or actual changes made by a task. However, sometimes, Ansible is either incapable or just needs some fine-tuning based on the situation. To facilitate this, a set of task constructs exist for playbook authors to utilize. Additionally, task blocks provide a method to gracefully recover from errors so that cleanup routines can be performed, and the rest of the play(s) can be completed. In the next chapter, we'll explore the use of Roles to organize tasks, files, variables, and other content.

5

Composing Reusable Ansible Content with Roles

For many projects, a simple, single Ansible playbook may suffice. As time goes on and projects grow, additional playbooks and variable files are added and task files may be split out. Other projects within an organization may want to reuse some of the content; either the projects get added to the directory tree or the desired content may get copied between multiple projects. As the complexity and size of the scenario grows, something more than a loosely organized handful of playbooks, task files, and variable files are highly desired. Creating such a hierarchy can be daunting and may explain why many uses of Ansible start off simple and only grow into a better organization once the scattered files become unwieldy and a hassle to maintain. Making the migration can be difficult and may require rewriting significant portions of playbooks, which can further delay reorganization efforts.

In this chapter, we will cover the best practices for compostable, reusable, and well-organized content within Ansible. Lessons learned in this chapter will help developers design Ansible content that grows well with the project, avoiding the need for difficult redesign work later. The following is an outline of what we will cover:

- Task, handler, variable, and playbook, include concepts
- Roles (structures, defaults, dependencies)
- Designing top level playbooks to utilize roles (tags and other things roles lack)
- Sharing roles across projects (dependencies via git, galaxy-like repos)

Task, handler, variable, and playbook include concepts

The first step to understanding how to efficiently organize an Ansible project structure is to master the concept of including files. The act of including files allows content to be defined in a topic specific file that can be included into other files one or more times within a project. This inclusion feature supports the concept of **Don't Repeat Yourself (DRY)**.

Including tasks

Task files are YAML files that define one or more tasks. These tasks are not directly tied to any particular play or playbook; they exist purely as a list of tasks. These files can be referenced by playbooks or other task files by way of the include operator. This operator takes a path to a task file, and as we learned in Chapter 1, *System Architecture and Design of Ansible*, the path can be relative from the file referencing it.

To demonstrate how to use the include operator to include tasks, let's create a simple play that includes a task file with some debug tasks within it. First, let's write our playbook file, and we'll call it includer.yaml:

```
---
- name: task inclusion
  hosts: localhost
  gather_facts: false

  tasks:
    - name: non-included task
      debug:
        msg: "I am not included"

    - include: more-tasks.yaml
```

Next, we'll create more-tasks.yaml in the same directory that holds includer.yaml:

```
---
- name: included task 1
  debug:
    msg: "I am the first included task"

- name: included task 2
  debug:
    msg: "I am the second included task"
```

Now, we can execute our playbook to observe the output:

```
● ● ●                    2. jkeating@serenity-2: ~/src/mastery (zsh)
~/src/mastery> ansible-playbook -i mastery-hosts includer.yaml -vv
No config file found; using defaults
statically included: /Users/jkeating/src/mastery/more-tasks.yaml

PLAYBOOK: includer.yaml ****************************************************
1 plays in includer.yaml

PLAY [task inclusion] ******************************************************

TASK [non-included task] ***************************************************
task path: /Users/jkeating/src/mastery/includer.yaml:6
ok: [localhost] => {
    "msg": "I am not included"
}

TASK [included task 1] *****************************************************
task path: /Users/jkeating/src/mastery/more-tasks.yaml:1
ok: [localhost] => {
    "msg": "I am the first included task"
}

TASK [included task 2] *****************************************************
task path: /Users/jkeating/src/mastery/more-tasks.yaml:5
ok: [localhost] => {
    "msg": "I am the second included task"
}

PLAY RECAP *****************************************************************
localhost                  : ok=3    changed=0    unreachable=0    failed=0

~/src/mastery> _
```

We can clearly see our tasks from the `include` file execution. Because the `include` operator was used within the play's tasks section, the included tasks were executed within that play. In fact, if we were to add a task to the play after the `include` operator, we would see that the order of execution follows as if all the tasks from the included file existed at the spot the `include` operator was used:

```
tasks:
    - name: non-included task
      debug:
        msg: "I am not included"
```

```
- include: more-tasks.yaml

- name: after-included tasks
  debug:
    msg: "I run last"
```

If we run our modified playbook, we will see the task order we expect:

```
2. jkeating@serenity-2: ~/src/mastery (zsh)

~/src/mastery> ansible-playbook -i mastery-hosts includer.yaml -vv
No config file found; using defaults
statically included: /Users/jkeating/src/mastery/more-tasks.yaml

PLAYBOOK: includer.yaml *********************************************************
1 plays in includer.yaml

PLAY [task inclusion] **********************************************************

TASK [non-included task] ******************************************************
task path: /Users/jkeating/src/mastery/includer.yaml:6
ok: [localhost] => {
    "msg": "I am not included"
}

TASK [included task 1] ********************************************************
task path: /Users/jkeating/src/mastery/more-tasks.yaml:1
ok: [localhost] => {
    "msg": "I am the first included task"
}

TASK [included task 2] ********************************************************
task path: /Users/jkeating/src/mastery/more-tasks.yaml:5
ok: [localhost] => {
    "msg": "I am the second included task"
}

TASK [after-included tasks] ***************************************************
task path: /Users/jkeating/src/mastery/includer.yaml:12
ok: [localhost] => {
    "msg": "I run last"
}

PLAY RECAP ********************************************************************
localhost                  : ok=4    changed=0    unreachable=0    failed=0

~/src/mastery>
```

By breaking these tasks into their own file, we could include them multiple times or in multiple playbooks. If we ever have to alter one of the tasks, we only have to alter a single file, no matter how many places this file gets referenced.

Passing variable values to included tasks

Sometimes, we want to split out a set of tasks but have those tasks act slightly differently depending on variable data. The `include` operator allows us to define and override variable data at the time of inclusion. The scope of the definition is only within the included task file (and any other files that file may itself include). To illustrate this capability, let's create a new scenario in which we need to touch a couple of files, each in their own directory path. Instead of writing two file tasks for each file (one to create the directory and another to touch the file), we'll create a task file with each task that will use variable names in the tasks. Then, we'll include the task file twice, each time passing different data in. First, we'll do this with the task file `files.yaml`:

```
---
- name: create leading path
  file:
    path: "{{ path }}"
    state: directory

- name: touch the file
  file:
    path: "{{ path + '/' + file }}"
    state: touch
```

Next, we'll create the play to include the task file we've just created, passing along variable data for the path and file variables:

```
---
- name: touch files
  hosts: localhost
  gather_facts: false

  tasks:
    - include: files.yaml       vars:
        path: /tmp/foo
        file: herp

    - include: files.yaml       vars:
        path: /tmp/foo
        file: derp
```

Variable definitions provided when including files can either be in the inline format of `key=value` or in the illustrated YAML format of `key:value` inside of a `vars` hash.

When we run this playbook, we'll see four tasks get executed, the two tasks from within `files.yaml` twice. The second set should result in only one change, as the path is the same for both sets:

```
2. jkeating@serenity-2: ~/src/mastery (zsh)
~/src/mastery> ansible-playbook -i mastery-hosts includer.yaml -vv
No config file found; using defaults
statically included: /Users/jkeating/src/mastery/files.yaml
statically included: /Users/jkeating/src/mastery/files.yaml

PLAYBOOK: includer.yaml ****************************************************
1 plays in includer.yaml

PLAY [task inclusion] *****************************************************

TASK [create leading path] ***********************************************
task path: /Users/jkeating/src/mastery/files.yaml:1
changed: [localhost] => {"changed": true, "gid": 0, "group": "wheel", "mode": "0
755", "owner": "jkeating", "path": "/tmp/foo", "size": 68, "state": "directory",
 "uid": 501}

TASK [touch the file] ****************************************************
task path: /Users/jkeating/src/mastery/files.yaml:6
changed: [localhost] => {"changed": true, "dest": "/tmp/foo/herp", "gid": 0, "gr
oup": "wheel", "mode": "0644", "owner": "jkeating", "size": 0, "state": "file",
"uid": 501}

TASK [create leading path] ***********************************************
task path: /Users/jkeating/src/mastery/files.yaml:1
ok: [localhost] => {"changed": false, "gid": 0, "group": "wheel", "mode": "0755"
, "owner": "jkeating", "path": "/tmp/foo", "size": 102, "state": "directory", "u
id": 501}

TASK [touch the file] ****************************************************
task path: /Users/jkeating/src/mastery/files.yaml:6
changed: [localhost] => {"changed": true, "dest": "/tmp/foo/derp", "gid": 0, "gr
oup": "wheel", "mode": "0644", "owner": "jkeating", "size": 0, "state": "file",
"uid": 501}

PLAY RECAP ***************************************************************
localhost                  : ok=4    changed=3    unreachable=0    failed=0

~/src/mastery>
```

Passing complex data to included tasks

When wanting to pass complex data to included tasks, such as a list or hash, an alternative syntax can be used when including the file. Let's repeat the last scenario, only this time instead of including the task file twice, we'll include it once and pass a hash of the paths and files in. First, we'll work the task file:

```
---
- name: create leading path
  file:
    path: "{{ item.value.path }}"
    state: directory
  with_dict: "{{ files }}"

- name: touch the file
  file:
    path: "{{ item.value.path + '/' + item.key }}"
    state: touch
  with_dict: "{{ files }}"
```

Now, we'll alter our playbook to provide the `files` hash in a single `include` statement:

```
---
- name: touch files
  hosts: localhost
  gather_facts: false

  tasks:
    - include: files.yaml
      vars:
        files:
          herp:
            path: /tmp/foo
          derp:
            path: /tmp/foo
```

If we run this new playbook and task file, we should see similar but slightly different output, the end result of which is the /tmp/foo directory already in place and the two files herp and derp being touched within:

```
● ● ●                  2. jkeating@serenity-2: ~/src/mastery (zsh)
~/src/mastery> ansible-playbook -i mastery-hosts includer.yaml -vv
No config file found; using defaults
statically included: /Users/jkeating/src/mastery/files.yaml

PLAYBOOK: includer.yaml *********************************************************
1 plays in includer.yaml

PLAY [task inclusion] **********************************************************

TASK [create leading path] ****************************************************
task path: /Users/jkeating/src/mastery/files.yaml:1
ok: [localhost] => (item={'key': u'herp', 'value': {u'path': u'/tmp/foo'}}) => {
"changed": false, "gid": 0, "group": "wheel", "item": {"key": "herp", "value": {
"path": "/tmp/foo"}}, "mode": "0755", "owner": "jkeating", "path": "/tmp/foo", "
size": 136, "state": "directory", "uid": 501}
ok: [localhost] => (item={'key': u'derp', 'value': {u'path': u'/tmp/foo'}}) => {
"changed": false, "gid": 0, "group": "wheel", "item": {"key": "derp", "value": {
"path": "/tmp/foo"}}, "mode": "0755", "owner": "jkeating", "path": "/tmp/foo", "
size": 136, "state": "directory", "uid": 501}

TASK [touch the file] *********************************************************
task path: /Users/jkeating/src/mastery/files.yaml:7
changed: [localhost] => (item={'key': u'herp', 'value': {u'path': u'/tmp/foo'}})
 => {"changed": true, "dest": "/tmp/foo/herp", "gid": 0, "group": "wheel", "item
": {"key": "herp", "value": {"path": "/tmp/foo"}}, "mode": "0644", "owner": "jke
ating", "size": 0, "state": "file", "uid": 501}
changed: [localhost] => (item={'key': u'derp', 'value': {u'path': u'/tmp/foo'}})
 => {"changed": true, "dest": "/tmp/foo/derp", "gid": 0, "group": "wheel", "item
": {"key": "derp", "value": {"path": "/tmp/foo"}}, "mode": "0644", "owner": "jke
ating", "size": 0, "state": "file", "uid": 501}

PLAY RECAP ********************************************************************
localhost                  : ok=2    changed=1    unreachable=0    failed=0

~/src/mastery>
```

Using this manner of passing in a hash of data allows for the growth of the set of things created without having to grow the number of include statements in the main playbook.

Conditional task includes

Similar to passing data into included files, conditionals can also be passed into included files. This is accomplished by attaching a `when` statement to the include operator. This conditional does not cause Ansible to evaluate the test to determine whether or not the file should be included; rather, it instructs Ansible to add the conditional to each and every task within the included file (and any other files said file may include).

> It is not possible to conditionally include a file. Files will always be included; however, a task conditional can be applied to every task within.

Let's demonstrate this by modifying our first example that includes simple debug statements. We'll add a conditional and pass along some data for the conditional to use. First, let's modify the playbook:

```
---
- name: task inclusion
  hosts: localhost
  gather_facts: false

  tasks:
    - include: more-tasks.yaml
      when: item | bool        vars:
        a_list:
          - true
          - false
```

Next, let's modify `more-tasks.yaml` to loop over the `a_list` variable in each task:

```
---
- name: included task 1
  debug:
    msg: "I am the first included task"
  with_items: "{{ a_list }}"

- name: include task 2
  debug:
    msg: "I am the second included task"
  with_items: "{{ a_list }}"
```

Now, let's run the playbook and see our new output:

```
● ● ●                    2. jkeating@serenity-2: ~/src/mastery (zsh)
~/src/mastery> ansible-playbook -i mastery-hosts includer.yaml -vv
No config file found; using defaults
statically included: /Users/jkeating/src/mastery/more-tasks.yaml

PLAYBOOK: includer.yaml ***************************************************
1 plays in includer.yaml

PLAY [task inclusion] *****************************************************

TASK [included task 1] ****************************************************
task path: /Users/jkeating/src/mastery/more-tasks.yaml:1
ok: [localhost] => (item=True) => {
    "item": true,
    "msg": "I am the first included task"
}
skipping: [localhost] => (item=False)  => {"changed": false, "item": false, "ski
p_reason": "Conditional check failed", "skipped": true}

TASK [included task 2] ****************************************************
task path: /Users/jkeating/src/mastery/more-tasks.yaml:6
ok: [localhost] => (item=True) => {
    "item": true,
    "msg": "I am the second included task"
}
skipping: [localhost] => (item=False)  => {"changed": false, "item": false, "ski
p_reason": "Conditional check failed", "skipped": true}

PLAY RECAP ****************************************************************
localhost                  : ok=2    changed=0    unreachable=0    failed=0

~/src/mastery> _
```

We can see a skipped iteration per task, the iteration where the item evaluated to a Boolean false. It's important to remember that all hosts will evaluate all included tasks. There is no way to influence Ansible to not include a file for a subset of hosts. At most, a conditional can be applied to every task within an include hierarchy so that included tasks may be skipped. One method to include tasks based on host facts is to utilize the group_by action plugin to create dynamic groups based on host facts. Then, you can give the groups their own plays to include specific tasks. This is an exercise left up to the reader.

Tagging included tasks

When including task files, it is possible to tag all the tasks within the file. The `tags` key is used to define one or more tags to apply to all the tasks within the include hierarchy. The ability to tag at include time can keep the task file itself un-opinionated about how the tasks should be tagged and can allow for a set of tasks to be included multiple times but with different data and tags passed along.

> Tags can be defined at the `include` statement or at the play itself to cover all includes (and other tasks) in a given play.

Let's create a simple demonstration to illustrate how tags can be used. We'll start with a playbook that includes a task file twice, each with a different tag name and different variable data:

```
---
- name: task inclusion
  hosts: localhost
  gather_facts: false

  tasks:
    - include: more-tasks.yaml          vars:
        data: first
      tags: first

    - include: more-tasks.yaml          vars:
        data: second
      tags: second
```

Now, we'll update `more-tasks.yaml` to do something with the data being provided:

```
---
- name: included task
  debug:
    msg: "My data is {{ data }}"
```

If we run this playbook without selecting tags, we'll see this task run twice:

```
2. jkeating@serenity-2: ~/src/mastery (zsh)
~/src/mastery> ansible-playbook -i mastery-hosts includer.yaml -vv
No config file found; using defaults
statically included: /Users/jkeating/src/mastery/more-tasks.yaml
statically included: /Users/jkeating/src/mastery/more-tasks.yaml

PLAYBOOK: includer.yaml ******************************************************
1 plays in includer.yaml

PLAY [task inclusion] ********************************************************

TASK [included task] ********************************************************
task path: /Users/jkeating/src/mastery/more-tasks.yaml:11
ok: [localhost] => {
    "msg": "My data is first"
}

TASK [included task] ********************************************************
task path: /Users/jkeating/src/mastery/more-tasks.yaml:11
ok: [localhost] => {
    "msg": "My data is second"
}

PLAY RECAP ******************************************************************
localhost                  : ok=2    changed=0    unreachable=0    failed=0

~/src/mastery> _
```

Now, if we select which tag to run, say the second tag, by altering our `ansible-playbook` arguments, we should see only that occurrence of the included task being run:

```
~/src/mastery> ansible-playbook -i mastery-hosts includer.yaml -vv --tags second

No config file found; using defaults
statically included: /Users/jkeating/src/mastery/more-tasks.yaml
statically included: /Users/jkeating/src/mastery/more-tasks.yaml

PLAYBOOK: includer.yaml ****************************************************************
1 plays in includer.yaml

PLAY [task inclusion] ****************************************************************

TASK [included task] ****************************************************************
task path: /Users/jkeating/src/mastery/more-tasks.yaml:11
ok: [localhost] => {
    "msg": "My data is second"
}

PLAY RECAP ****************************************************************
localhost                  : ok=1    changed=0    unreachable=0    failed=0

~/src/mastery> _
```

Our example used the `--tags` command line argument to indicate which tagged tasks to run. A different argument, `--skip-tags`, allows expressing the opposite, which tagged tasks to not run.

Task includes with loops

Task inclusions can be combined with loops as well. When adding a `with_` loop to a task include, the tasks inside the file will be executed with the `item` variable which holds the place of the current loop value. The entire include file will be executed repeatedly until the loop runs out of items. Let's update our example play to demonstrate this:

```
- name: task inclusion
  hosts: localhost
  gather_facts: false

  tasks:
    - include: more-tasks.yaml
      with_items:
        - one
        - two
```

We also need to update our `more-tasks.yaml` file to make use of the loop `item`:

```
---
- name: included task 1
  debug:
    msg: "I am the first included task with {{ item }}"
- name: included task 2
  debug:
    msg: "I am the second included task with {{ item }}"
```

When executed, we can tell that tasks 1 and 2 are executed a single time for each `item` in the loop:

```
● ● ●                    2. jkeating@serenity-2: ~/src/mastery (zsh)
~/src/mastery> ansible-playbook -i mastery-hosts includer.yaml -vv
No config file found; using defaults

PLAYBOOK: includer.yaml ******************************************************
1 plays in includer.yaml

PLAY [task inclusion] ********************************************************

TASK [include] **************************************************************
task path: /Users/jkeating/src/mastery/includer.yaml:15
included: /Users/jkeating/src/mastery/more-tasks.yaml for localhost
included: /Users/jkeating/src/mastery/more-tasks.yaml for localhost

TASK [included task 1] ******************************************************
task path: /Users/jkeating/src/mastery/more-tasks.yaml:1
ok: [localhost] => {
    "msg": "I am the first included task with one"
}

TASK [included task 2] ******************************************************
task path: /Users/jkeating/src/mastery/more-tasks.yaml:6
ok: [localhost] => {
    "msg": "I am the second included task with one"
}

TASK [included task 1] ******************************************************
task path: /Users/jkeating/src/mastery/more-tasks.yaml:1
ok: [localhost] => {
    "msg": "I am the first included task with two"
}

TASK [included task 2] ******************************************************
task path: /Users/jkeating/src/mastery/more-tasks.yaml:6
ok: [localhost] => {
    "msg": "I am the second included task with two"
}

PLAY RECAP ******************************************************************
localhost                  : ok=6    changed=0    unreachable=0    failed=0

~/src/mastery>
```

Looping on inclusion is a powerful concept, but it does introduce one complexity. What is there were tasks inside the included file that have their own loops? There will be a collision of the `item` variable, creating unexpected outcomes. For this reason, the `loop_control` feature was added to Ansible in version 2.1. Among other things, this feature provides a method to name the variable used for the loop, instead of the default of `item`. Using this, we can distinguish between the `item` that comes outside of the include from any `items` used inside of the include. To demonstrate this, we'll add a `loop_var` loop control to our outer include:

```
- include: more-tasks.yaml
  with_items:
    - one
    - two
  loop_control:
    loop_var: include_item
```

Inside `more-tasks.yaml` we'll have a task with its own loop, making use of the `include_item` and the local `item`:

```
---
- name: included task 1
  debug:
    msg: "I combine {{ item }} and {{ include_item }}"
  with_items:
    - a
    - b
```

When executed, we see that task 1 is executed twice per inclusion loop and that the two loop variables are used:

```
                    2. jkeating@serenity-2: ~/src/mastery (zsh)
~/src/mastery> ansible-playbook -i mastery-hosts includer.yaml -vv
No config file found; using defaults

PLAYBOOK: includer.yaml ********************************************************
1 plays in includer.yaml

PLAY [task inclusion] *********************************************************

TASK [include] ***************************************************************
task path: /Users/jkeating/src/mastery/includer.yaml:15
included: /Users/jkeating/src/mastery/more-tasks.yaml for localhost
included: /Users/jkeating/src/mastery/more-tasks.yaml for localhost

TASK [included task 1] *******************************************************
task path: /Users/jkeating/src/mastery/more-tasks.yaml:2
ok: [localhost] => (item=a) => {
    "item": "a",
    "msg": "I combine a and one"
}
ok: [localhost] => (item=b) => {
    "item": "b",
    "msg": "I combine b and one"
}

TASK [included task 1] *******************************************************
task path: /Users/jkeating/src/mastery/more-tasks.yaml:2
ok: [localhost] => (item=a) => {
    "item": "a",
    "msg": "I combine a and two"
}
ok: [localhost] => (item=b) => {
    "item": "b",
    "msg": "I combine b and two"
}

PLAY RECAP *******************************************************************
localhost                  : ok=4    changed=0    unreachable=0    failed=0

~/src/mastery> _
```

Other loop controls exist as well, such as label, which will define what is shown on screen in the task output for the item value (useful to prevent large data structures from cluttering the screen) and pause, providing the ability to pause for a defined number of seconds between each loop.

Including handlers

Handlers are essentially tasks. They're a set of potential tasks triggered by way of notifications from other tasks. As such, handler tasks can be included just like regular tasks can. The `include` operator is legal within the `handlers` block.

Unlike with task includes, variable data cannot be passed along when including handler tasks. However, it is possible to attach a conditional to a handler inclusion, to apply the conditional to every handler within the file.

Let's create an example to demonstrate. First, we'll create a playbook that has a task that will always change, and that includes a handler task file and attaches a conditional to that inclusion:

```
---
- name: touch files
  hosts: localhost
  gather_facts: false

  tasks:
    - name: a task
      debug:
        msg: "I am a changing task"
      changed_when: true
      notify: a handler

  handlers:
    - include: handlers.yaml
      when: foo | default('true') | bool
```

 When evaluating a variable that may be defined outside of a playbook, it's best to use the `bool` filter to ensure that strings are properly converted to their Boolean meaning.

Next, we'll create `handlers.yaml` to define our handler task:

```
---
- name: a handler
  debug:
    msg: "handling a thing"
```

If we execute this playbook without providing any further data, we should see our handler trigger:

```
● ● ●                2. jkeating@serenity-2: ~/src/mastery (zsh)
~/src/mastery> ansible-playbook -i mastery-hosts includer.yaml -vv
No config file found; using defaults
statically included: /Users/jkeating/src/mastery/handlers.yaml

PLAYBOOK: includer.yaml ***********************************************************
1 plays in includer.yaml

PLAY [task inclusion] *************************************************************

TASK [a task] ********************************************************************
task path: /Users/jkeating/src/mastery/includer.yaml:6
NOTIFIED HANDLER a handler
ok: [localhost] => {
    "msg": "I am a changing task"
}

RUNNING HANDLER [a handler] ******************************************************
ok: [localhost] => {
    "msg": "handling a thing"
}

PLAY RECAP ***********************************************************************
localhost                  : ok=2    changed=1    unreachable=0    failed=0

~/src/mastery> _
```

Now, let's run the playbook again; this time we'll define `foo` as false and as an `extra-var` in our `ansible-playbook` execution arguments:

```
● ● ●                2. jkeating@serenity-2: ~/src/mastery (zsh)
~/src/mastery> ansible-playbook -i mastery-hosts includer.yaml -vv -e foo=false
No config file found; using defaults
statically included: /Users/jkeating/src/mastery/handlers.yaml

PLAYBOOK: includer.yaml ***********************************************************
1 plays in includer.yaml

PLAY [task inclusion] ************************************************************

TASK [a task] *******************************************************************
task path: /Users/jkeating/src/mastery/includer.yaml:6
NOTIFIED HANDLER a handler
ok: [localhost] => {
    "msg": "I am a changing task"
}

RUNNING HANDLER [a handler] *****************************************************
skipping: [localhost] => {"changed": false, "skip_reason": "Conditional check fa
iled", "skipped": true}

PLAY RECAP **********************************************************************
localhost                  : ok=1    changed=1    unreachable=0    failed=0

~/src/mastery> _
```

This time, since `foo` evaluates to `false`, our included handler gets skipped.

Including variables

Variable data can also be separated into loadable files. This allows for sharing variables across multiple plays or playbooks or including variable data that lives outside the project directory (such as secret data). Variable files are simple YAML formatted files providing keys and values. Unlike task include files, variable include files cannot further include more files.

Variables can be included in three different ways; via `vars_files`, via `include_vars`, or via `--extra-vars` (`-e`).

vars_files

The `vars_files` key is a play directive. It defines a list of files to read from to load variable data. These files are read and parsed at the time the playbook itself is parsed. Just as with including tasks and handlers, the path is relative to the file referencing the file.

Here is an example play that loads variables from a file:

```
---
- name: vars
  hosts: localhost
  gather_facts: false

  vars_files:
    - variables.yaml

  tasks:
    - name: a task
      debug:
        msg: "I am a {{ name }}"
```

Now, we need to create `variables.yaml` in the same directory as our playbook:

```
name: derp
```

Running the playbook will show that the name variable value is properly sourced from the `variables.yaml` file:

```
~/src/mastery> ansible-playbook -i mastery-hosts includer.yaml -vv
No config file found; using defaults

PLAYBOOK: includer.yaml ****************************************************
1 plays in includer.yaml

PLAY [vars] ****************************************************************

TASK [a task] **************************************************************
task path: /Users/jkeating/src/mastery/includer.yaml:9
ok: [localhost] => {
    "msg": "I am a derp"
}

PLAY RECAP *****************************************************************
localhost                  : ok=1    changed=0    unreachable=0    failed=0

~/src/mastery>
```

Dynamic vars_files inclusion

In certain scenarios, it may be desirable to parameterize the variable files to be loaded. It is possible to do this by using a variable as part of the filename; however, the variable must have a value defined at the time the playbook is parsed, just like when using variables in task names. Let's update our example play to load a variable file based on the data provided at execution time:

```
---
- name: vars
  hosts: localhost
  gather_facts: false

  vars_files:
    - "{{ varfile }}"

  tasks:
    - name: a task
      debug:
        msg: "I am a {{ name }}"
```

Now, when we execute the playbook, we'll provide the value for `varfile` with the `-e` argument:

```
~/src/mastery> ansible-playbook -i mastery-hosts includer.yaml -vv -e varfile=va
riables.yaml
No config file found; using defaults

PLAYBOOK: includer.yaml ***************************************************
1 plays in includer.yaml

PLAY [vars] **************************************************************

TASK [a task] ************************************************************
task path: /Users/jkeating/src/mastery/includer.yaml:9
ok: [localhost] => {
    "msg": "I am a derp"
}

PLAY RECAP ***************************************************************
localhost                  : ok=1    changed=0    unreachable=0    failed=0

~/src/mastery> _
```

In addition to the variable value needing to be defined at execution time, the file to be loaded must also exist at execution time. Even if a reference to a file is four plays down in a playbook and the file itself is generated by the first play, unless the file exists at execution time, `ansible-playbook` will report an error.

include_vars

The second method to include variable data from files is the `include_vars` module. This module will load variables as a task action and will be done for each host. Unlike most modules, this module is executed locally on the Ansible host; therefore, all paths are still relative to the play file itself. Because the variable loading is done as a task, evaluation of variables in the filename happens when the task is executed. Variable data in the `file name` can be host-specific and defined in a preceding task. Additionally, the file itself does not have to exist at execution time; it can be generated by a preceding task, as well. This is a very powerful and flexible concept that can lead to very dynamic playbooks if used properly.

Before getting ahead of ourselves, let's demonstrate a simple usage of `include_vars` by modifying our existing play to load the variable file as a task:

```
---
- name: vars
  hosts: localhost
  gather_facts: false

  tasks:
    - name: load variables
      include_vars: "{{ varfile }}"

    - name: a task
      debug:
        msg: "I am a {{ name }}"
```

Execution of the playbook remains the same and our output differs only slightly from previous iterations:

```
●  ●  ●                2. jkeating@serenity-2: ~/src/mastery (zsh)
~/src/mastery> ansible-playbook -i mastery-hosts includer.yaml -vv -e varfile=va
riables.yaml
No config file found; using defaults

PLAYBOOK: includer.yaml ********************************************************
1 plays in includer.yaml

PLAY [vars] *******************************************************************

TASK [load variables] *********************************************************
task path: /Users/jkeating/src/mastery/includer.yaml:9
ok: [localhost] => {"ansible_facts": {"name": "derp"}, "changed": false}

TASK [a task] *****************************************************************
task path: /Users/jkeating/src/mastery/includer.yaml:12
ok: [localhost] => {
    "msg": "I am a derp"
}

PLAY RECAP ********************************************************************
localhost                  : ok=2    changed=0    unreachable=0    failed=0

~/src/mastery> _
```

Just like with other tasks, looping can be done to load more than one file in a single task.
This is particularly effective when using the special `with_first_found` loop to iterate
through a list of increasingly more generic file names until a file is found to be loaded. Let's
demonstrate this by changing our play to use gathered host facts to try and load a variable
file specific to the distribution, specific to the distribution family, or finally, a default file:

```
---
- name: vars
  hosts: localhost
  gather_facts: true

  tasks:
    - name: load variables
      include_vars: "{{ item }}"
      with_first_found:
        - "{{ ansible_distribution }}.yaml"
        - "{{ ansible_os_family }}.yaml"
        -  variables.yaml

    - name: a task
      debug:
        msg: "I am a {{ name }}"
```

Execution should look very similar to previous runs, only this time we'll see a fact-gathering task, and we will not pass along extra variable data in the execution:

```
2. jkeating@serenity-2: ~/src/mastery (zsh)
~/src/mastery> ansible-playbook -i mastery-hosts includer.yaml -vv -e varfile=va
riables.yaml
No config file found; using defaults

PLAYBOOK: includer.yaml **********************************************************
1 plays in includer.yaml

PLAY [vars] *********************************************************************

TASK [setup] *******************************************************************
ok: [localhost]

TASK [load variables] **********************************************************
task path: /Users/jkeating/src/mastery/includer.yaml:9
ok: [localhost] => (item=/Users/jkeating/src/mastery/variables.yaml) => {"ansibl
e_facts": {"name": "derp"}, "item": "/Users/jkeating/src/mastery/variables.yaml"
}

TASK [a task] ******************************************************************
task path: /Users/jkeating/src/mastery/includer.yaml:16
ok: [localhost] => {
    "msg": "I am a derp"
}

PLAY RECAP *********************************************************************
localhost                  : ok=3    changed=0    unreachable=0    failed=0

~/src/mastery> _
```

We can also see from the output which file was found to load. In this case, `variables.yaml` was loaded, as the other two files did not exist. This practice is commonly used to load variables that are operating system specific to the host in question. Variables for a variety of operating systems can be written out to appropriately named files. By utilizing the variable `ansible_distribution`, which is populated by fact gathering, variable files that use `ansible_distribution` values as part of their name can be loaded by way of a `with_first_found` argument. A default set of variables can be provided in a file that does not use any variable data as a failsafe.

extra-vars

The final method to load variable data from a file is to reference a file path with the `--extra-vars` (or `-e`) argument to `ansible-playbook`. Normally, this argument expects a set of `key=value` data; however, if a file path is provided and prefixed with the @ symbol, Ansible will read the entire file to load variable data. Let's alter one of our earlier examples where we used `-e` and instead of defining a variable directly on the command line, we'll include the variable file we've already written out:

```
---
- name: vars
  hosts: localhost
  gather_facts: false

  tasks:
    - name: a task
      debug:
        msg: "I am a {{ name }}"
```

When we provide a path after the @ symbol, the path is relative to the current working directory, regardless of where the playbook itself lives. Let's execute our playbook and provide a path to `variables.yaml`:

```
~/src/mastery> ansible-playbook -i mastery-hosts includer.yaml -vv -e @variables
.yaml
No config file found; using defaults

PLAYBOOK: includer.yaml ***********************************************************
1 plays in includer.yaml

PLAY [vars] ***********************************************************************

TASK [a task] *********************************************************************
task path: /Users/jkeating/src/mastery/includer.yaml:16
ok: [localhost] => {
    "msg": "I am a derp"
}

PLAY RECAP ************************************************************************
localhost                  : ok=1    changed=0    unreachable=0    failed=0

~/src/mastery> _
```

When including a variable file with the `--extra-vars` argument, the file must exist at `ansible-playbook` execution time.

Including playbooks

Playbook files can include other whole playbook files. This construct can be useful to tie together a few independent playbooks in a larger, more comprehensive playbook. Playbook inclusion is a bit more primitive than task inclusion. You cannot perform variable substitution when including a playbook, you cannot apply conditionals, and you cannot apply tags, either. The playbook files to be included must exist at the time of execution as well.

Roles

With a functional understanding of the inclusion of variables, tasks, handlers, and playbooks, we can move on to the more advanced topic of **Roles**. Roles move beyond the basic structure of a few playbooks and a few broken out files to reference. Roles provide a framework for fully independent, or interdependent, collections of variables, tasks, files, templates, and modules. Each role is typically limited to a particular theme or desired end result, with all the necessary steps to reach that result either within the role itself or in other roles listed as dependencies. Roles themselves are not playbooks. There is no way to directly execute a role. Roles have no setting for which host the role will apply to. Top-level playbooks are the glue that binds the hosts from your inventory to roles that should be applied to those hosts.

Role structure

Roles have a structured layout on the file system. This structure exists to provide automation around including tasks, handlers, variables, modules, and role dependencies. The structure also allows for easy reference of files and templates from anywhere within the role.

Roles all live in a subdirectory of a playbook archive, in the `roles/` directory. This is, of course, configurable by way of the `roles_path` general configuration key, but let's stick to the defaults. Each role is itself a directory tree. The role name is the directory name within `roles/`. Each role can have a number of subdirectories with special meaning that are processed when a role is applied to a set of hosts.

A role may contain all these elements, or as few as just one of them. Missing elements are simply ignored. Some roles exist just to provide common handlers across a project. Other roles exist as a single dependency point that in turn just depends on numerous other roles.

Tasks

The task file is the main meat of a role. If `roles/<role_name>/tasks/main.yaml` exists, all the tasks therein and any other files it includes will be embedded in the play and executed.

Handlers

Similar to tasks, handlers are automatically loaded from `roles/<role_name>/handlers/main.yaml`, if the file exists. These handlers can be referenced by any task within the role, or by any tasks within any other role that lists this role as a dependency.

Variables

There are two types of variables that can be defined in a role. There are role variables, loaded from `roles/<role_name>/vars/main.yaml`, and there are role defaults that are loaded from `roles/<role_name>/defaults/main.yaml`. The difference between `vars` and `defaults` has to do with precedence order. Refer to `Chapter 1`, *System Architecture and Design of Ansible,* for a detailed description of the order. Role defaults are the lowest order variables. Literally, any other definition of a variable will take precedence over a role default. Role defaults can be thought of as place holders for actual data, a reference of what variables a developer may be interested in defining with site-specific values. Role variables, on the other hand, have a higher order precedence. Role variables can be overridden, but generally they are used when the same data set is referenced more than once within a role. If the data set is to be redefined with site-local values, then the variable should be listed in the role defaults rather than the role variables.

Modules and plugins

A role can include custom modules as well as plugins. While the Ansible project is quite good at reviewing and accepting submitted modules, there are certain cases where it may not be advisable or even legal to submit a custom module upstream. In those cases, delivering the module with the role may be a better option. Modules can be loaded from `roles/<role_name>/library/` and can be used by any task in the role, or any later role. Modules provided in this path will override any other copies of the same module name anywhere else on the file system, which can be a way to distribute added functionality to a core module before the functionality has been accepted upstream and released with a new version of Ansible.

Likewise, plugins are often used to tweak Ansible behavior in a way that makes sense for a particular environment, and are unsuitable for upstream contribution. Plugins can be distributed as part of a role, which may be easier than explicitly installing plugins on every host that will act as an Ansible control host. Plugins will automatically be loaded if found inside of a role, in one of the following subdirectories:

- `action_plugins`
- `lookup_plugins`
- `callback_plugins`
- `connection_plugins`
- `filter_plugins`
- `strategy_plugins`
- `cache_plugins`
- `test_plugins`
- `shell_plugins`

Dependencies

Roles can express a dependency upon another role. It is common practice for sets of roles to all depend on a common role such as tasks, handlers, modules, and so on. Those roles may depend upon only having to be defined once. When Ansible processes a role for a set of hosts, it will first look for any dependencies listed in `roles/<role_name>/meta/main.yaml`. If any are defined, those roles will be processed and the tasks within will be executed (after checking for any dependencies listed within, too) until all dependencies have been completed before starting on the initial role tasks. We will describe role dependencies more in depth later in this chapter.

Files and templates

Task and handler modules can reference files relatively within roles/<role_name>/files/. The filename can be provided without any prefix and will be sourced from roles/<role_name>/files/<file_name>. Relative prefixes are allowed as well, in order to access files within subdirectories of roles/<role_name>/files/. Modules such as template, copy, and script may take advantage of this.

Similarly, templates used by the template module can be referenced relatively within roles/<role_name>/templates/. This sample code uses a relative path to load the template derp.j2 from the full roles/<role_name>/templates/herp/derp.j2 path:

```
- name: configure herp
  template:
    src: herp/derp.j2
    dest: /etc/herp/derp.j2
```

Putting it all together

To illustrate what full role structure might look like, here is an example role by the name of demo:

```
roles/demo
├── defaults
│   └── main.yaml
├── files
│   └── foo
├── handlers
│   └── main.yaml
├── library
│   └── samplemod.py
├── meta
│   └── main.yaml
├── tasks
│   └── main.yaml
├── templates
│   └── bar.j2
└── vars
    └── main.yaml
```

When creating a role, not every directory or file is required. Only the files that exist will be processed.

Role dependencies

As stated before, roles can depend on other roles. These relationships are called dependencies and they are described in a role's meta/main.yaml file. This file expects a top-level data hash with a key of dependencies; the data within is a list of roles:

```
---
dependencies:
  - role: common
  - role: apache
```

In this example, Ansible will fully process the common role first (and any dependencies it may express) before continuing with the apache role and then finally starting on the role's tasks.

Dependencies can be referenced by name without any prefix, if they exist within the same directory structure or live within the configured roles_path. Otherwise, full paths can be used to locate roles:

```
role: /opt/ansible/site-roles/apache
```

When expressing a dependency, it is possible to pass along data to the dependency. The data can be variables, tags, or even conditionals.

Role dependency variables

Variables that are passed along when listing a dependency will override values for matching variables defined in defaults/main.yaml or vars/main.yaml. This can be useful for using a common role like an apache role as a dependency while providing site-specific data such as what ports to open in the firewall or what apache modules to enable. Variables are expressed as additional keys to the role listing. Let's update our example to add simple and complex variables to our two dependencies:

```
---
dependencies:
  - role: common
    simple_var_a: True
    simple_var_b: False
  - role: apache
    complex_var:
```

```
key1: value1
key2: value2
short_list:
  - 8080
  - 8081
```

When providing dependency variable data, two names are reserved and should not be used as role variables: `tags` and `when`. The former is used to pass tag data into a role, and the latter is used to pass a conditional into the role.

Tags

Tags can be applied to all the tasks found within a dependency role. This functions much in the same way that tags can be applied to included task files, as described earlier in this chapter. The syntax is simple; the `tags` key can be a single item or a list. To demonstrate, let's add some tags to our example dependency list:

```
---
dependencies:
  - role: common
    simple_var_a: True
    simple_var_b: False
    tags: common_demo
  - role: apache
    complex_var:
      key1: value1
      key2: value2
    short_list:
      - 8080
      - 8081
    tags:
      - apache_demo
      - 8080
      - 8181
```

As with adding tags to included task files, all the tasks found within a dependency (and any dependency within that hierarchy) will gain the provided tags.

Role dependency conditionals

While it is not possible to prevent the processing of a dependency role with a conditional, it is possible to skip all the tasks within a dependency role hierarchy by applying a conditional to a dependency. This mirrors the functionality of task inclusion with conditionals, as well. The `when` key is used to express the conditional. Once again, we'll grow our example by adding a dependency to demonstrate the syntax:

```
---
dependencies:
  - role: common
    simple_var_a: True
    simple_var_b: False
    tags: common_demo
  - role: apache
    complex_var:
      key1: value1
      key2: value2
    short_list:
      - 8080
      - 8081
    tags:
      - apache_demo
      - 8080
      - 8181
    when: backend_server == 'apache'
```

Role application

Roles are not plays. They do not possess any opinions about which hosts the role tasks should run on, what connection methods to use, whether or not to operate serially, or any other play behaviors described in `Chapter 1`, *System Architecture and Design of Ansible*. Roles must be applied inside of a play within a playbook, where all these opinions can be expressed.

To apply a role within a play, the `roles` operator is used. This operator expects a list of roles to apply to the hosts in the play. Much like describing role dependencies, when describing roles to apply, data can be passed along, such as variables, tags, and conditionals. The syntax is exactly the same.

To demonstrate applying roles within a play, let's create a simple role and apply it in a simple playbook. First, let's build the role named `simple`, which will have a single `debug` task in `roles/simple/tasks/main.yaml` that prints the value of a role default variable defined in `roles/simple/defaults/main.yaml`. First, let's work the task file:

```
---
- name: print a variable
  debug:
    var: derp
```

Next, we'll write our default file with a single variable, `derp`:

```
---
derp: herp
```

To execute this role, we'll write a playbook with a single play to apply the role. We'll call our playbook `roleplay.yaml`, and it'll live at the same directory level as the `roles/` directory:

```
---
- hosts: localhost
  gather_facts: false

  roles:
    - role: simple
```

 If no data is provided with the role, an alternative syntax that just lists the roles to apply can be used, instead of the shown hash. However, for consistency, I feel it's best to always use the same syntax within a project.

We'll re-use our `mastery-hosts` inventory from earlier chapters and execute the playbook:

```
2. jkeating@serenity-2: ~/src/mastery (zsh)
~/src/mastery> ansible-playbook -i mastery-hosts roleplay.yaml -vv
No config file found; using defaults

PLAYBOOK: roleplay.yaml **********************************************************
1 plays in roleplay.yaml

PLAY [localhost] ****************************************************************

TASK [simple : print a variable] ***********************************************
task path: /Users/jkeating/src/mastery/roles/simple/tasks/main.yaml:2
ok: [localhost] => {
    "derp": "herp"
}

PLAY RECAP *********************************************************************
localhost                  : ok=1    changed=0    unreachable=0    failed=0

~/src/mastery> _
```

Thanks to the magic of roles, the `derp` variable value was automatically loaded from the role defaults. Of course, we can override the default value when applying the role. Let's modify our playbook and supply a new value for `derp`:

```
---
- hosts: localhost
  gather_facts: false

  roles:
    - role: simple
      derp: newval
```

This time when we execute, we'll see `newval` as the value for `derp`:

```
2. jkeating@serenity-2: ~/src/mastery (zsh)
~/src/mastery> ansible-playbook -i mastery-hosts roleplay.yaml -vv
No config file found; using defaults

PLAYBOOK: roleplay.yaml ********************************************************
1 plays in roleplay.yaml

PLAY [localhost] **************************************************************

TASK [simple : print a variable] *********************************************
task path: /Users/jkeating/src/mastery/roles/simple/tasks/main.yaml:2
ok: [localhost] => {
    "derp": "newval"
}

PLAY RECAP ********************************************************************
localhost                  : ok=1    changed=0    unreachable=0    failed=0

~/src/mastery> _
```

Multiple roles can be applied within a single play. The `roles:` key expects a list value. Just add more roles to apply more roles:

```
---
- hosts: localhost
  gather_facts: false

  roles:
    - role: simple
      derp: newval
    - role: second_role
      othervar: value
    - role: third_role
    - role: another_role
```

Mixing roles and tasks

Plays that use roles are not limited to just roles. These plays can have `tasks` of their own, as well as two other blocks of tasks: `pre_tasks` and `post_tasks`. The order in which these are executed is not dependent upon which order these sections are listed in the play itself; rather, there is a strict order to block execution within a play. See `Chapter 1`, *System Architecture and Design of Ansible,* for details on the playbook order of operations.

Handlers for a play are flushed at multiple points. If there is a `pre_tasks` block, handlers are flushed after all `pre_tasks` are executed. Then, the `roles` and `tasks` blocks are executed (roles first, then tasks, regardless of the order they are written in the playbook), after which handlers will be flushed again. Finally, if a `post_tasks` block exists, handlers will be flushed once again after all `post_tasks` have executed. Of course, handlers can be flushed at any time with the `meta: flush_handlers` call. Let's expand on our `roleplay.yaml` to demonstrate all the different times handlers can be triggered:

```
---
- hosts: localhost
  gather_facts: false

  pre_tasks:
    - name: pretask
      debug:
          msg="a pre task"
      changed_when: true
      notify: say hi

  roles:
    - role: simple
      derp: newval

  tasks:
    - name: task
      debug:
          msg: "a task"
      changed_when: true
      notify: say hi

  post_tasks:
    - name: posttask
      debug:
          msg: "a post task"
      changed_when: true
      notify: say hi

  handlers:
    - name: say hi
      debug:
          msg="hi"
```

We'll also modify our simple role's tasks to notify the `say hi` handler, as well:

```
---
- name: print a variable
  debug:
```

```
    var: derp
  changed_when: true
  notify: say hi
```

 This only works because the say hi handler has been defined in the play that is calling the simple role. If the handler is not defined, an error will occur. It's best practice to only notify handlers that exist within the same role or any role marked as a dependency.

Running our playbook should result in the say hi handler being called a total of three of times: once for pre_tasks, once for roles and tasks, and once for post_tasks:

```
2. jkeating@serenity-2: ~/src/mastery (zsh)

~/src/mastery} ansible-playbook -i mastery-hosts roleplay.yaml -vv
No config file found; using defaults

PLAYBOOK: roleplay.yaml ****************************************************
1 plays in roleplay.yaml

PLAY [localhost] **********************************************************

TASK [pretask] ***********************************************************
task path: /Users/jkeating/src/mastery/roleplay.yaml:6
NOTIFIED HANDLER say hi
ok: [localhost] => {
    "msg": "a pre task"
}

RUNNING HANDLER [say hi] **************************************************
ok: [localhost] => {
    "msg": "hi"
}

TASK [simple : print a variable] *****************************************
task path: /Users/jkeating/src/mastery/roles/simple/tasks/main.yaml:2
NOTIFIED HANDLER say hi
ok: [localhost] => {
    "derp": "newval"
}

TASK [task] **************************************************************
task path: /Users/jkeating/src/mastery/roleplay.yaml:16
ok: [localhost] => {
    "msg": "a task"
}

RUNNING HANDLER [say hi] **************************************************
ok: [localhost] => {
    "msg": "hi"
}

TASK [posttask] **********************************************************
task path: /Users/jkeating/src/mastery/roleplay.yaml:23
NOTIFIED HANDLER say hi
ok: [localhost] => {
    "msg": "a post task"
}

RUNNING HANDLER [say hi] **************************************************
ok: [localhost] => {
    "msg": "hi"
}

PLAY RECAP ***************************************************************
localhost                  : ok=7    changed=4    unreachable=0    failed=0

~/src/mastery>
```

While the order in which `pre_tasks`, `roles`, `tasks`, and `post_tasks` are written into a play does not impact the order in which those sections are executed, it's a best practice to write them in the order that they will be executed. This is a visual cue to help remember the order and to avoid confusion when reading the playbook later.

Role includes

With Ansible version 2.2, a new action plugin is made available as a technical preview, `include_role`. This plugin is used in a task to include and execute an entire role directly from a task. This is an interesting concept that is still being evaluated, and is not guaranteed to remain available in future releases. Reliance on this functionality should be avoided.

Role sharing

One of the advantages of using roles is the ability to share the role across plays, playbooks, entire project spaces, and even across organizations. Roles are designed to be self-contained (or to clearly reference dependent roles) so that they can exist outside of a project space where the playbook that applies the role lives. Roles can be installed in shared paths on an Ansible host, or they can be distributed via source control.

Ansible Galaxy

Ansible Galaxy (`https://galaxy.ansible.com/`) is a community hub for finding and sharing Ansible roles. Anybody can visit the website to browse the roles and reviews; plus, users who create a login can provide reviews of the roles they've tested. Roles from Galaxy can be downloaded using the `ansible-galaxy` utility provided with Ansible.

The `ansible-galaxy` utility can connect to and install roles from the Ansible Galaxy website. This utility will default to installing roles into `/etc/ansible/roles`. If `roles_path` is configured, or if a run-time path is provided with the `--roles-path` (or `-p`) option, the roles will be installed there instead. If any roles have been installed to the `roles_path` or the provided path, `ansible-galaxy` can list those and show information about those, as well. To demonstrate the usage of `ansible-galaxy`, let's use it to install a role for managing `known_hosts` for `ssh` from Ansible Galaxy into the roles directory we've been working with. Installing roles from Ansible Galaxy requires a `username.rolename`, as multiple users may have uploaded roles with the same name. In this case, we want the `docker_ubuntu` role from the user `angstwad`:

```
● ● ●          2. jkeating@serenity-2: ~/src/mastery (zsh)
~/src/mastery> ansible-galaxy install -p roles/ angstwad.docker_ubuntu
- downloading role 'docker_ubuntu', owned by angstwad
- downloading role from https://github.com/angstwad/docker.ubuntu/archive/v2.1.0
.tar.gz
- extracting angstwad.docker_ubuntu to roles/angstwad.docker_ubuntu
- angstwad.docker_ubuntu was installed successfully
~/src/mastery>
```

Now we can make use of this role by referencing `angstwad.docker_ubuntu` in a play or another role's dependencies block. We can also list it and gain information about it using the `ansible-galaxy` utility:

```
● ● ●          2. jkeating@serenity-2: ~/src/mastery (zsh)
~/src/mastery> ansible-galaxy list -p roles/
- angstwad.docker_ubuntu, v2.1.0
~/src/mastery> ansible-galaxy info -p roles/ angstwad.docker_ubuntu |head -n 36
[DEPRECATION WARNING]: The comma separated role spec format, use the
yaml/explicit format instead..
This feature will be removed in a future release.
 Deprecation warnings can be disabled by setting deprecation_warnings=False in
ansible.cfg.

Role: angstwad.docker_ubuntu
	description: Docker on Ubuntu greater than 12.04
	active: True
	commit: 0af1f02708abe8101940efe565c5dafd4c12032e
	commit_message: Merge pull request #122 from lhoss/configurable_proxy
Configurable proxy in the docker config
	commit_url: https://github.com/angstwad/docker.ubuntu/commit/0af1f02708a
be8101940efe565c5dafd4c12032e
	company:
	created: 2014-01-28T03:13:44.951Z
	dependencies: []
	download_count: 18598
	forks_count: 125
	galaxy_info:
		author: Paul Durivage
		categories: ['development', 'packaging', 'system']
		license: Apache v2.0
		min_ansible_version: 1.2
		platforms: [{'name': 'Debian', 'versions': ['jessie']}, {'name':
'Ubuntu', 'versions': ['precise', 'raring', 'saucy', 'trusty']}]
	github_branch:
	github_repo: docker.ubuntu
	github_user: angstwad
	id: 292
	install_date: Fri Dec 30 22:47:22 2016
	intalled_version: v2.1.0
	is_valid: True
	issue_tracker_url: https://github.com/angstwad/docker.ubuntu/issues
	license: Apache v2.0
	min_ansible_version: 1.2
	modified: 2016-12-30T22:39:54.000Z
	namespace: angstwad
	open_issues_count: 7
	path: [u'roles/']
	readme: docker_ubuntu
********
~/src/mastery>
```

The output was capped at 37 lines, to avoid displaying the entire README.md contents. Some of the data being displayed by the info command lives within the role itself, in the meta/main.yaml file. Previously, we've only seen dependency information in this file and it may not have made much sense to name the directory meta, but now we see that other metadata lives in this file, as well:

```
                          2. jkeating@serenity-2: ~/src/mastery (zsh)
~/src/mastery> cat roles/angstwad.docker_ubuntu/meta/main.yml
---
galaxy_info:
  author: Paul Durivage
  description: Docker on Ubuntu greater than 12.04
  license: Apache v2.0
  min_ansible_version: 1.2
  platforms:
    - name: Debian
      versions:
        - jessie
    - name: Ubuntu
      versions:
        - precise
        - raring
        - saucy
        - trusty
  categories:
    - development
    - packaging
    - system
dependencies: []
  # List your role dependencies here, one per line. Only
  # dependencies available via galaxy should be listed here.
  # Be sure to remove the '[]' above if you add dependencies
  # to this list.
~/src/mastery>
```

The ansible-galaxy utility can also help in the creation of new roles. The init method will create a skeleton directory tree for the role, as well as populate the meta/main.yaml file with placeholders for Galaxy-related data. The init method takes a variety of options, as shown in the help output:

```
● ● ●                2. jkeating@serenity-2: ~/src/mastery (zsh)
~/src/mastery> ansible-galaxy init --help
Usage: ansible-galaxy init [options] role_name

Options:
  -f, --force          Force overwriting an existing role
  -h, --help           show this help message and exit
  -c, --ignore-certs   Ignore SSL certificate validation errors.
  -p INIT_PATH, --init-path=INIT_PATH
                       The path in which the skeleton role will be created.
                       The default is the current working directory.
  --offline            Don't query the galaxy API when creating roles
  -s API_SERVER, --server=API_SERVER
                       The API server destination
  -v, --verbose        verbose mode (-vvv for more, -vvvv to enable
                       connection debugging)
  --version            show program's version number and exit
~/src/mastery>
```

Let's demonstrate this capability by creating a new role in our working directory named
autogen:

```
● ● ●                2. jkeating@serenity-2: ~/src/mastery (zsh)
~/src/mastery> ansible-galaxy init -p roles/ autogen
- autogen was created successfully
~/src/mastery> tree roles/autogen
roles/autogen
├── README.md
├── defaults
│   └── main.yml
├── files
├── handlers
│   └── main.yml
├── meta
│   └── main.yml
├── tasks
│   └── main.yml
├── templates
├── tests
│   ├── inventory
│   └── test.yml
└── vars
    └── main.yml

8 directories, 8 files
~/src/mastery>
```

For roles that are not suitable for Ansible Galaxy, such as roles dealing with in-house systems, `ansible-galaxy` can install directly from a git URL. Instead of just providing a role name to the install method, a full git URL with an optional version can be provided instead. For example, if we wanted to install the `foowhiz` role from our internal git server, we could simply do the following:

```
2. jkeating@serenity-2: ~/src/mastery (zsh)
~/src/mastery> ansible-galaxy install -p /opt/ansible/roles git+git@git.internal
.site:ansible-roles/foowhiz_
```

Without version info, the `master` branch will be used. Without name data, the name will be determined from the URL itself. To provide a version, append a comma and the version string that git can understand, such as a tag or branch name, like `v1`:

```
2. jkeating@serenity-2: ~/src/mastery (zsh)
~/src/mastery> ansible-galaxy install -p /opt/ansible/roles git+git@git.internal
.site:ansible-roles/foowhiz,v1_
```

A name for the role can be added with another comma followed by the name string. If you need to supply a name but do not wish to supply a version, an empty slot is still required for the version. For example:

```
2. jkeating@serenity-2: ~/src/mastery (zsh)
~/src/mastery> ansible-galaxy install -p /opt/ansible/roles git+git@git.internal
.site:ansible-roles/foowhiz,,foo-whiz-common_
```

Roles can also be installed directly from tarballs, as well, by providing a URL to the tarball in lieu of a full git URL or a role name to fetch from Ansible Galaxy.

When you need to install many roles for a project, it's possible to define multiple roles to download and install in a YAML formatted file that ends with `.yaml` (or `.yml`). The format of this file allows you to specify multiple roles from multiple sources and retain the ability to specify versions and role names. In addition, the source control method can be listed (currently only `git` and `hg` are supported):

```
---
- src: <name or url>
  version: <optional version>
  name: <optional name override>
  scm: <optional defined source control mechanism>
```

To install all the roles within a file, use the `--roles-file` (`-r`) option with the install method:

```
●●●                    2. jkeating@serenity-2: ~/src/mastery (zsh)
~/src/mastery> ansible-galaxy install -r foowhiz-reqs.yaml
```

Summary

Ansible provides the capability to divide content logically into separate files. This capability helps project developers to not repeat the same code over and over again. Roles within Ansible take this capability a step further and wrap some magic around the paths to the content. Roles are tunable, reusable, portable, and shareable blocks of functionality. Ansible Galaxy exists as a community hub for developers to find, rate, and share roles. The `ansible-galaxy` command-line tool provides a method to interact with the Ansible Galaxy site or other role sharing mechanisms. These capabilities and tools help with the organization and utilization of common code.

In the next chapter, we'll cover different deployment and upgrade strategies and the Ansible features useful for each strategy.

6
Minimizing Downtime with Rolling Deployments

Application deployments and upgrades can be approached in a variety of different strategies. The best approach depends on the application itself, the capabilities of the infrastructure the application runs on, and any promised service-level agreements with the users of the application. Whatever strategy you use, Ansible is well suited to facilitate the deployment. In this chapter, we'll walk through a couple of common deployment strategies and showcase the Ansible features that will be useful within those strategies. We'll also discuss a couple of other deployment considerations that are common across both deployment strategies which are:

- In-place upgrades
- Expanding and contracting
- Failing fast
- Minimizing disruptive actions
- Serializing single tasks

In-place upgrades

The first type of deployment we'll cover is in-place upgrades. This style of deployment operates on infrastructure that already exists in order to upgrade the existing application. This model can be seen as a traditional model that existed when the creation of new infrastructure was a costly endeavor in terms of both time and money.

To minimize the downtime during this type of an upgrade, a general design pattern is to deploy the application across multiple hosts behind a load balancer. The load balancer will act as a gateway between users of the application and the servers that run the application. Requests for the application will come to the load balancer, and depending on configuration, the load balancer will decide which backend server to direct the request to.

To perform a rolling in-place upgrade of an application deployed with this pattern, each server (or a small subset of the servers) will be disabled at the load balancer, upgraded, and then re-enabled to take on new requests. This process will be repeated for the remaining servers in the pool until all servers have been upgraded. As only a portion of the available application servers is taken offline to be upgraded, the application as a whole remains available for requests. Of course, this assumes that an application can perform well with mixed versions running at the same time.

Let's build a playbook to upgrade a fictional application. Our fictional application will run on servers `foo-app01` through `foo-app08`, which exist in the group `foo-app`. These servers will have a simple website being served via the `nginx` webserver, with the content coming from a `foo-app` git repository, defined by the variable `foo-app.repo`. A load balancer server, `foo-lb`, running the `haproxy` software, will front these app servers.

In order to operate on a subset of our `foo-app` servers, we need to employ the serial mode. This mode changes how Ansible will execute a play. By default, Ansible will execute tasks of a play across each host in the order that the tasks are listed. Each task of the play is executed across every host before moving on to the next task. If we were to use the default method, our first task would remove every server from the load balancer, which would result in complete outage of our application. The serial mode, instead, lets us operate on a subset so that the application as a whole stays available even if some of the members are offline. In our example, we'll use a serial amount of two in order to keep the majority of the application members online:

```
---
- name: Upgrade foo-app in place
  hosts: foo-app
  serial: 2
```

 Ansible 2.2 introduced the concept of `serial` batches, a list of numbers that could increase the amount of hosts addressed serially each time through the play. This allows for increasing the size of the hosts addressed as confidence increases. The last number provided will be the size of any remaining batch until all hosts have been completed.

Now, we can start creating our tasks. The first task will be to disable the host from the load balancer. The load balancer runs on the `foo-lb` host; however, we're operating on the `foo-app` hosts. Therefore, we need to delegate the task using the `delegate_to` task operator. This operator redirects where Ansible will connect in order to execute the task, but keeps all the variable context of the original host. We'll use the `haproxy` module to disable the current host from the `foo-app` backend pool:

```
tasks:
  - name: disable member in balancer
    haproxy:
      backend: foo-app
      host: "{{ inventory_hostname }}"
      state: disabled
    delegate_to: foo-lb
```

With the host disabled, we can now update the `foo-app` content. We'll use the git module to update the content path with the desired version defined as `foo-version`. We'll add a `notify` handler to this task to reload the `nginx` server if the content update results in a change. This can be done every time, but we're using this as an example usage of notify:

```
  - name: pull stable foo-app
    git:
      repo: "{{ foo-app.repo }}"
      dest: /srv/foo-app/
      version: "{{ foo-version }}"
    notify:
      - reload nginx
```

Our next step would be to re-enable the host in the load balancer; however, if we did that task next, we'd put the old version back in place, as our notified handler hasn't run yet. So, we need to trigger our handlers early by way of the `meta: flush_handlers` call, which we learned about in the previous chapter:

```
  - meta: flush_handlers
```

Now, we can re-enable the host in the load balancer. We can just enable it straight away and rely on the load balancer to wait until the host is healthy before sending requests to it. However, because we are running with a reduced number of available hosts, we need to ensure that all the remaining hosts are healthy. We can make use of a `wait_for` task to wait until the `nginx` service is once again serving connections. The `wait_for` module will wait for a condition on either a port or a file path. In our example, we will wait for the port `80` and the condition that port should be in. If it is started (the default), this means it is accepting connections:

```
- name: ensure healthy service
  wait_for:
    port: 80
```

Finally, we can re-enable the member within `haproxy`. Once again, we'll delegate the task to `foo-lb`:

```
- name: enable member in balancer
  haproxy:
    backend: foo-app
    host: "{{ inventory_hostname }}"
    state: enabled
  delegate_to: foo-lb
```

Of course, we still need to define our `reload nginx` handler:

```
handlers:
  - name: reload nginx
    service:
      name: nginx
      state: restarted
```

This playbook, when run, will now perform a rolling in-place upgrade of our application.

Expanding and contracting

An alternative to the in-place upgrade strategy is the expand and contract strategy. This strategy has become popular of late thanks to the self-service nature of on-demand infrastructure, such as cloud computing or virtualization pools. The ability to create new servers on demand from a large pool of available resources means that every deployment of an application can happen on brand new systems. This strategy avoids a host of issues, such as a build up of cruft on long running systems, such as:

- The configuration files no longer managed by Ansible are left behind
- The run-away processes consume resources in the background
- Things manually changed by humans with shell access to the server

Starting afresh each time also removes differences between an initial deployment and an upgrade. The same code path can be used, reducing the risk of surprises while upgrading an application. This type of an install can also make it extremely easy to roll back if the new version does not perform as expected. In addition to this, as new systems are created to replace old systems, the application does not need to go into a degraded state during the upgrade.

Let's re-approach our previous upgraded playbook with the expand and contract strategy. Our pattern will be to create new servers, deploy our application, verify our application, add new servers to the load balancer, and remove old servers from the load balancer. First, let's start with creating new servers. For this example, we'll make use of an OpenStack Compute Cloud to launch new instances:

```yaml
---
- name: Create new foo servers
  hosts: localhost

  tasks:
    - name: launch instances
      os_server:
        name: foo-appv{{ version }}-{{ item }}
        image: foo-appv{{ version }}
        flavor: 4
        key_name: ansible-prod
        security_groups: foo-app
        auto_floating_ip: false
        state: present
        auth:
          auth_url: https://me.openstack.blueboxgrid.com:5001/v2.0
          username: jlk
          password: FAKEPASSWORD
          project_name: mastery
      register: launch
      with_sequence: count=8
```

In this task, we're looping over a count of 8 using `with_sequence`. Each loop in the item variable will be replaced with a number. This allows us to create eight new server instances with a name based on the version of our application and the number of the loop. We're also assuming a prebuilt image to use so that we do not need to do any further configuration of the instance. In order to use the servers in future plays, we need to add their details to the inventory. To accomplish this, we register the results of the run in the launch variable, which we'll use next to create runtime inventory entries:

```
- name: add hosts
  add_host:
    name: "{{ item.openstack.name }}"
    ansible_ssh_host: "{{ item.openstack.private_v4 }}"
    groups: new-foo-app
  with_items: launch.results
```

This task will create new inventory items with the same name as that of our server instance. To help Ansible know how to connect, we'll set `ansible_ssh_host` to the IP address that our cloud provider assigned to the instance (this is assuming that the address is reachable by the host running Ansible). Finally, we'll add the hosts to the group `new-foo-app`. As our launch variable comes from a task with a loop, we need to iterate over the results of that loop by accessing the results key. This allows us to loop over each launch action to access the data specific to that task.

Next, we'll operate on the servers to ensure that the new service is ready for use. We'll use `wait_for` again, just as we did earlier, as a part of a new play on our `new-foo-app` group:

```
- name: Ensure new app
  hosts: new-foo-app
  tasks:
    - name: ensure healthy service
      wait_for:
        port: 80
```

Once they're all ready to go, we can reconfigure the load balancer to make use of our new servers. For the sake of simplicity, we will assume a template for the `haproxy` configuration that expects hosts in a `new-foo-app` group, and the end result will be a configuration that knows all about our new hosts and forgets about our old hosts. This means that we can simply call a template task on the load balancer system itself rather than attempting to manipulate the running state of the balancer:

```
- name: Configure load balancer
  hosts: foo-lb
  tasks:
    - name: haproxy config
      template:
```

```
          dest: /etc/haproxy/haproxy.cfg
          src: templates/etc/haproxy/haproxy.cfg

    - name: reload haproxy
      service:
        name: haproxy
        state: reloaded
```

Once the new configuration file is in place, we can issue a reload of the haproxy service. This will parse the new configuration file and start a new listening processes for new incoming connections. The existing connections will eventually close and the old processes will terminate. All new connections will be routed to the new servers running our new application version.

This playbook can be extended to decommission the old version of the servers, or that action may happen at a different time, when it has been decided that a rollback to the old version capability is no longer necessary.

The expand and contract strategy can involve more tasks, and even separate playbooks for creating a golden image set, but the benefits of fresh infrastructure for every release far outweigh the extra tasks or added complexity of creation followed by deletion.

Failing fast

When performing an upgrade of an application, it may be desirable to fully stop the deployment at any sign of error. A partially upgraded system with mixed versions may not work at all, so continuing with part of the infrastructure while leaving the failed systems behind can lead to big problems. Fortunately, Ansible provides a mechanism to decide when to reach a fatal error scenario.

By default, when Ansible is running through a playbook and encounters an error, Ansible will remove the failed host from the list of play hosts and continue with the tasks or plays. Ansible will stop executing once either all the requested hosts for a play have failed, or all the plays have been completed. To change this behavior, there are a couple of play controls that can be employed. Those controls are any_errors_fatal and max_fail_percentage.

The any_errors_fatal option

This setting instructs Ansible to consider the entire operation to be fatal and stop executing immediately if any host encounters an error. To demonstrate this, we'll add a new group to our `mastery-hosts` inventory using a pattern that will expand up to ten new hosts:

```
[failtest]
failer[01:10]
```

Then we'll create a play on this group with `any_errors_fatal` set to true. We'll also turn off fact gathering since these hosts do not exist:

```
---
- name: any errors fatal
  hosts: failtest
  gather_facts: false
  any_errors_fatal: true
```

We want a task that will fail for one of the hosts but not the others. Then, we'll want a second task as well, just to demonstrate how it will not run:

```
  tasks:
    - name: fail last host
      fail:
        msg: "I am last"
      when: inventory_hostname == play_hosts[-1]
    - name: never ran
      debug:
        msg: "I should never be ran"
      when: inventory_hostname == play_hosts[-1]
```

Now when we execute, we'll see one host fail but the entire play will stop after the first task:

```
●  ●  ●                2. jkeating@serenity-2: ~/src/mastery (zsh)
~/src/mastery> ansible-playbook -i mastery-hosts failtest.yaml

PLAY [any errors fatal] ********************************************************

TASK [fail last host] **********************************************************
skipping: [failer04]
skipping: [failer03]
skipping: [failer05]
skipping: [failer01]
skipping: [failer02]
skipping: [failer06]
skipping: [failer07]
skipping: [failer09]
skipping: [failer08]
fatal: [failer10]: FAILED! => {"changed": false, "failed": true, "msg": "I am la
st"}

NO MORE HOSTS LEFT *************************************************************
         to retry, use: --limit @/Users/jkeating/src/mastery/failtest.retry

PLAY RECAP *********************************************************************
failer01                   : ok=0    changed=0    unreachable=0    failed=0
failer02                   : ok=0    changed=0    unreachable=0    failed=0
failer03                   : ok=0    changed=0    unreachable=0    failed=0
failer04                   : ok=0    changed=0    unreachable=0    failed=0
failer05                   : ok=0    changed=0    unreachable=0    failed=0
failer06                   : ok=0    changed=0    unreachable=0    failed=0
failer07                   : ok=0    changed=0    unreachable=0    failed=0
failer08                   : ok=0    changed=0    unreachable=0    failed=0
failer09                   : ok=0    changed=0    unreachable=0    failed=0
failer10                   : ok=0    changed=0    unreachable=0    failed=1

exit 2
~/src/mastery>
```

We can see that just one host failed, however, Ansible reported all hosts to have failed, and aborted the playbook before getting to the next play.

The max_fail_percentage option

This setting allows play developers to define a percentage of hosts that can fail before the whole operation is aborted. At the end of each task, Ansible will perform a math operation to determine the number of the hosts targeted by the play that have reached a failure state, and if that number is greater than the number allowed, Ansible will abort the playbook. This is similar to `any_errors_fatal`, in fact, `any_errors_fatal` internally just expresses a `max_fail_percentage` parameter of `0`, where any failure is considered fatal. Let's edit our play from the preceding and change our `max_fail_percentage` parameter to `20`:

```
---
- name: any errors fatal
  hosts: failtest
```

```
gather_facts: false
max_fail_percentage: 20
```

By making that change, our play should complete both tasks without aborting:

```
● ● ●                 2. jkeating@serenity-2: ~/src/mastery (zsh)
~/src/mastery> ansible-playbook -i mastery-hosts failtest.yaml

PLAY [any errors fatal] *************************************************

TASK [fail last host] **************************************************
skipping: [failer01]
skipping: [failer03]
skipping: [failer04]
skipping: [failer06]
skipping: [failer09]
skipping: [failer07]
skipping: [failer08]
skipping: [failer02]
skipping: [failer05]
fatal: [failer10]: FAILED! => {"changed": false, "failed": true, "msg": "I am la
st"}

TASK [never ran] ******************************************************
skipping: [failer02]
skipping: [failer04]
skipping: [failer03]
skipping: [failer05]
skipping: [failer07]
skipping: [failer06]
skipping: [failer01]
skipping: [failer08]
ok: [failer09] => {
    "msg": "I should never be ran"
}
        to retry, use: --limit @/Users/jkeating/src/mastery/failtest.retry

PLAY RECAP ************************************************************
failer01                   : ok=0    changed=0    unreachable=0    failed=0
failer02                   : ok=0    changed=0    unreachable=0    failed=0
failer03                   : ok=0    changed=0    unreachable=0    failed=0
failer04                   : ok=0    changed=0    unreachable=0    failed=0
failer05                   : ok=0    changed=0    unreachable=0    failed=0
failer06                   : ok=0    changed=0    unreachable=0    failed=0
failer07                   : ok=0    changed=0    unreachable=0    failed=0
failer08                   : ok=0    changed=0    unreachable=0    failed=0
failer09                   : ok=1    changed=0    unreachable=0    failed=0
failer10                   : ok=0    changed=0    unreachable=0    failed=1

exit 2
~/src/mastery>
```

Now, if we change our conditional so that we fail on over 20 percent of the hosts, we'll see the playbook abort early:

```
- name: fail last host
  fail:
    msg: "I am last"
  when: inventory_hostname in play_hosts[0:3]
```

We're setting up three hosts to fail, which will give us a failure rate of greater than 20 percent. The `max_fail_percentage` setting is the maximum allowed, so our setting of 20 would allow 2 out of the 10 hosts to fail. With three hosts failing, we will see a fatal error before the second task:

```
~/src/mastery> ansible-playbook -i mastery-hosts failtest.yaml

PLAY [any errors fatal] ****************************************************

TASK [fail last host] ******************************************************
fatal: [failer02]: FAILED! => {"changed": false, "failed": true, "msg": "I am last"}
skipping: [failer05]
skipping: [failer04]
fatal: [failer03]: FAILED! => {"changed": false, "failed": true, "msg": "I am last"}
skipping: [failer06]
fatal: [failer01]: FAILED! => {"changed": false, "failed": true, "msg": "I am last"}
skipping: [failer08]
skipping: [failer07]
skipping: [failer09]
skipping: [failer10]

NO MORE HOSTS LEFT *********************************************************

NO MORE HOSTS LEFT *********************************************************
        to retry, use: --limit @/Users/jkeating/src/mastery/failtest.retry

PLAY RECAP *****************************************************************
failer01                   : ok=0    changed=0    unreachable=0    failed=1
failer02                   : ok=0    changed=0    unreachable=0    failed=1
failer03                   : ok=0    changed=0    unreachable=0    failed=1
failer04                   : ok=0    changed=0    unreachable=0    failed=0
failer05                   : ok=0    changed=0    unreachable=0    failed=0
failer06                   : ok=0    changed=0    unreachable=0    failed=0
failer07                   : ok=0    changed=0    unreachable=0    failed=0
failer08                   : ok=0    changed=0    unreachable=0    failed=0
failer09                   : ok=0    changed=0    unreachable=0    failed=0
failer10                   : ok=0    changed=0    unreachable=0    failed=0

exit 2
~/src/mastery>
```

Forcing handlers

Normally, when Ansible fails a host, it stops executing anything on that host. This means that any pending handlers will not be run. This can be undesirable, and there is a play control that will force Ansible to process pending handlers for failed hosts. This play control is force_handlers, which must be set to the Boolean true.

Let's modify our preceding example a little to demonstrate this functionality. We'll remove our max_fail_percentage parameter add a new first task. We need to create a task that returns successfully with a change. We can do this with the debug module using the changed_when task control, even though the debug module will never register a change by default. We'll revert our fail task conditional to what we originally started with as well:

```
---
- name: any errors fatal
  hosts: failtest
  gather_facts: false
    tasks:     - name: run first
      debug:
        msg: "I am a change"
      changed_when: true
      when: inventory_hostname == play_hosts[-1]
      notify: critical handler
    - name: change a host
      fail:
        msg: "I am last"
      when: inventory_hostname == play_hosts[-1]
```

Our third task remains unchanged, but we will define our critical handler:

```
    - name: never ran
      debug:
        msg: "I should never be ran"
      when: inventory_hostname == play_hosts[-1]
  handlers:
  - name: critical handler
    debug:
      msg: "I really need to run"
```

Let's run this new play to show the default behavior of the handler not being executed. In the interest of reduced output, we'll limit execution to just one of the hosts:

```
● ● ●                  2. jkeating@serenity-2: ~/src/mastery (zsh)
~/src/mastery> ansible-playbook -i mastery-hosts failtest.yaml --limit failer01:
failer01

PLAY [any errors fatal] *********************************************************

TASK [run first] ****************************************************************
ok: [failer01] => {
    "msg": "I am a change"
}

TASK [fail last host] ***********************************************************
fatal: [failer01]: FAILED! => {"changed": false, "failed": true, "msg": "I am la
st"}

RUNNING HANDLER [critical handler] **********************************************
        to retry, use: --limit @/Users/jkeating/src/mastery/failtest.retry

PLAY RECAP **********************************************************************
failer01                   : ok=1    changed=1    unreachable=0    failed=1

exit 2
~/src/mastery> _
```

Now, we add the force_handlers play control and set it to true:

```
---
- name: any errors fatal
  hosts: failtest
  gather_facts: false
  max_fail_percentage: 0
  force_handlers: true
```

This time when we run the playbook, we should see the handler run even for the failed hosts:

```
2. jkeating@serenity-2: ~/src/mastery (zsh)
~/src/mastery> ansible-playbook -i mastery-hosts failtest.yaml --limit failer01:
failer01

PLAY [any errors fatal] ********************************************************

TASK [run first] **************************************************************
ok: [failer01] => {
    "msg": "I am a change"
}

TASK [fail last host] *********************************************************
fatal: [failer01]: FAILED! => {"changed": false, "failed": true, "msg": "I am la
st"}

RUNNING HANDLER [critical handler] ********************************************
ok: [failer01] => {
    "msg": "I really need to run"
}
        to retry, use: --limit @/Users/jkeating/src/mastery/failtest.retry

PLAY RECAP ********************************************************************
failer01                   : ok=2    changed=1    unreachable=0    failed=1

exit 2
~/src/mastery> _
```

Forcing handlers can be a runtime decision as well, using the `--force-handlers` command line argument to `ansible-playbook`.

Forcing handlers to run can be really useful for repeated playbook runs. The first run may result in some changes but if a fatal error is encountered before the handlers are flushed, those handler calls will be lost. Repeated runs will not result in the same changes so the handler will never run without manual interaction. Forcing handlers to execute will make some attempt at ensuring that those handler calls are not lost.

Minimizing disruptions

During deployments, there are often tasks that can be considered disruptive or destructive. These tasks may include restarting services, performing database migrations, and so on. Disruptive tasks should be clustered together to minimize the overall impact on an application, while destructive tasks should only be performed once.

Delaying a disruption

Restarting services for a new code version is a very common need. When viewed in isolation, a single service can be restarted whenever the code and configuration for the application has changed, without concern for the overall distributed system health. Typically, a distributed system will have roles for each part of the system, and each role will operate essentially in isolation on the hosts targeted to perform those roles. When deploying an application for the first time, there is no existing uptime of the whole system to worry about; so, services can be restarted at will. However, during an upgrade, it may be desirable to delay all service restarts until every service is ready to minimize interruptions.

Reuse of role code is strongly encouraged rather than designing a completely separate upgrade code path. To accommodate a coordinated reboot, the role code for a particular service needs protection around the service restart. A common pattern is to put a conditional statement on the disruptive tasks that check a variable's value. When performing an upgrade, this variable can be defined at runtime to trigger this alternative behavior. This variable can also trigger a coordinated restart of services at the end of the main playbook once all roles have completed, to cluster the disruption and minimize the total outage.

Let's create a fictional application upgrade that involves two roles with simulated service restarts. We'll call these roles `microA` and `microB`:

```
roles/microA
├── handlers
│   └── main.yaml
└── tasks
    └── main.yaml
roles/microB
├── handlers
│   └── main.yaml
└── tasks
    └── main.yaml
```

For both of these roles, we'll have a simple debug task that simulates the installation of a package. We'll notify a handler to simulate the restart of a service. And, to ensure that the handler will trigger, we'll force the task to always register as changed:

```
roles/microA/tasks/main.yaml:
---

- name: install microA package
  debug:
    msg: "This is installing A"
  changed_when: true
  notify: restart microA
roles/microB/tasks/main.yaml:
---

- name: install microB package
  debug:
    msg: "This is installing B"
  changed_when: true
  notify: restart microB
```

The handlers for these roles will be debug actions as well, and we'll attach a conditional to the handler task to only restart if the upgrade variable evaluates to the Boolean `false`. We'll also use the default filter to give this variable a default value of `false`:

```
roles/microA/handlers/main.yaml:
---

- name: restart microA
  debug:
    msg: "microA is restarting"
  when: not upgrade | default(false) | bool
roles/microB/handlers/main.yaml:
---

- name: restart microB
  debug:
    msg: "microB is restarting"
  when: not upgrade | default(false) | bool
```

For our top-level playbook, we'll create four plays. The first two plays will apply each of the micro roles and the last two plays will do the restarts. The last two plays will only be executed if performing an upgrade; so, they will make use of the upgrade variable as a condition. Let's have a look at the following code snippet:

```yaml
micro.yaml:
---

- name: apply microA
  hosts: localhost
  gather_facts: false

  roles:
    - role: microA

- name: apply microB
  hosts: localhost
  gather_facts: false

  roles:
    - role: microB

- name: restart microA
  hosts: localhost
  gather_facts: false

  tasks:
    - name: restart microA for upgrade
      debug:
        msg: "microA is restarting"
      when: upgrade | default(false) | bool

- name: restart microB
  hosts: localhost
  gather_facts: false

  tasks:
    - name: restart microB for upgrade
      debug:
        msg: "microB is restarting"
      when: upgrade | default(false) |bool
```

If we execute this playbook without defining the upgrade module, we will see the execution of each role and the handlers within. The final two plays will just have skipped tasks:

```
● ● ●                2. jkeating@serenity-2: ~/src/mastery (zsh)
~/src/mastery> ansible-playbook -i mastery-hosts micro.yaml

PLAY [apply microA] ********************************************************

TASK [microA : install microA package] ************************************
ok: [localhost] => {
    "msg": "This is installing A"
}

RUNNING HANDLER [microA : restart microA] *********************************
ok: [localhost] => {
    "msg": "microA is restarting"
}

PLAY [apply microB] ********************************************************

TASK [microB : install microB package] ************************************
ok: [localhost] => {
    "msg": "This is installing B"
}

RUNNING HANDLER [microB : restart microB] *********************************
ok: [localhost] => {
    "msg": "microB is restarting"
}

PLAY [restart microA] *****************************************************

TASK [restart microA for upgrade] *****************************************
skipping: [localhost]

PLAY [restart microB] *****************************************************

TASK [restart microB for upgrade] *****************************************
skipping: [localhost]

PLAY RECAP ****************************************************************
localhost                  : ok=4    changed=2    unreachable=0    failed=0

~/src/mastery>
```

Now, let's execute the playbook again, and this time, we'll define the upgrade as `true` at runtime:

```
● ● ●                    2. jkeating@serenity-2: ~/src/mastery (zsh)
~/src/mastery> ansible-playbook -i mastery-hosts micro.yaml -e upgrade=true

PLAY [apply microA] ***********************************************************

TASK [microA : install microA package] ***************************************
ok: [localhost] => {
    "msg": "This is installing A"
}

RUNNING HANDLER [microA : restart microA] ************************************
skipping: [localhost]

PLAY [apply microB] ***********************************************************

TASK [microB : install microB package] ***************************************
ok: [localhost] => {
    "msg": "This is installing B"
}

RUNNING HANDLER [microB : restart microB] ************************************
skipping: [localhost]

PLAY [restart microA] ********************************************************

TASK [restart microA for upgrade] ********************************************
ok: [localhost] => {
    "msg": "microA is restarting"
}

PLAY [restart microB] ********************************************************

TASK [restart microB for upgrade] ********************************************
ok: [localhost] => {
    "msg": "microB is restarting"
}

PLAY RECAP *******************************************************************
localhost                  : ok=4    changed=2    unreachable=0    failed=0

~/src/mastery> _
```

This time, we can see that our handlers are skipped but the final two plays have tasks that execute. In a real world scenario, where many more things are happening in the microA and microB roles, and potentially other micro-service roles on other hosts, the difference could be of many minutes or more. Clustering the restarts at the end can reduce the interruption period significantly.

Running destructive tasks only once

Destructive tasks come in many flavors. They can be one-way tasks that are extremely difficult to roll back, one-time tasks that cannot easily be rerun, or they can be race condition tasks that if performed in parallel would result in catastrophic failure. For these reasons and more, it is essential that these tasks be performed only once from a single host. Ansible provides a mechanism to accomplish this by way of the run_once task control.

The run_once task control will ensure that the task only executes a single time from a single host, regardless of how many hosts happen to be in a play. While there are other methods to accomplish this goal, such as using a conditional to make the task only execute on the first host of a play, the run_once control is the most simple and direct way to express this desire. Additionally, any variable data registered from a task controlled by run_once will be made available to all hosts of the play, not just the host that was selected by Ansible to perform the action. This can simplify later retrieval of the variable data.

Let's create an example playbook to demonstrate this functionality. We'll reuse our failtest hosts created in an earlier example to have a pool of hosts, and select two of them using a host pattern. We'll do a debug task set to run_once and register the results, then access the result in a different task by a different host:

```
---
- name: run once test
  hosts: failtest[0:1]
  gather_facts: false

  tasks:
    - name: do a thing
      debug:
        msg: "I am groot"
      register: groot
      run_once: true

    - name: what is groot
      debug:
        var: groot
      when: inventory_hostname == play_hosts[-1]
```

When we run this play, we'll pay special attention to the hostnames listed for each task operation:

```
2. jkeating@serenity-2: ~/src/mastery (zsh)
~/src/mastery> ansible-playbook -i mastery-hosts runonce.yaml

PLAY [run once test] *********************************************************

TASK [do a thing] ***********************************************************
ok: [failer01] => {
    "msg": "I am groot"
}

TASK [what is groot] ********************************************************
skipping: [failer01]
ok: [failer02] => {
    "groot": {
        "changed": false,
        "msg": "I am groot"
    }
}

PLAY RECAP ******************************************************************
failer01                   : ok=1    changed=0    unreachable=0    failed=0
failer02                   : ok=1    changed=0    unreachable=0    failed=0

~/src/mastery> _
```

We can see that the do a thing task is executed on the host failer01, while the what is groot task, which examines the data from the do a thing task, operates on host failer02.

Serializing single tasks

Certain applications that run multiple copies of a service may not react well to all of those services being restarted at once. Typically, when upgrading this type of application, a serial play is used. However, if the application is of large enough scale, serializing the entire play may be wildly inefficient. A different approach can be used, which is to serialize just the sensitive task(s), often the handlers to restart services.

To serialize a specific handler task, we can make use of a built in variable, `play_hosts`. This variable holds the list of hosts that should be used for a given task, as part of the play. It is kept up to date with hosts that have failed or are unreachable. Using this variable, we can construct a loop to iterate over each host that could potentially run a handler task. Instead of using the `item` in the module arguments, we'll use the `item` in `when` conditional and a `delegate_to` directive, so that we can run the handler task if the host notified the handler and delegate the handler task to the host in the loop, rather than the original host. However, if we just use this as the list for a `with_items` directive, we'll end up executing the task for every host, for each of the hosts that trigger a handler. That's obviously unwanted, so we can use a task directive, `run_once`, to change behavior. The `run_once` directive instructs Ansible to only execute the task for one host, instead of for every host that it would normally target. Combining `run_once` and our `with_items` of `play_hosts` creates a scenario where Ansible will run through the loop, only once. Finally, we want to wait a small amount of time between each loop so that the restarted service can become functional before we restart the next one. We can make use of a `loop_control` of `pause` (introduced with Ansible version 2.2) to insert a pause between each iteration of the loop.

To demonstrate how this serialization will work, we'll write a play using a few hosts from our `failtest` group, with a task that creates a change, registers the output (so we can check in the handler task) and a serialized handler task:

```
---
- name: parallel and serial
  hosts: failtest[0:3]
  gather_facts: false

  tasks:
    - name: do a thing
      debug:
        msg: "I am groot"
      changed_when: inventory_hostname in play_hosts[0:2]
      register: groot
      notify: restart groot

  handlers:
    - name: restart groot
      debug:
        msg: "I am groot?"
      with_items: "{{ play_hosts }}"
      delegate_to: "{{ item }}"
      run_once: true
      when: hostvars[item]['groot']['changed'] | bool
      loop_control:
        pause: 2
```

Upon execution of this playbook we can see the handler notification (thanks to double verbosity −vv), and in the handler task we can see the loop, conditional, and delegation. Unfortunately, we cannot see the delay happen as that information is not part of the output:

```
● ● ●                    2. jkeating@serenity-2: ~/src/mastery (zsh)
~/src/mastery> ansible-playbook -i mastery-hosts forserial.yaml -vv
No config file found; using defaults

PLAYBOOK: forserial.yaml ***********************************************
1 plays in forserial.yaml

PLAY [parallel and serial] *********************************************

TASK [do a thing] ******************************************************
task path: /Users/jkeating/src/mastery/forserial.yaml:7
NOTIFIED HANDLER restart groot
ok: [failer01] => {
    "msg": "I am groot"
}
ok: [failer04] => {
    "msg": "I am groot"
}
ok: [failer03] => {
    "msg": "I am groot"
}
NOTIFIED HANDLER restart groot
ok: [failer02] => {
    "msg": "I am groot"
}

RUNNING HANDLER [restart groot] ****************************************
ok: [failer01 -> failer01] => (item=failer01) => {
    "item": "failer01",
    "msg": "I am groot?"
}
ok: [failer01 -> failer02] => (item=failer02) => {
    "item": "failer02",
    "msg": "I am groot?"
}
skipping: [failer01] => (item=failer03) => {"changed": false, "item": "failer03
", "skip_reason": "Conditional check failed", "skipped": true}
skipping: [failer01] => (item=failer04) => {"changed": false, "item": "failer04
", "skip_reason": "Conditional check failed", "skipped": true}

PLAY RECAP *************************************************************
failer01                   : ok=2    changed=1    unreachable=0    failed=0
failer02                   : ok=1    changed=1    unreachable=0    failed=0
failer03                   : ok=1    changed=0    unreachable=0    failed=0
failer04                   : ok=1    changed=0    unreachable=0    failed=0

~/src/mastery> _
```

Summary

Deployment and upgrade strategies are a matter of taste. Each comes with distinct advantages and disadvantages. Ansible does not possess an opinion on which is better, and therefore is well suited to perform deployments and upgrades regardless of the strategy. Ansible provides features and design patterns that facilitate a variety of styles with ease. Understanding the nature of each strategy and how Ansible can be tuned for that strategy will empower you to decide and design deployments for each of your applications. Task controls and built in variables provide methods to efficiently upgrade large scale applications while treating specific tasks carefully.

In Chapter 7, *Troubleshooting Ansible,* we'll cover topics that will help for when things don't quite go as expected when executing Ansible playbooks.

7
Troubleshooting Ansible

Ansible is simple but powerful. The simplicity of Ansible means that the operation is easy to understand and follow. Being able to understand and follow is critically important when debugging unexpected behavior. In this chapter, we will explore the various methods that can be employed to examine, introspect, modify, and, otherwise debug the operation of Ansible:

- Playbook logging and verbosity
- Variable introspection
- Playbook debugging
- Ansible console
- Debugging local code execution
- Debugging remote code execution

Playbook logging and verbosity

Increasing the verbosity of Ansible output can solve many problems. From invalid module arguments to incorrect connection commands, increased verbosity can be critical to pinpointing the source of an error. Playbook logging and verbosity were briefly discussed in Chapter 2, *Protecting Your Secrets with Ansible*, with regards to protecting secret values while executing playbooks. This section will cover verbosity and logging further in-depth.

Verbosity

When executing playbooks with `ansible-playbook`, the output is displayed on standard out. With the default level of verbosity, very little information is displayed. As a play is executed, `ansible-playbook` will print a PLAY header with the name of the play. Then for each task, a TASK header is printed with the name of the task. As each host executes the task, the name of the host is displayed along with the task state, which can be `ok`, `fatal`, or `changed`. No further information about the task is displayed, such as the module being executed, the arguments provided to the module, or the return data from the execution. While this is fine for well-established playbooks, I tend to want a little more information about my plays. In most previous examples in this book, we've used a verbosity level of 2 (-vv) so that we can see the location of the task and return data. There are five total levels of verbosity: none, which is the default level, 1 (-v), where the return data and conditional information is displayed, 2 (-vv) for task location and handler notification information, 3 (-vvv), which provides details of the connection attempts, task invocation information, and 4 (-vvvv), which will pass along extra verbosity options to the connection plugins (such as passing -vvv to the `ssh` commands). Increasing the verbosity can help pinpoint where errors might be occurring as well as providing extra insight into how Ansible is performing its operations.

As mentioned in `Chapter 2`, *Protecting Your Secrets with Ansible*, verbosity beyond 1 can leak sensitive data to standard out and log files, so care should be taken when using increased verbosity in a potentially shared environment.

Logging

While the default is for `ansible-playbook` to log to standard out, the amount of output may be greater than the buffer of the terminal emulator being used; therefore it may be necessary to save all the output to a file. While various shells provide some mechanism to redirect output, a more elegant solution is to direct `ansible-playbook` to log to a file. This is accomplished by way of either a `log_path` definition in the `ansible.cfg` file or by setting `ANSIBLE_LOG_PATH` as an environment variable. The value of either should be the path to a file. If the path does not exist, Ansible will attempt to create the file. If the file does exist, Ansible will append to the file, allowing consolidation of multiple `ansible-playbook` execution logs.

The use of a log file is not mutually exclusive with logging to standard output. Both can happen at the same time, and the verbosity level provided has an effect on both.

Variable introspection

A common set of problems encountered when developing Ansible playbooks is the improper use or invalid assumption of the value of variables. This is particularly common when registering the results of one task in a variable and later using that variable in a task or template. If the desired element of the result is not accessed properly, the end result will be unexpected or perhaps even harmful.

To troubleshoot improper variable usage, inspection of the variable value is the key. The easiest way to inspect a variable's value is with the debug module. The debug module allows for displaying free form text on screen, and like with other tasks, the arguments to the module can take advantage of the Jinja2 template syntax as well. Let's demonstrate this usage by creating a sample play that executes a task, registers the result, and then shows the result in a debug statement using the Jinja2 syntax to render the variable:

```
---
- name: variable introspection demo
  hosts: localhost
  gather_facts: false

  tasks:
    - name: do a thing
      uri:
        url: https://derpops.bike
      register: derpops

    - name: show derpops
      debug:
        msg: "derpops value is {{ derpops }}"
```

Now when we run this play, we'll see displayed value for `derpops`:

```
● ● ●                    2. jkeating@serenity: ~/src/mastery (zsh)
~/src/mastery> ansible-playbook -i mastery-hosts vintro.yaml -vv

PLAY [variable introspection demo] ***********************************

TASK: [do a thing] ***************************************************
<localhost> REMOTE_MODULE uri url=https://derpops.bike
ok: [localhost] => {"changed": false, "content_location": "https://derpops.bike"
, "content_type": "text/html; charset=UTF-8", "date": "Sun, 31 May 2015 04:57:56
 GMT", "link": "<http://wp.me/4H3Bf>; rel=shortlink", "redirected": false, "serv
er": "Apache/2.4.6 (CentOS) OpenSSL/1.0.1e-fips PHP/5.4.16", "status": 200, "tra
nsfer_encoding": "chunked", "x_pingback": "https://derpops.bike/xmlrpc.php", "x_
powered_by": "PHP/5.4.16"}

TASK: [show derpops] *************************************************
ok: [localhost] => {
    "msg": "derpops value is {'status': 200, 'changed': False, 'x_pingback': 'ht
tps://derpops.bike/xmlrpc.php', 'transfer_encoding': 'chunked', 'x_powered_by':
'PHP/5.4.16', 'server': 'Apache/2.4.6 (CentOS) OpenSSL/1.0.1e-fips PHP/5.4.16',
'date': 'Sun, 31 May 2015 04:57:56 GMT', 'link': '<http://wp.me/4H3Bf>; rel=shor
tlink', 'content_type': 'text/html; charset=UTF-8', 'content_location': 'https:/
/derpops.bike', 'invocation': {'module_name': u'uri', 'module_args': ''}, 'redir
ected': False}"
}

PLAY RECAP **********************************************************
localhost                  : ok=2    changed=0    unreachable=0    failed=0

~/src/mastery> []
```

The debug module has a different option that may be useful as well. Instead of printing a free form string to debug template usage, the module can simply print the value of any variable. This is done using the `var` argument instead of the `msg` argument. Let's repeat our example, but this time, we'll use the `var` argument, and we'll access just the `server` subelement of the `derpops` variable:

```
---
- name: variable introspection demo
  hosts: localhost
  gather_facts: false
```

```
tasks:
  - name: do a thing
    uri:
      url: https://derpops.bike
    register: derpops

  - name: show derpops
    debug:
      var: derpops.server
```

Running this modified play will show just the `server` portion of the `derpops` variable:

```
2. jkeating@serenity: ~/src/mastery (zsh)
~/src/mastery> ansible-playbook -i mastery-hosts vintro.yaml -vv

PLAY [variable introspection demo] ********************************************

TASK: [do a thing] ************************************************************
<localhost> REMOTE_MODULE uri url=https://derpops.bike
ok: [localhost] => {"changed": false, "content_location": "https://derpops.bike"
, "content_type": "text/html; charset=UTF-8", "date": "Sun, 31 May 2015 05:20:13
 GMT", "link": "<http://wp.me/4H3Bf>; rel=shortlink", "redirected": false, "serv
er": "Apache/2.4.6 (CentOS) OpenSSL/1.0.1e-fips PHP/5.4.16", "status": 200, "tra
nsfer_encoding": "chunked", "x_pingback": "https://derpops.bike/xmlrpc.php", "x_
powered_by": "PHP/5.4.16"}

TASK: [show derpops] **********************************************************
ok: [localhost] => {
    "var": {
        "derpops.server": "Apache/2.4.6 (CentOS) OpenSSL/1.0.1e-fips PHP/5.4.16"
    }
}

PLAY RECAP ********************************************************************
localhost                  : ok=2    changed=0    unreachable=0    failed=0

~/src/mastery> []
```

In our example that used the `msg` argument to `debug`, the variable needed to be expressed inside of mustache brackets, but when using `var`, it did not. This is because `msg` expects a string, and so Ansible needs to render the variable as a string via the template engine. However, `var` expects a single unrendered variable.

Variable sub elements

Another frequent mistake in playbooks is to improperly reference a subelement of a **complex variable**. A complex variable is one that is more than simply a string; it is either a list or a hash. Often the wrong subelement will be referenced, or the element will be improperly referenced expecting a different type.

While lists are fairly easy to work with, hashes present some unique challenges. A hash is an unordered key-value set of potentially mixed types, which could also be nested. A hash can have one element that is a single string, while another element can be list of strings, and a third element can be a another hash with further elements inside of it. Knowing how to properly access the right subelement is critical to success.

For an example, let's modify our previous play a bit more. This time we'll allow Ansible to gather facts, and then we'll show the value of `ansible_default_ipv4`:

```
---
- name: variable introspection demo
  hosts: localhost

  tasks:
    - name: show a complex hash
      debug:
        var: ansible_default_ipv4
```

The output is shown in the following screenshot:

```
●  ●  ●                  2. jkeating@serenity: ~/src/mastery (zsh)
~/src/mastery> ansible-playbook -i mastery-hosts vintro.yaml -vv

PLAY [variable introspection demo] ********************************************

GATHERING FACTS ***************************************************************
<localhost> REMOTE_MODULE setup
ok: [localhost]

TASK: [show a complex hash] ***************************************************
ok: [localhost] => {
    "var": {
        "ansible_default_ipv4": {
            "address": "192.168.10.101",
            "broadcast": "192.168.10.255",
            "device": "en0",
            "flags": [
                "UP",
                "BROADCAST",
                "SMART",
                "RUNNING",
                "SIMPLEX",
                "MULTICAST"
            ],
            "gateway": "192.168.10.10",
            "interface": "en0",
            "macaddress": "6c:40:08:a5:b9:92",
            "media": "Unknown",
            "media_select": "autoselect",
            "mtu": "1500",
            "netmask": "255.255.255.0",
            "network": "192.168.10.0",
            "options": [
                "PERFORMNUD"
            ],
            "status": "active",
            "type": "unknown"
        }
    }
}

PLAY RECAP ********************************************************************
localhost                  : ok=2    changed=0    unreachable=0    failed=0

~/src/mastery> []
```

Using debug to display the entire complex variable is a great way to learn all the names of the subelements.

This variable has elements that are strings along with elements that are lists of strings. Let's access the last item in the list of flags:

```
---
- name: variable introspection demo
  hosts: localhost

  tasks:
    - name: show a complex hash
      debug:
        var: ansible_default_ipv4.flags[-1]
```

The output is shown in the following screenshot:

```
2. jkeating@serenity: ~/src/mastery (zsh)
~/src/mastery> ansible-playbook -i mastery-hosts vintro.yaml -vv

PLAY [variable introspection demo] ********************************************

GATHERING FACTS ***************************************************************
<localhost> REMOTE_MODULE setup
ok: [localhost]

TASK: [show a complex hash] ***************************************************
ok: [localhost] => {
    "var": {
        "ansible_default_ipv4.flags[-1]": "MULTICAST"
    }
}

PLAY RECAP ********************************************************************
localhost                  : ok=2    changed=0    unreachable=0    failed=0

~/src/mastery> []
```

Because `flags` is a list, we can use the list index method to select a specific item from the list. In this case, `-1` will give us the very last item in the list.

Subelement versus Python object method

A less common but confusing gotcha comes from a quirk of the Jinja2 syntax. Complex variables within Ansible playbooks and templates can be referenced in two ways. The first style is to reference the base element by the name followed by a bracket and the subelement within quotes inside the brackets. This is the standard subscript syntax, for example, to access the `herp` subelement of the `derp` variable, we will use the following:

```
{{ derp['herp'] }}
```

The second style is a convenience method that Jinja2 provides, which is to use a period to separate the elements. This is called **dot notation**:

```
{{ derp.herp }}
```

There is a subtle difference in how these styles work that has to do with Python objects and object methods. As Jinja2 is at its heart a Python utility, variables in Jinja2 have access to their native Python methods. A string variable has access to Python string methods, a list has access to list methods, and a dictionary has access to dictionary methods. When using the first style, Jinja2 will first search the element for a subelement of the provided name. If none is found, Jinja2 will then attempt to access a Python method of the provided name. However, the order is reversed when using the second style; first a Python object method is searched for and if not found, then a subelement is searched for. This difference matters when there is a name collision between a subelement and a method. Imagine a variable named `derp`, which is a complex variable. This variable has a subelement named `keys`. Using each style to access the `keys` element will result in different values. Let's build a playbook to demonstrate this:

```yaml
---
- name: sub-element access styles
  hosts: localhost
  gather_facts: false
  vars:
    - derp:
        keys:
          - c
          - d
  tasks:
    - name: subscript style
      debug:
        var: derp['keys']
    - name: dot notation style
      debug:
        var: derp.keys
```

When running this play, we clearly see the difference between the two styles. The first style successfully references the `keys` subelement, while the second style references the `keys` method of Python dictionaries:

```
● ● ●                    2. jkeating@serenity: ~/src/mastery (zsh)
~/src/mastery> ansible-playbook -i mastery-hosts objmethod.yaml -vv

PLAY [sub-element access styles] ********************************************

TASK: [subscript style] ****************************************************
ok: [localhost] => {
    "var": {
        "derp['keys']": [
            "c",
            "d"
        ]
    }
}

TASK: [dot notation style] *************************************************
ok: [localhost] => {
    "var": {
        "derp.keys": "<built-in method keys of dict object at 0x7fa7cb30edf0>"
    }
}

PLAY RECAP *****************************************************************
localhost                  : ok=2    changed=0    unreachable=0    failed=0

~/src/mastery> []
```

Generally, it's best to avoid using subelement names that conflict with Python object methods. However, if that's not possible, the next best thing to do is to be aware of the difference in subelement reference styles and choose the appropriate one.

Debugging code execution

Sometimes logging and inspection of variable data is not enough to troubleshoot a problem. When this happens, it can be necessary to interactively debug the playbook, or to dig deeper into the internals of Ansible code. There are two main sets of Ansible code, the code that runs locally on the Ansible host and the module code that runs remotely on the target host.

Playbook debugging

Playbooks can be interactively debugged, using an execution strategy introduced in Ansible 2.1, the debug strategy. If a play uses this strategy, when an error state is encountered an interactive debugging session starts. This interactive session can be used to display variable data, display task arguments, update task arguments, update variables, redo task execution, continue execution, or exit the debugger.

Let's demonstrate this with a play that has a successful task followed by a task with an error, followed by a final successful task. We'll re-use the playbook we've been using but update it a bit:

```
---
- name: sub-element access styles
  hosts: localhost
  gather_facts: false
  strategy: debug

  vars:
    - derp:
        keys:
          - c
          - d

  tasks:
    - name: subscript style
      debug:
        var: derp['keys']

    - name: failing task
      debug:
        msg: "this is {{ derp['missing'] }}"

    - name: final task
      debug:
        msg: "my only friend the end"
```

Upon execution, Ansible will encounter an error in our `failing task`, and present the `(debug)` prompt:

```
● ● ●        2. ansible-playbook -i mastery-hosts objmethod.yaml -vv (python)
~/src/mastery> ansible-playbook -i mastery-hosts objmethod.yaml -vv
No config file found; using defaults

PLAYBOOK: objmethod.yaml *********************************************
1 plays in objmethod.yaml

PLAY [sub-element access styles] *************************************

TASK [subscript style] **********************************************
task path: /Users/jkeating/src/mastery/objmethod.yaml:14
ok: [localhost] => {
    "derp['keys']": [
        "c",
        "d"
    ]
}

TASK [failing task] *************************************************
task path: /Users/jkeating/src/mastery/objmethod.yaml:18
fatal: [localhost]: FAILED! => {"failed": true, "msg": "the field 'args' has an
invalid value, which appears to include a variable that is undefined. The error
was: 'dict object' has no attribute 'missing'\n\nThe error appears to have been
in '/Users/jkeating/src/mastery/objmethod.yaml': line 18, column 7, but may\nbe
elsewhere in the file depending on the exact syntax problem.\n\nThe offending li
ne appears to be:\n\n\n   - name: failing task\n        ^ here\n"}
Debugger invoked
(debug)
```

From this prompt, we can display the task, and the arguments to the task, using the `p` command:

```
● ● ●        2. ansible-playbook -i mastery-hosts objmethod.yaml -vv (python)
Debugger invoked
(debug) p task
TASK: failing task
(debug) p task.args
{u'msg': u"this is {{ derp['missing'] }}"}
(debug)
```

We can also change the playbook on the fly in order to try different arguments or variable values. Let's define the `missing` key of the `derp` variable, and then retry the execution. All the variables are within the top level `vars` dictionary. We can directly set variable data using Python syntax, and then retry with the `r` command:

```
●  ●  ●                    2. jkeating@serenity-2: ~/src/mastery (zsh)
Debugger invoked
(debug) p task
TASK: failing task
(debug) p task.args
{u'msg': u"this is {{ derp['missing'] }}"}
(debug) vars['derp']['missing'] = "the end"
(debug) r
ok: [localhost] => {
    "msg": "this is the end"
}

TASK [final task] ***********************************************************
task path: /Users/jkeating/src/mastery/objmethod.yaml:22
ok: [localhost] => {
    "msg": "my only friend the end"
}

PLAY RECAP *****************************************************************
localhost                  : ok=3    changed=0    unreachable=0    failed=0

~/src/mastery>
```

The `debug` execution strategy is a handy tool for quickly iterating through different task argument and variable combinations in order to figure out the correct path forward. However, because errors result in interactive consoles, the `debug` strategy is inappropriate for automated executions of playbooks, as there is no human on the console to manipulate the debugger.

Changing data within the debugger will not save the changes to backing files. Always remember to update playbook files to reflect discoveries made during debugging.

Debugging local code

The local Ansible code is the lion's share of the code that comes with Ansible. All the playbook, play, role, and task parsing code live locally. All the task result processing code and transport code live locally. All the code except for the assembled module code that is transported to the remote host lives locally.

Local Ansible code can be broken down into three major sections: inventory, playbook, and executor. Inventory code deals with parsing inventory data from host files, dynamic inventory scripts, or combinations of the two in directory trees. Playbook code is used to parse the playbook YAML code into Python objects within Ansible. Executor code is the core API and deals with forking processes, connecting to hosts, executing modules, handling results, and most other things. Learning the general area to start debugging comes with practice, but the general areas described here are a starting point.

As Ansible is written in Python, the tool for debugging local code execution is the Python debugger, pdb. This tool allows us to insert break points inside the Ansible code and interactively walk through the execution of the code, line by line. This is very useful for examining the internal state of Ansible as the local code executes. There are many books and websites that cover the usage of pdb, and can by found with a simple web search for an introduction to Python pdb, so we will not repeat them here. The basics are to edit the source file to be debugged, insert a new line of code to create a break point, and then execute the code. Code execution will stop where the breakpoint was created and a prompt will be provided to explore the code state.

Debugging inventory code

Inventory code deals with finding inventory sources, reading or executing the discovered files, parsing the inventory data into inventory objects, and loading variable data for the inventory. To debug how Ansible will deal with an inventory, a breakpoint must be added inside `inventory/__init__.py` or one of the other files within the `inventory/` subdirectory. This directory will be located on the local filesystem wherever Ansible has been installed. On a Linux system, this is typically stored in the path `/usr/lib/python2.7/site-packages/ansible/inventory/`. This path may be inside of a Python virtual environment if Ansible has been installed that way. To discover where Ansible is installed, simply type `which ansible` from the command line. This command will show where the `ansible` executable is installed, and may indicate a Python virtual environment. For this book, Ansible has been installed in a Python virtual environment with the path `/Users/jkeating/.virtualenvs/ansible/`.

To discover the path to the ansible python code, simply type `python -c "import ansible; print(ansible)"`. On my system this shows `<module 'ansible' from '/Users/jkeating/.virtualenvs/ansible/lib/python2.7/site-packages/ansible/__init__.pyc'>`, from which we can deduce that the inventory subdirectory is located at `/Users/jkeating/.virtualenvs/ansible/lib/python2.7/site-packages/ansible/inventory/`.

Within `inventory/__init__.py`, there is a class definition for the `Inventory` class. This is the inventory object that will be used throughout a playbook run, and it is created when `ansible-playbook` parses the options provided to it for an inventory source. The `__init__` method of the `Inventory` class does all the inventory discovery, parsing, and variable loading. To troubleshoot an issue in those three areas, a breakpoint should be added within the `__init__()` method. A good place to start would be after all of the class variables are given an initial value and just before any data is processed. In version 2.2.0.0 of Ansible, this would be line 98 of `inventory/__init__.py`, where the `parse_inventory` function is called.

We can skip down to the `parse_inventory` function definition, on line 107 to insert our breakpoint. To insert a breakpoint we must first import the `pdb` module and then call the `set_trace()` function:

```
3. vim (vim)
        # clear the cache here, which is only useful if more than
        # one Inventory objects are created when using the API directly
        self.clear_pattern_cache()
        self.clear_group_dict_cache()

        self.parse_inventory(host_list)

def serialize(self):
        data = dict()
        return data

def deserialize(self, data):
        pass

def parse_inventory(self, host_list):

        import pdb; pdb.set_trace()
        if isinstance(host_list, string_types):
            if "," in host_list:
                host_list = host_list.split(",")
                host_list = [ h for h in host_list if h and h.strip() ]
                                                               109,9        10%
```

To start debugging, save the source file and then execute `ansible-playbook` as normal. When the breakpoint is reached, the execution will stop and a `pdb` prompt will be displayed:

```
2. ansible-playbook -i mastery-hosts objmethod.yaml -vv (python)
~/src/mastery> ansible-playbook -i mastery-hosts objmethod.yaml -vv
> /Users/jkeating/.virtualenvs/ansible/lib/python2.7/site-packages/ansible/inven
tory/__init__.py(71)__init__()
-> if isinstance(host_list, basestring):
(Pdb) []
```

From here, we can issue any number of debugger commands, such as the `help` command:

```
  ●  ●  ●      2. ansible-playbook -i mastery-hosts objmethod.yaml -vv (python)
> /Users/jkeating/.virtualenvs/ansible/lib/python2.7/site-packages/ansible/inven
tory/__init__.py(71)__init__()
-> if isinstance(host_list, basestring):
(Pdb) help

Documented commands (type help <topic>):
========================================
EOF    bt         cont       enable  jump  pp       run      unt
a      c          continue   exit    l     q        s        until
alias  cl         d          h       list  quit     step     up
args   clear      debug      help    n     r        tbreak   w
b      commands   disable    ignore  next  restart  u        whatis
break  condition  down       j       p     return   unalias  where

Miscellaneous help topics:
==========================
exec  pdb

Undocumented commands:
======================
retval  rv

(Pdb) []
```

The `where` and the `list` commands can help us determine where we are in the stack, and where we are in the code:

```
●  ●  ●        3. ansible-playbook -i mastery-hosts objmethod.yaml -vv (python)

(Pdb) where
  /Users/jkeating/.virtualenvs/ansible/bin/ansible-playbook(103)<module>()
-> exit_code = cli.run()
  /Users/jkeating/.virtualenvs/ansible/lib/python2.7/site-packages/ansible/cli/p
laybook.py(132)run()
-> inventory = Inventory(loader=loader, variable_manager=variable_manager, host_
list=self.options.inventory)
  /Users/jkeating/.virtualenvs/ansible/lib/python2.7/site-packages/ansible/inven
tory/__init__.py(97)__init__()
-> self.parse_inventory(host_list)
> /Users/jkeating/.virtualenvs/ansible/lib/python2.7/site-packages/ansible/inven
tory/__init__.py(109)parse_inventory()
-> if isinstance(host_list, string_types):
(Pdb) list
104                     pass
105
106          def parse_inventory(self, host_list):
107
108                  import pdb; pdb.set_trace()
109  ->             if isinstance(host_list, string_types):
110                      if "," in host_list:
111                          host_list = host_list.split(",")
112                          host_list = [ h for h in host_list if h and h.strip() ]
113
114                  self.parser = None
(Pdb) _
```

The `where` command showed us that we're in `inventory/__init__.py` in the `parse_inventory()` method. The next frame up is the same file, the `__init__()` function. Before that is a different file, the `playbook.py` file, and the function in that file is `run()`; this line calls to `ansible.inventory.Inventory` to create the `inventory` object. Before that is the original file, `ansible-playbook`, calling `cli.run()`.

The `list` command shows the source code around our current point of execution, five lines before and five lines after.

From here, we can guide `pdb` through the function line by line with the `next` command. And, if we chose to, we can trace into other function calls with the `step` command. We can also print variable data to inspect values:

```
3. ansible-playbook -i mastery-hosts objmethod.yaml -vv (python)
108                     import pdb; pdb.set_trace()
109   ->                if isinstance(host_list, string_types):
110                         if "," in host_list:
111                             host_list = host_list.split(",")
112                         host_list = [ h for h in host_list if h and h.strip() ]
113
114                     self.parser = None
(Pdb) p host_list
u'mastery-hosts'
(Pdb)
```

We can see that the `host_list` variable has a value of `mastery-hosts`, which is the string we gave `ansible-playbook` for our inventory data. We can continue to walk through or jump around, or just use the `continue` command to run until the next breakpoint or the completion of the code.

Debugging playbook code

Playbook code is responsible for loading, parsing, and executing playbooks. The main entry point for playbook handling is `playbook/__init__.py`, inside of which lives the `PlayBook` class. A good starting point for debugging playbook handling is line `76`:

```
                                    3. fg (vim)
    self._file_name = file_name

    # dynamically load any plugins from the playbook directory
    for name, obj in get_all_plugin_loaders():
        if obj.subdir:
            plugin_path = os.path.join(self._basedir, obj.subdir)
            if os.path.isdir(plugin_path):
                obj.add_directory(plugin_path)

    import pdb; pdb.set_trace()
    ds = self._loader.load_from_file(os.path.basename(file_name))
    if not isinstance(ds, list):
        # restore the basedir in case this error is caught and handled
                                                        76,9          68%
```

Putting a breakpoint here will allow us to trace through finding the playbook file and parsing it. Specifically, stepping into the `self._loader.load_from_file()` function call, we will be able to follow the parsing in action.

The `PlayBook` class `load()` function just does the initial parsing. Other classes within other directories are used for execution of plays and tasks. A particularly interesting directory is the `ansible/executor/` directory, which holds files with classes to execute playbooks, plays, and tasks. The `run()` function within the `PlaybookExecutor` class defined in the `ansible/executor/playbook_executor.py` file will loop through all of the plays in the playbook and execute the plays, which will, in turn, execute the individual tasks. This is the function to walk through if facing an issue related to play parsing, play or task callbacks, tags, play host selection, serial operation, handler running, or anything in between.

Debugging executor code

Executor code in Ansible is the connector code that binds together inventory data, playbooks, plays, tasks, and the connection methods. While each of those other code bits can be individually debugged, how they interact can be examined within executor code.

The executor classes are defined in various files within `executor/`. One such class is the `PlaybookExecutor` class. This class handles executing all the plays and the tasks within a given playbook. The class creation function, `__init__()`, creates a series of `placeholder` attributes, as well as setting some default values, while the `run()` function is where most of the fun happens.

Debugging can often take you from one file to another, jumping around the code base. For example, in the `__init__()` function of the `PlaybookExecutor` class, there is code to cache whether or not the default `ssh` executable supports control persist. `ControlPersist` is the feature of `ssh` that keeps sockets to remote hosts open for a period of time for fast reuse. Let's put a break point here and follow the code:

```
                self._tqm = TaskQueueManager(inventory=inventory, variable_manager=v
ariable_manager, loader=loader, options=options, passwords=self.passwords)


        # Note: We run this here to cache whether the default ansible ssh
        # executable supports control persist.  Sometime in the future we may
        # need to enhance this to check that ansible_ssh_executable specified
        # in inventory is also cached.  We can't do this caching at the point
        # where it is used (in task_executor) because that is post-fork and
        # therefore would be discarded after every task.
        import pdb; pdb.set_trace()
        check_for_controlpersist(C.ANSIBLE_SSH_EXECUTABLE)

    def run(self):

        '''
        Run the given playbook, based on the settings in the play which
        may limit the runs to serialized groups, etc.
        '''
```

```
67,9                    21%
```

Now we can run our `objmethod.yml` playbook again to get into a debugging state:

```
● ● ●      3. ansible-playbook -i mastery-hosts objmethod.yaml -vv (python)
~/src/mastery> ansible-playbook -i mastery-hosts objmethod.yaml -vv
No config file found; using defaults
> /Users/jkeating/.virtualenvs/ansible/lib/python2.7/site-packages/ansible/execu
tor/playbook_executor.py(68)__init__()
-> check_for_controlpersist(C.ANSIBLE_SSH_EXECUTABLE)
(Pdb) _
```

We'll need to step into the function to follow the execution. Stepping into the function will take us to a different file:

```
● ● ●      3. ansible-playbook -i mastery-hosts objmethod.yaml -vv (python)
-> check_for_controlpersist(C.ANSIBLE_SSH_EXECUTABLE)
(Pdb) step
--Call--
> /Users/jkeating/.virtualenvs/ansible/lib/python2.7/site-packages/ansible/utils
/ssh_functions.py(29)check_for_controlpersist()
-> def check_for_controlpersist(ssh_executable):
(Pdb) _
```

From here we can use list to see the code in our new file:

```
                3. ansible-playbook -i mastery-hosts objmethod.yaml -vv (python)
(Pdb) list
 24
 25
 26     _HAS_CONTROLPERSIST = {}
 27
 28
 29  -> def check_for_controlpersist(ssh_executable):
 30         try:
 31             # If we've already checked this executable
 32             return _HAS_CONTROLPERSIST[ssh_executable]
 33         except KeyError:
 34             pass
(Pdb) _
```

Walking a few more lines down, we come to a block of code that will execute an ssh command and check the output to determine if ControlPersist is supported:

```
                3. ansible-playbook -i mastery-hosts objmethod.yaml -vv (python)
(Pdb) l
 32             return _HAS_CONTROLPERSIST[ssh_executable]
 33         except KeyError:
 34             pass
 35
 36         has_cp = True
 37  ->     try:
 38             cmd = subprocess.Popen([ssh_executable,'-o','ControlPersist'], stdout=subprocess.PIPE, stderr=subprocess.PIPE)
 39             (out, err) = cmd.communicate()
 40             if b"Bad configuration option" in err or b"Usage:" in err:
 41                 has_cp = False
 42         except OSError:
(Pdb) _
```

Let's walk through the next couple of lines and then print out what the value of `err` is. This will show us the result of the `ssh` execution and the whole string that Ansible will be searching within:

```
● ● ●      3. ansible-playbook -i mastery-hosts objmethod.yaml -vv (python)
37  ->      try:
38              cmd = subprocess.Popen([ssh_executable,'-o','ControlPersist'], s
tdout=subprocess.PIPE, stderr=subprocess.PIPE)
39              (out, err) = cmd.communicate()
40              if b"Bad configuration option" in err or b"Usage:" in err:
41                  has_cp = False
42          except OSError:
(Pdb) n
> /Users/jkeating/.virtualenvs/ansible/lib/python2.7/site-packages/ansible/utils
/ssh_functions.py(38)check_for_controlpersist()
-> cmd = subprocess.Popen([ssh_executable,'-o','ControlPersist'], stdout=subproc
ess.PIPE, stderr=subprocess.PIPE)
(Pdb) n
> /Users/jkeating/.virtualenvs/ansible/lib/python2.7/site-packages/ansible/utils
/ssh_functions.py(39)check_for_controlpersist()
-> (out, err) = cmd.communicate()
(Pdb) n
> /Users/jkeating/.virtualenvs/ansible/lib/python2.7/site-packages/ansible/utils
/ssh_functions.py(40)check_for_controlpersist()
-> if b"Bad configuration option" in err or b"Usage:" in err:
(Pdb) p err
'command-line line 0: Missing ControlPersist argument.\r\n'
(Pdb) _
```

As we can see, the search string is not within the `err` variable, so the value of `has_cp` remains the default of `True`.

 A quick note on forks and debugging: when Ansible uses multiprocessing for multiple forks, debugging becomes difficult. A debugger may be attached to one fork and not another, which will make it very difficult to debug the code. Unless specifically debugging the multiprocessing code, best practice is to stick to a single fork.

Debugging remote code

The remote code is the code that Ansible transports to a remote host in order to execute. This is typically module code, or in the case of action_plugins, other snippets of code. Using the debugging method discussed in the previous section to debug module execution will not work, as Ansible simply copies the code over and then executes it. There is no terminal attached to the remote code execution, and thus, no way to attach to a debugging prompt, that is, without editing the module code.

To debug module code, we need to edit the module code itself to insert a debugger break point. Instead of directly editing the installed module file, create a copy of the file in a library/ directory relative to the playbooks. This copy of the module code will be used instead of the installed file, which makes it easy to temporarily edit a module without disrupting other users of modules on the system.

Unlike with other Ansible code, module code cannot be directly debugged with pdb, because the module code is assembled and then transported to a remote host. Thankfully, there is a solution in the form of a slightly different debugger named rpdb - **The Remote Python Debugger**. This debugger has the ability to start a listening service on a provided port in order to allow remote connections into the Python process. Connecting to the process remotely will allow debugging the code line by line, just as we did with other Ansible code.

To demonstrate how this debugger works, first we're going to need a remote host. For this example, we're using a remote host by the name of debug.example.com, and setting the IP address to a host that is already set up and waiting. Next, we need a playbook to execute a module that we'd like to debug:

```
---
- name: remote code debug
  hosts: debug.example.com
  gather_facts: false

  tasks:
    - name: a remote module execution
      systemd:
        name: dnsmasq
        state: stopped
        enabled: no
```

This play simply calls the systemd module to ensure that the dnsmasq service is stopped and will not start up upon boot. As stated above, we need to make a copy of the service module and place it in library/. The location of the service module to copy from will vary based on the way Ansible is installed. Typically, this module will be located in the modules/core/system/ subdirectory of where the Ansible Python code lives, like /Users/jkeating/.virtualenvs/ansible/lib/python2.7/site-packages/ansible/modules/core/system/systemd.py on my system. Then, we can edit it to put in our break point:

```
                enabled = dict(type='bool'),
                masked = dict(type='bool'),
                daemon_reload= dict(type='bool', default=False, aliases=['daemon
-reload']),
                user= dict(type='bool', default=False),
        ),
        supports_check_mode=True,
        required_one_of=[['state', 'enabled', 'masked', 'daemon_reload']],
    )

# initialize
import rpdb; rpdb.set_trace(addr="0.0.0.0")
systemctl = module.get_bin_path('systemctl')
if module.params['user']:
    systemctl = systemctl + " --user"
unit = module.params['name']
rc = 0
out = err = ''
result = {
                                              248,5          64%
```

We'll put the break point just before the systemctl variable value gets created, near line 248. First, the rpdb module must be imported (meaning that the rpdb Python library needs to exist on the remote host), then the break point needs to be created with set_trace(). Unlike the regular debugger, this function will open a port and listen for external connections. By default, the function will listen for connections to port 4444 on the address 127.0.0.1. However, that address is not exposed over the network, so in my example I've instructed rpdb to listen on address 0.0.0.0, effectively every address on the host. Now, we can run this playbook to set up the server that will wait for a client connection:

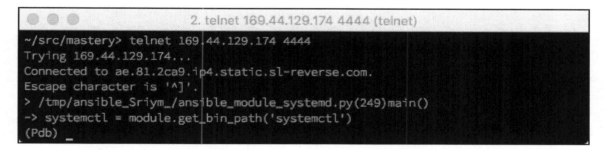

```
●  ●  ●              3. ansible-playbook -i mastery-debug rpdb.yml -vv (python)
~/src/mastery> ansible-playbook -i mastery-debug rpdb.yml -vv
No config file found; using defaults

PLAYBOOK: rpdb.yml ***********************************************************
1 plays in rpdb.yml

PLAY [remote code debug] ****************************************************

TASK [a remote module execution] *******************************************
task path: /Users/jkeating/src/mastery/rpdb.yml:7
```

Now that the server is running, we can connect to it from another terminal. Connecting to the running process can be accomplished with the `telnet` program:

```
●  ●  ●                       2. telnet 169.44.129.174 4444 (telnet)
~/src/mastery> telnet 169.44.129.174 4444
Trying 169.44.129.174...
Connected to ae.81.2ca9.ip4.static.sl-reverse.com.
Escape character is '^]'.
> /tmp/ansible_Sriym_/ansible_module_systemd.py(249)main()
-> systemctl = module.get_bin_path('systemctl')
(Pdb) _
```

From this point on, we can debug as normal. The commands we've used before still exist, such as `list` to show where in the code the current frame is:

```
● ● ●                    2. telnet 169.44.129.174 4444 (telnet)
(Pdb) list
244                    required_one_of=[['state', 'enabled', 'masked', 'daemon_relo
ad']],
245            )
246
247        # initialize
248        import rpdb; rpdb.set_trace(addr="0.0.0.0")
249  ->    systemctl = module.get_bin_path('systemctl')
250        if module.params['user']:
251            systemctl = systemctl + " --user"
252        unit = module.params['name']
253        rc = 0
254        out = err = ''
(Pdb)
```

Using the debugger, we can walk through the `systemd` module to track how it determines the path to the underlying tool, trace which commands are executed on the host, determine how a change is computed, and so on. The entire file can be stepped through, including any other external libraries the module may make use of, allowing debugging of other non-module code on the remote host as well.

If the debugging session allows the module to exit cleanly, the playbook execution will return as normal. However, if the debugging session is disconnected from before the module completes, the playbook will error:

```
  ● ● ●                3. jkeating@serenity-2: ~/src/mastery (zsh)
TASK [a remote module execution] ***************************************
task path: /Users/jkeating/src/mastery/rpdb.yml:7
fatal: [debug.example.com]: FAILED! => {"changed": false, "failed": true, "modul
e_stderr": "", "module_stdout": "pdb is running on 0.0.0.0:4444\r\nTraceback (mo
st recent call last):\r\n  File \"/tmp/ansible_yWg_v/ansible_module_systemd.py\
", line 386, in <module>\r\n    main()\r\n  File \"/tmp/ansible_yWg_v/ansible_m
odule_systemd.py\", line 249, in main\r\n    systemctl = module.get_bin_path('sy
stemctl')\r\n  File \"/tmp/ansible_yWg_v/ansible_module_systemd.py\", line 249,
 in main\r\n    systemctl = module.get_bin_path('systemctl')\r\n  File \"/usr/li
b64/python2.7/bdb.py\", line 49, in trace_dispatch\r\n    return self.dispatch_l
ine(frame)\r\n  File \"/usr/lib64/python2.7/bdb.py\", line 68, in dispatch_line\
r\n    if self.quitting: raise BdbQuit\r\nbdb.BdbQuit\r\n", "msg": "MODULE FAILU
RE"}
        to retry, use: --limit @/Users/jkeating/src/mastery/rpdb.retry

PLAY RECAP ****************************************************************
debug.example.com          : ok=0    changed=0    unreachable=0    failed=1

exit 2
~/src/mastery>
```

Because of this side-effect, it is best to not exit the debugger early, and instead issue a `continue` command when your debugging is finished.

Debugging the action plugins

Some modules are actually action plugins. These are tasks that will execute some code locally before transporting code to the remote host. Some example action plugins include `copy`, `fetch`, `script`, and `template`. The source to these plugins can be found in `plugins/action/`. Each plugin will have its own file in this directory that can be edited to have break points inserted to debug the code executed prior to (or in lieu of) sending code to the remote host. Debugging these is typically done with `pdb`, as most of the code is executed locally.

Summary

Ansible is software, and software breaks. It's not a matter of if, but when. Invalid input, improper assumptions, unexpected environments – all things that can lead to a frustrating situation when tasks and plays are just not performing as expected. Introspection and debugging are troubleshooting techniques that can quickly turn frustration into elation when a root cause is discovered.

In the next chapter, we will learn how to extend the functionality of Ansible by writing our own modules, plugins, and inventory sources.

8

Extending Ansible

Ansible takes the kitchen sink approach to functionality. There are over 800 modules available for use within Ansible at the time of writing this. In addition, there are numerous callback plugins, lookup plugins, filter plugins, and dynamic inventory plugins. Even with all of that functionality, there can still exist a need to add new functionality.

This chapter will explore the following ways in which new capabilities can be added to Ansible:

- Developing modules
- Developing plugins
- Developing dynamic inventory plugins
- Contributing code to the Ansible project

Developing modules

Modules are the workhorse of Ansible. They provide just enough abstraction that enables playbooks to be stated simply and clearly. There are over 100 modules maintained by the core Ansible development team covering clouds, commands, databases, files, network, packaging, source control, system, utilities, web infrastructure, and so on. In addition, there are nearly 700 other modules maintained by community contributors that expand functionality in many of these categories. The real magic happens inside the module code, which takes in the arguments passed to it and works to establish the desired outcome.

Modules in Ansible are the bits of code that get transported to the remote host to be executed. They can be written in any language that the remote host can execute; however, Ansible provides some very useful shortcuts if writing the module in Python.

The basic module construct

A module exists to satisfy a need – the need to do a piece of work on a host. Modules usually, but not always, expect input, and will return some sort of output. Modules also strive to be idempotent, allowing rerunning the module over and over again without having a negative impact. In Ansible, the input is in the form of command-line arguments to the module, and output is delivered as JSON to standard out.

Input is generally provided in the space-separated `key=value` syntax and it's up to the module to deconstruct these into the usable data. If using Python, there are convenience functions to manage this, and if using a different language, then it is up to the module code to fully process the input.

The output is JSON formatted. Convention dictates that in a success scenario, the JSON output should have at least one key, changed, which is a Boolean to indicate whether the module execution resulted in a change or not. Additional data can be returned as well, which may be useful to define specifically what changed, or provide important information back to the playbook for later use. Additionally, host facts can be returned in the JSON data to automatically create host variables based on the module execution results. We will see more on this later.

Custom modules

Ansible provides an easy mechanism to utilize custom modules outside of what comes with Ansible. As we learned in Chapter 1, *System Architecture and Design of Ansible*, Ansible will search many locations to find a requested module. One such location, the first location, is the `library/` subdirectory of the path where the top-level playbook resides. This is where we will place our custom module so that we can use it in our example playbook.

Modules can also be embedded within roles to deliver the added functionality that a role may depend upon. These modules are only available to the role that contains it or any other roles or tasks executed after the role containing the module. To deliver a module with a role, place the module in the `library/` subdirectory of the role's root.

Simple module

To demonstrate the ease of writing Python-based modules, let's create a simple module. The purpose of this module will be to remotely copy a source file to a destination file; a simple task that we can build up from. To start our module, we need to create the module file. For easy access to our new module, we'll create the file in the `library/` subdirectory of the working directory we've already been using. We'll call this module `remote_copy.py`, and to start it off, we'll need to put in a `sha-bang` line to indicate that this module is to be executed with Python:

```
#!/usr/bin/python
#
```

For Python-based modules, the convention is to use `/usr/bin/python` as the listed executable. When executed on a remote system, the configured Python interpreter for the remote host is used to execute the module, so fret not if your Python doesn't exist in this path. Next, we'll import a Python library we'll use later in the module, called `shutil`:

```
import shutil
```

Now, we're ready to create our main function. The main function is essentially the entry point to the module, where the arguments to the module will be defined and where the execution will start. When creating modules in Python, we can take some shortcuts in this main function to bypass a lot of boilerplate code, and get straight to the argument definitions. We do this by creating an `AnsibleModule` object and giving it an `argument_spec` dictionary for the arguments:

```
def main():
    module = AnsibleModule(
        argument_spec = dict(
            source=dict(required=True, type='str'),
            dest=dict(required=True, type='str')
        )
    )
```

In our module, we're providing two arguments. The first argument is `source`, which we'll use to define the source file for the copy. The second argument is `dest`, the destination for the copy. Both of these arguments are marked as required, which will raise an error when executed if one of the two are not provided. Both arguments are of the type `string`. The location of the `AnsibleModule` class has not yet been defined, as that happens later in the file.

With a module object at our disposal, we can now create the code that will do the actual work on the remote host. We'll make use of `shutil.copy` and our provided arguments to accomplish the copy:

```
shutil.copy(module.params['source'],
            module.params['dest'])
```

The `shutil.copy` function expects a source and a destination, which we've provided by accessing `module.params`. The `module.params` dictionary holds all of the parameters for the module. Having completed the copy, we are now ready to return the results to Ansible. This is done via another `AnsibleModule` method, `exit_json`. This method expects a set of `key=value` arguments and will format it appropriately for a JSON return. Since we're always performing a copy, we will always return a change for simplicity's sake:

```
module.exit_json(changed=True)
```

This line will exit the function, and thus the module. This function assumes a successful action and will exit the module with the appropriate return code for success: `0`. We're not done with our module's code though, we still have to account for the `AnsibleModule` location. This is where a bit of magic happens, where we tell Ansible what other code to combine with our module to create a complete work that can be transported:

```
from ansible.module_utils.basic import *
```

That's all it takes! That one line gets us access to all of the basic `module_utils`, a decent set of helper functions and classes. There is one last thing we should put into our module, a couple of lines of code telling the interpreter to execute the `main()` function when the module file is executed:

```
if __name__ == '__main__':
    main()
```

Now our module file is complete and we can test it with a playbook. We'll call our playbook `simple_module.yaml`, and store it in the same directory as the `library/` directory where we've just written our module file. We'll run the play on `localhost` for simplicity's sake and use a couple of filenames in `/tmp` for the source and destination. We'll also use a task to ensure that we have a source file to begin with:

```
---
- name: test remote_copy module
  hosts: localhost
  gather_facts: false

  tasks:
    - name: ensure foo
```

```
file:
  path: /tmp/foo
  state: touch

- name: do a remote copy
  remote_copy:
    source: /tmp/foo
    dest: /tmp/bar
```

To run this playbook, we'll reference our `mastery-hosts` file. If the `remote_copy` module file is written to the correct location, everything will work just fine, and the screen output will look as follows:

```
● ● ●                    2. jkeating@serenity: ~/src/mastery (zsh)
~/src/mastery> ansible-playbook -i mastery-hosts simple_module.yaml -vv

PLAY [test remote_copy module] ********************************************

TASK: [ensure foo] ********************************************************
<localhost> REMOTE_MODULE file state=touch path=/tmp/foo
changed: [localhost] => {"changed": true, "dest": "/tmp/foo", "gid": 0, "group":
 "wheel", "mode": "0644", "owner": "jkeating", "size": 0, "state": "file", "uid"
 : 501}

TASK: [do a remote copy] **************************************************
<localhost> REMOTE_MODULE remote_copy source=/tmp/foo dest=/tmp/bar
changed: [localhost] => {"changed": true}

PLAY RECAP ****************************************************************
localhost                  : ok=2    changed=2    unreachable=0    failed=0

~/src/mastery> []
```

Our first task touches the /tmp/foo path to ensure that it exists, and then our second task makes use of `remote_copy` to copy /tmp/foo to /tmp/bar. Both tasks are successful, resulting in a change each time.

Module documentation

No module should be considered complete unless it contains documentation on how to operate the module. Documentation for modules exists within the module itself, in special variables called DOCUMENTATION, EXAMPLES, and RETURN.

The DOCUMENTATION variable contains a specially formatted string describing the module name, the version it was added to Ansible (if it is in Ansible proper), a short description of the module, a longer description, a description of the module arguments, author and license information, additional requirements, and any extra notes useful to users of the module. Let's add a DOCUMENTATION string to our module:

```
import shutil

DOCUMENTATION = '''
---
module: remote_copy
version_added: future
short_description: Copy a file on the remote host
description:
  - The remote_copy module copies a file on the remote host from a given
source to a provided destination.
options:
  source:
    description:
      - Path to a file on the source file on the remote host
    required: True
  dest:
    description:
      - Path to the destination on the remote host for the copy
    required: True
author:
  - Jesse Keating
'''
```

The format of the string is essentially YAML, with some top-level keys containing hash structures within (same as the options key). Each option has subelements to describe the option, indicate whether the option is required, list any aliases for the option, list static choices for the option, or indicate a default value for the option. With this string saved to the module, we can test our formatting to ensure that the documentation will render correctly. This is done via the ansible-doc tool with an argument to indicate where to search for modules. If we run it from the same place as our playbook, the command will be ansible-doc -M library/ remote_copy, and the output will be as follows:

```
2. jkeating@serenity: ~/src/mastery (zsh)
~/src/mastery> ansible-doc -M library/ remote_copy |cat -
> REMOTE_COPY

    The remote_copy module copies a file on the remote host from a given
    source to a provided destination.

Options (= is mandatory):

= dest
        Path to the destination on the remote host for the copy

= source
        Path to a file on the source file on the remote host


~/src/mastery> []
```

In this example, I've piped the output into `cat` to prevent the pager from hiding the execution line. Our documentation string appears to be formatted correctly, and provides the user with important information regarding the usage of the module.

The EXAMPLES string is used to provide one or more example uses of the module, snippets of the task code that one would use in a playbook. Let's add an example task to demonstrate the usage. This variable definition traditionally goes after the DOCUMENTATION definition:

```
EXAMPLES = '''
# Example from Ansible Playbooks
- name: backup a config file
  remote_copy:
    source: /etc/herp/derp.conf
    dest: /root/herp-derp.conf.bak
'''
```

With this variable defined, our `ansible-doc` output will now include the example, as we can see in the following screenshot:

```
● ● ●                2. jkeating@serenity: ~/src/mastery (zsh)
~/src/mastery> ansible-doc -M library/ remote_copy |cat -
> REMOTE_COPY

    The remote_copy module copies a file on the remote host from a given
    source to a provided destination.

Options (= is mandatory):

= dest
        Path to the destination on the remote host for the copy

= source
        Path to a file on the source file on the remote host

EXAMPLES:
# Example from Ansible Playbooks
- name: backup a config file
  remote_copy:
    source: /etc/herp/derp.conf
    dest: /root/herp-derp.conf.bak


~/src/mastery> []
```

The last documentation variable, RETURN, is a relatively new feature of module documentation. This variable is used to describe the return data from a module execution. Return data is often useful as a registered variable for later usage, and having documentation of what return data to expect can aid in playbook development. Our module doesn't have any return data yet; so before we can document return data, we first have to add return data. This can be done by modifying the `module.exit_json` line to add more information. Let's add the `source` and `dest` data into the return output:

```
module.exit_json(changed=True, source=module.params['source'],
                 dest=module.params['dest'])
```

Rerunning the playbook will show extra data being returned, as shown in the following screenshot:

```
● ● ●                    2. jkeating@serenity: ~/src/mastery (zsh)
~/src/mastery> ansible-playbook -i mastery-hosts simple_module.yaml -vv

PLAY [test remote_copy module] ********************************************

TASK: [ensure foo] ********************************************************
<localhost> REMOTE_MODULE file state=touch path=/tmp/foo
changed: [localhost] => {"changed": true, "dest": "/tmp/foo", "gid": 0, "group":
 "wheel", "mode": "0644", "owner": "jkeating", "size": 0, "state": "file", "uid"
: 501}

TASK: [do a remote copy] **************************************************
<localhost> REMOTE_MODULE remote_copy source=/tmp/foo dest=/tmp/bar
changed: [localhost] => {"changed": true, "dest": "/tmp/bar", "gid": 0, "group":
 "wheel", "mode": "0644", "owner": "jkeating", "size": 0, "source": "/tmp/foo",
"state": "file", "uid": 501}

PLAY RECAP ****************************************************************
localhost                  : ok=2    changed=2    unreachable=0    failed=0

~/src/mastery> []
```

Looking closely at the return data, we can see more data than we put in our module. This is actually a bit of a helper functionality within Ansible; when a return data set includes a dest variable Ansible will gather more information about the destination file. The extra data gathered is gid (group ID), group (group name), mode (permissions), uid (owner ID), owner (owner name), size, and state (file, link, or directory). We can document all of these return items in our RETURN variable, which is added after the EXAMPLES variable:

```
RETURN = '''
source:
  description: source file used for the copy
  returned: success
  type: string
  sample: "/path/to/file.name"
dest:
  description: destination of the copy
  returned: success
  type: string
  sample: "/path/to/destination.file"
```

```
gid:
  description: group ID of destination target
  returned: success
  type: int
  sample: 502
group:
  description: group name of destination target
  returned: success
  type: string
  sample: "users"
uid:
  description: owner ID of destination target
  returned: success
  type: int
  sample: 502
owner:
  description: owner name of destination target
  returned: success
  type: string
  sample: "fred"
mode:
  description: permissions of the destination target
  returned: success
  type: int
  sample: 0644
size:
  description: size of destination target
  returned: success
  type: int
  sample: 20
state:
  description: state of destination target
  returned: success
  type: string
  sample: "file"
'''
```

Each return item is listed with a description, the cases when the item would be in the return data, the type of item it is, and a sample of the value. The RETURN string is essentially repeated verbatim in the `ansible-doc` output, as shown in the following (abbreviated) example:

```
● ● ●                    2. jkeating@serenity: ~/src/mastery (zsh)
~/src/mastery> ansible-doc -M library/ remote_copy |cat -
> REMOTE_COPY

    The remote_copy module copies a file on the remote host from a given
    source to a provided destination.

Options (= is mandatory):

= dest
        Path to the destination on the remote host for the copy

= source
        Path to a file on the source file on the remote host

EXAMPLES:
# Example from Ansible Playbooks
- name: backup a config file
  remote_copy:
    source: /etc/herp/derp.conf
    dest: /root/herp-derp.conf.bak

RETURN VALUES:
source:
  description: source file used for the copy
  returned: success
  type: string
  sample: "/path/to/file.name"
dest:
  description: destination of the copy
  returned: success
  type: string
  sample: "/path/to/destination.file"
```

Providing fact data

Similar to data returned as part of a module `exit`, a module can directly create facts for a host by returning data in a key named `ansible_facts`. Providing facts directly from a module eliminates the need to register the return of a task with a subsequent `set_fact` task. To demonstrate this usage, let's modify our module to return the `source` and `dest` data as facts. Because these facts will become top-level host variables, we'll want to use more descriptive fact names than `source` and `dest`:

```
facts = {'rc_source': module.params['source'],
         'rc_dest': module.params['dest']}

module.exit_json(changed=True, ansible_facts=facts)
```

We'll also add a task to our playbook to use one of the facts in a debug statement:

```
- name: show a fact
  debug:
    var: rc_dest
```

Now, running the playbook will show the new return data plus the use of the variable:

```
                  2. jkeating@serenity: ~/src/mastery (zsh)
~/src/mastery> ansible-playbook -i mastery-hosts simple_module.yaml -vv

PLAY [test remote_copy module] ****************************************

TASK: [ensure foo] ***************************************************
<localhost> REMOTE_MODULE file state=touch path=/tmp/foo
changed: [localhost] => {"changed": true, "dest": "/tmp/foo", "gid": 0, "group":
 "wheel", "mode": "0644", "owner": "jkeating", "size": 0, "state": "file", "uid"
: 501}

TASK: [do a remote copy] *********************************************
<localhost> REMOTE_MODULE remote_copy source=/tmp/foo dest=/tmp/bar
changed: [localhost] => {"ansible_facts": {"rc_dest": "/tmp/bar", "rc_source": "
/tmp/foo"}, "changed": true}

TASK: [show a fact] **************************************************
ok: [localhost] => {
    "var": {
        "rc_dest": "/tmp/bar"
    }
}

PLAY RECAP ***********************************************************
localhost                  : ok=3      changed=2    unreachable=0    failed=0

~/src/mastery> []
```

If our module does not return facts, we will have to register the output and use set_fact to create the fact for us, as shown in the following code:

```
- name: do a remote copy
  remote_copy:
    source: /tmp/foo
    dest: /tmp/bar
  register: mycopy

- name: set facts from mycopy
```

```
set_fact:
  rc_dest: "{{ mycopy.dest }}"
```

The check mode

Since version 1.1, Ansible has supported check mode, a mode of operation that will pretend to make changes to a system without actually changing the system. Check mode is useful for testing whether a change will actually happen, or if a system state has drifted since the last Ansible run. Check mode depends on modules to support check mode and return data as if it had actually completed the change. Supporting check mode in our module requires two changes; the first is to indicate that the module supports check mode, and the second is to detect when check mode is active and return data before execution.

Supporting the check mode

To indicate that a module supports check mode, an argument has to be set when creating the module object. This can be done before or after the `argument_spec` variable is defined in the module object; here, we will do it after it is defined:

```
module = AnsibleModule(
    argument_spec = dict(
        source=dict(required=True, type='str'),
        dest=dict(required=True, type='str')
    ),
    supports_check_mode=True
)
```

Handling check mode

Detecting when check mode is active is very easy. The module object will have a `check_mode` attribute, which will be set to Boolean value `true` when check mode is active. In our module, we want to detect whether check mode is active before performing the copy. We can simply move the copy action into an `if` statement to avoid copying when check mode is active. The return can happen without any changes:

```
if not module.check_mode:
    shutil.copy(module.params['source'],
                module.params['dest'])
```

Now, we can run our playbook and add the -C argument to our execution. This argument engages check mode. We'll also test to ensure that the playbook did not actually create and copy the files. Let's take a look at the following screenshot:

```
 ● ● ●                2. jkeating@serenity: ~/src/mastery (zsh)
~/src/mastery> file /tmp/foo /tmp/bar
/tmp/foo: cannot open `/tmp/foo' (No such file or directory)
/tmp/bar: cannot open `/tmp/bar' (No such file or directory)
~/src/mastery> ansible-playbook -i mastery-hosts simple_module.yaml -vv -C

PLAY [test remote_copy module] ********************************************

TASK: [ensure foo] ********************************************************
<localhost> REMOTE_MODULE file state=touch path=/tmp/foo CHECKMODE=True
changed: [localhost] => {"changed": true, "dest": "/tmp/foo", "state": "absent"}

TASK: [do a remote copy] **************************************************
<localhost> REMOTE_MODULE remote_copy source=/tmp/foo dest=/tmp/bar CHECKMODE=Tr
ue
changed: [localhost] => {"ansible_facts": {"rc_dest": "/tmp/bar", "rc_source": "
/tmp/foo"}, "changed": true}

TASK: [show a fact] *******************************************************
ok: [localhost] => {
    "var": {
        "rc_dest": "/tmp/bar"
    }
}

PLAY RECAP ****************************************************************
localhost                  : ok=3    changed=2    unreachable=0    failed=0

~/src/mastery> file /tmp/foo /tmp/bar
/tmp/foo: cannot open `/tmp/foo' (No such file or directory)
/tmp/bar: cannot open `/tmp/bar' (No such file or directory)
~/src/mastery> []
```

Although the module output looks like it created and copied files, we can see that the files referenced did not exist before execution and still do not exist after execution.

Developing plugins

Plugins are another way of extending or modifying the functionality of Ansible. While modules are executed as tasks, plugins are utilized in a variety of other places. Plugins are broken down into a few types, based on where they would plug in to the Ansible execution. Ansible ships some plugins for each of these areas, and end users can create their own to extend the functionality of these specific areas.

Connection type plugins

Any time Ansible makes a connection to a host to perform a task, a connection plugin is used. Ansible ships with a few connection plugins, including `ssh`, `docker`, `chroot`, `local`, and `smart`. Additional connection mechanisms can be utilized by Ansible to connect to remote systems by creating a connection plugin, which may be useful if faced with connecting to some new type of system, such as a network switch, or maybe your refrigerator some day. Creating connection plugins is a bit beyond the scope of this book; however, the easiest way to get started is to read through the existing plugins that ship with Ansible and pick one to modify as necessary. The existing plugins can be found in `plugins/connection/` wherever the Ansible Python libraries are installed on your system, such as `/Users/jkeating/.virtualenvs/ansible/lib/python2.7/site-packages/ansible/plugins/connection/` on my system.

Shell plugins

Much like connection plugins, Ansible makes use of shell plugins to execute things in a shell environment. Each shell has subtle differences that Ansible cares about in order to properly execute commands, redirect output, discover errors, and other such interactions. Ansible supports a number of shells, including `sh`, `csh`, `fish`, and `powershell`. We can add more shells by implementing a new shell plugin.

Lookup plugins

Lookup plugins are how Ansible accesses outside data sources from the host system, and implements language features, such as looping constructs (`with_*`). A lookup plugin can be created to access data from an existing data store, or to create a new looping mechanism. The existing lookup plugins can be found in `plugins/lookup/`. Lookup plugins can be added to introduce new ways of looping over content, or for looking up resources in external systems.

Vars plugins

Constructs to inject variable data exist in the form of vars plugins. Data such as `host_vars` and `group_vars` are implemented via plugins. While it's possible to create new variable plugins, most often, it is better to create a custom inventory source or a fact module instead.

The fact caching plugins

Recently (as of version 1.8), Ansible gained the ability to cache facts between playbook runs. Where the facts are cached depends on the configured cache plugin that is used. Ansible includes plugins to cache facts in `memory` (not actually cached between runs), `memcached`, `redis`, and `jsonfile`. Creating a fact caching plugin can enable additional caching mechanisms.

Filter plugins

While Jinja2 includes a number of filters, Ansible has made filters pluggable to extend the Jinja2 functionality. Ansible includes a number of filters that are useful to Ansible operations, and users of Ansible can add more. Existing plugins can be found in `plugins/filter/`.

To demonstrate the development of a filter plugin, we will create a simple filter plugin to do a silly thing to text strings. We will create a filter that will replace any occurrence of the cloud with somebody else's computer. We'll define our filter in a file within a new directory, `filter_plugins/`, in our existing working directory. The name of the file doesn't matter, as we'll define the name of the filter within the file; so, lets name our file `filter_plugins/sample_filter.py`. First, we need to define the function that will perform the translation, and provide the code to translate the strings:

```python
def cloud_truth(a):
    return a.replace("the cloud", "somebody else's computer")
```

Next, we'll need to construct a `FilterModule` object and define our filter within it. This object is what Ansible will load, and Ansible expects there to be a `filters` function within the object that returns a set of filter names to functions within the file:

```python
class FilterModule(object):
    '''Cloud truth filters'''
    def filters(self):
        return {'cloud_truth': cloud_truth}
```

Now, we can use this filter in a playbook, which we'll call `simple_filter.yaml`:

```
---
- name: test cloud_truth filter
  hosts: localhost
  gather_facts: false
  vars:
    statement: "I store my files in the cloud"
  tasks:
    - name: make a statement
      debug:
        msg: "{{ statement | cloud_truth }}"
```

Now, let's run our playbook and see our filter in action:

```
  ● ● ●                    2. jkeating@serenity: ~/src/mastery (zsh)
~/src/mastery> ansible-playbook -i mastery-hosts simple_filter.yaml -vv

PLAY [test cloud_truth filter] ************************************************

TASK: [make a statement] ******************************************************
ok: [localhost] => {
    "msg": "I store my files in somebody else's computer"
}

PLAY RECAP ********************************************************************
localhost                  : ok=1    changed=0    unreachable=0    failed=0

~/src/mastery> []
```

Our filter worked, and it turned the cloud into somebody else's computer. This is a silly example without any error handling, but it clearly demonstrates our capability to extend Ansible and Jinja2's filter capabilities.

 Although the file name a filter exists in can be whatever the developer wants to name it, a best practice is to name it after the filter itself so that it can easily be found in the future, potentially by other collaborators. This example did not follow this to demonstrate that the file name is not attached to the filter name.

Callback plugins

Callbacks are places in Ansible execution that can be plugged into for added functionality. There are expected callback points that can be registered against to trigger custom actions at those points. Here is a list of possible points to trigger functionality at the time of this writing:

- v2_on_any
- v2_runner_on_failed
- v2_runner_on_ok
- v2_runner_on_skipped
- v2_runner_on_unreachable
- v2_runner_on_no_hosts
- v2_runner_on_async_poll
- v2_runner_on_async_ok
- v2_runner_on_async_failed
- v2_runner_on_file_diff
- v2_playbook_on_start
- v2_playbook_on_notify
- v2_playbook_on_no_hosts_matched
- v2_playbook_on_no_hosts_remaining
- v2_playbook_on_task_start
- v2_playbook_on_cleanup_task_start
- v2_playbook_on_handler_task_start
- v2_playbook_on_vars_prompt
- v2_playbook_on_setup
- v2_playbook_on_import_for_host
- v2_playbook_on_not_import_for_host
- v2_playbook_on_play_start
- v2_playbook_on_stats
- v2_on_file_diff
- v2_playbook_on_include
- v2_runner_item_on_ok

- v2_runner_item_on_failed
- v2_runner_item_on_skipped
- v2_runner_retry

As an Ansible run reaches each of these states, any plugins that have code to run at these points will be executed. This provides a tremendous ability to extend Ansible without having to modify the base code

Callbacks can be utilized in a variety of ways; to change how things are displayed on screen, to update a central status system on progress, to implement a global locking system, or nearly anything imaginable. It's the most powerful way to extend the functionality of Ansible. To demonstrate our ability to develop a callback plugin, we'll create a simple plugin that will print something silly on the screen as a playbook executes:

1. First, we'll need to make a new directory to hold our callback. The location Ansible will look for is callback_plugins/. Unlike the filter plugin earlier, we do need to name our callback plugin file carefully as it will also have to be reflected in an ansible.cfg file.

2. We'll name ours callback_plugins/shrug.py. Inside this file, we'll need to create a CallbackModule class, subclassed from the CallbackModule defined in the default callback plugin found in ansible.plugins.callback.default, since we only need to change one aspect of normal output.

3. Within this class, we define variable values to indicate that it is a 2.0 version callback, and that it is an stdout type of callback, and finally that it has a name of shrug.

4. Also within this class, we define one or more of the callback points we'd like to plug into in order to make something happen.

5. We only have to define the points we want to plug in. In our case we'll plug into the v2_on_any point so that our plugin runs at every callback spot.

```
from ansible.plugins.callback import default
class CallbackModule(default.CallbackModule):
CALLBACK_VERSION = 2.0
CALLBACK_TYPE = 'stdout'
CALLBACK_NAME = 'shrug'
  def v2_on_any(self, *args, **kwargs):
    msg = '\xc2\xaf\\_(\xe3\x83\x84)_/\xc2\xaf'
      self._display.display(msg.decode('utf-8') * 8)
```

6. As this callback is a `stdout_callback`, we'll need to create an `ansible.cfg` file and within it indicate that the `shrug` stdout callback should be used. The `ansible.cfg` file can be in `/etc/ansible/` or in the same directory as the playbook.

```
[defaults]
stdout_callback = shrug
```

7. That's all we have to write into our callback. Once it's saved, we can rerun our previous playbook, which exercised our `sample_filter`, but this time we'll see something different on screen:

```
2. jkeating@serenity: ~/src/mastery (zsh)
~/src/mastery> ansible-playbook -i mastery-hosts simple_filter.yaml -vv
¯\_(ツ)_/¯¯\_(ツ)_/¯¯\_(ツ)_/¯¯\_(ツ)_/¯¯\_(ツ)_/¯¯\_(ツ)_/¯¯\_(ツ)_/¯¯\_(ツ)_/¯

PLAY [test cloud_truth filter] *******************************************
¯\_(ツ)_/¯¯\_(ツ)_/¯¯\_(ツ)_/¯¯\_(ツ)_/¯¯\_(ツ)_/¯¯\_(ツ)_/¯¯\_(ツ)_/¯¯\_(ツ)_/¯

TASK: [make a statement] *************************************************
¯\_(ツ)_/¯¯\_(ツ)_/¯¯\_(ツ)_/¯¯\_(ツ)_/¯¯\_(ツ)_/¯¯\_(ツ)_/¯¯\_(ツ)_/¯¯\_(ツ)_/¯
ok: [localhost] => {
    "msg": "I store my files in somebody else's computer"
}
¯\_(ツ)_/¯¯\_(ツ)_/¯¯\_(ツ)_/¯¯\_(ツ)_/¯¯\_(ツ)_/¯¯\_(ツ)_/¯¯\_(ツ)_/¯¯\_(ツ)_/¯

PLAY RECAP ***************************************************************
¯\_(ツ)_/¯¯\_(ツ)_/¯¯\_(ツ)_/¯¯\_(ツ)_/¯¯\_(ツ)_/¯¯\_(ツ)_/¯¯\_(ツ)_/¯¯\_(ツ)_/¯
localhost                  : ok=1    changed=0    unreachable=0    failed=0

~/src/mastery>
```

Very silly, but demonstrates the ability to plug into various points of a playbook execution. We chose to display a series of shrugs on screen, but we could have just as easily interacted with some internal audit and control system to record actions, or to report progress to an IRC or Slack channel.

Action plugins

Action plugins exist to hook into the task construct without actually causing a module to be executed, or to execute code locally on the Ansible host before executing a module on the remote host. A number of action plugins are included with Ansible and can be found in `plugins/action/`. One such action plugin is the `template` plugin used in place of a `template` module. When a playbook author writes a `template` task, that task will actually call the `template` plugin to do the work. The plugin, among other things, will render the template locally before copying the content to the remote host. Because actions have to happen locally, the work is done by an action plugin. Another action plugin we should be familiar with is the `debug` plugin, which we've used heavily in this book to print content. Creating a custom action plugin is useful when trying to accomplish both local work and remote work in the same task.

Distributing plugins

Much like distributing custom modules, there are standard places to store custom plugins alongside playbooks that expect to use plugins. The default locations for plugins are the locations that are shipped with the Ansible code install, subdirectories within `~/.ansible/plugins/`, and subdirectories of the project root (the place where the top-level playbook is stored). Plugins can be distributed within the same subdirectories of a role as well. To utilize plugins from any other location, we need to define the location to find the plugin for the plugin type in an `ansible.cfg` file.

When distributing plugins inside the project root, each plugin type gets its own top-level directory:

- `action_plugins/`
- `cache_plugins/`
- `callback_plugins/`
- `connection_plugins/`
- `shell_plugins/`
- `lookup_plugins/`
- `vars_plugins/`
- `filter_plugins/`

As with other Ansible constructs, the first plugin with a given name found will be used, and just like with modules, the paths relative to the project root are checked first, allowing a local override of an existing plugin. Simply place the filter file into the appropriate subdirectory, and it will automatically get used when referenced.

Developing dynamic inventory plugins

Inventory plugins are bits of code that will create inventory data for an Ansible execution. In many environments, the simple `ini` file style inventory source and variable structure is not sufficient to represent the actual infrastructure being managed. In such cases, a dynamic inventory source is desired, one that will discover the inventory and data at runtime at every execution of Ansible. A number of these dynamic sources ship with Ansible, primarily to operate Ansible with the infrastructure built into one cloud computing platform or another. A short, incomplete list of dynamic inventory plugins that ship with Ansible includes:

- `apache-libcloud`
- `cobbler`
- `console_io`
- `digital_ocean`
- `docker`
- `ec2`
- `gce`
- `libvirt_lxc`
- `linode`
- `openshift`
- `openstack`
- `rax`
- `vagrant`
- `vmware`
- `windows_azure`

An inventory plugin is essentially an executable script. Ansible calls the script with set arguments (`--list` or `--host <hostname>`) and expects JSON formatted output on standard out. When the `--list` argument is provided, Ansible expects a list of all the groups to be managed. Each group can list host membership, child group membership, and group variable data. When the script is called with the `--host <hostname>` argument, Ansible expects host-specific data to be returned (or an empty JSON dictionary).

Using a dynamic inventory source is easy. A source can be used directly by referring to it with the `-i` (`--inventory-file`) option to `ansible` and `ansible-playbook`, or by placing the plugin file in the `ansible.cfg` configured inventory path, or by putting the plugin file inside the directory referred to by either the inventory path in `ansible.cfg` or by the `-i` runtime option.

Before creating an inventory plugin, we must understand the expected format for when `--list` or `--host` is used with our script.

Listing hosts

When the `--list` argument is passed to an inventory script, Ansible expects the JSON output data to have a set of top-level keys. These keys are named for the groups in the inventory. Each group gets its own key. The structure within a group key varies depending on what data needs to be represented in the group. If a group just has hosts and no group level variables, the data within the key can simply be a list of host names. If the group has variables or children (group of groups), then the data needs to be a hash, which can have one or more keys named `hosts`, `vars`, or `children`. The hosts and children subkeys have a list value, a list of the hosts that exist in the group, or a list of the child groups. The `vars` subkey has a hash value, where each variable's name and value is represented by a key and value.

Listing host variables

When the `--host <hostname>` argument is passed to an inventory script, Ansible expects the JSON output data to simply be a hash of the variables, where each variable name and value is represented by a key and a value. If there are no variables for a given host, an empty hash is expected.

Simple inventory plugin

To demonstrate developing an inventory plugin, we'll create one that simply prints the same host data we've been using in our `mastery-hosts` file. Integrating with a custom asset management system or an infrastructure provider is a bit beyond the scope of this book, so we'll simply code the systems into the plugin itself. We'll write our inventory plugin to a file in the top level of our project root named `mastery-inventory.py`, and make it executable. We'll use Python for this file for the ease of handling execution arguments and JSON formatting:

1. First, we'll need to add a `sha-bang` line to indicate that this script is to be executed with Python:

```
#!/usr/bin/env python
#
```

2. Next, we'll need to import a couple of Python modules that we will need later in our plugin:

```
import json
import argparse
```

3. Now, we'll create a Python dictionary to hold all of our groups. Some of our groups just have hosts, while others have variables or children. We'll format each group accordingly:

```
inventory = {}
inventory['web'] = {'hosts': ['mastery.example.name'],
                    'vars': {'http_port': 80,
                             'proxy_timeout': 5}}
inventory['dns'] = {'hosts': ['backend.example.name']}
inventory['database'] = {'hosts': ['backend.example.name'],
                         'vars': {'ansible_ssh_user': 'database'}}
inventory['frontend'] = {'children': ['web']}
inventory['backend'] = {'children': ['dns', 'database'],
                        'vars': {'ansible_ssh_user': 'blotto'}}
inventory['errors'] = {'hosts': ['scsihost']}
inventory['failtest'] = {'hosts': ["failer%02d" % n for n in
                                   range(1,11)]}
```

4. To recreate our `failtest` group, which in our inventory file was represented as `failer[01:10]`, we used a Python list comprehension to produce the list for us, formatting the items in the list just the same as our original inventory file. Every other group entry is self-explanatory.

5. Our original inventory also had an `all` group variable that provided a default variable `ansible_ssh_user` to all groups (which groups could override) that we'll define here and make use of later in the file:

```
allgroupvars = {'ansible_ssh_user': 'otto'}
```

6. Next, we need to enter the host-specific variables into their own dictionary. Only two nodes in our original inventory have host-specific variables:

```
hostvars = {}
hostvars['web'] = {'ansible_ssh_host': '192.168.10.25'}
hostvars['scsihost'] = {'ansible_ssh_user': 'jkeating'}
```

7. With all our data defined, we can now move on to the code that will handle argument parsing. This is done via the `argparse` module we imported earlier in the file:

```
parser = argparse.ArgumentParser(description='Simple Inventory')
parser.add_argument('--list', action='store_true',
                    help='List all hosts')
parser.add_argument('--host', help='List details of a host')
args = parser.parse_args()
```

8. After parsing the arguments, we can deal with either the `--list` or `--host` actions. If a list is requested, we simply print a JSON representation of our inventory. This is where we'll take into account the `allgroupvars` data, the default `ansible_ssh_user` for each group. We'll loop through each group, create a copy of the `allgroupvars` data, update that data with any data that may already exist in the group, then replace the group's variable data with the newly updated copy. Finally, we'll print out the end result:

```
if args.list:
    for group in inventory:
        ag = allgroupvars.copy()
        ag.update(inventory[group].get('vars', {}))
        inventory[group]['vars'] = ag
    print(json.dumps(inventory))
```

9. Finally, we'll handle the `--host` action by printing the JSON formatted variable data for the provided host, or an empty hash if there is no host-specific variable data for the provided host:

```
elif args.host:
    print(json.dumps(hostvars.get(args.host, {})))
```

Now, our inventory is ready to test! We can execute it directly and pass the `--help` argument we get for free using `argparse`. This will show us the usage of our script based on the `argparse` data we provided earlier in the file:

```
2. jkeating@serenity: ~/src/mastery (zsh)
~/src/mastery> ./mastery-inventory.py --help
usage: mastery-inventory.py [-h] [--list] [--host HOST]

Simple Inventory

optional arguments:
  -h, --help   show this help message and exit
  --list       List all hosts
  --host HOST  List details of a host
~/src/mastery> []
```

If we pass `--list`, we'll get the output of all our groups; and, if we pass `--host` with a couple of hosts, we'll get either the host data or an empty set:

```
2. jkeating@serenity: ~/src/mastery (zsh)
~/src/mastery> ./mastery-inventory.py --list
{"web": {"hosts": ["mastery.example.name"], "vars": {"ansible_ssh_user": "otto",
"http_port": 80, "proxy_timeout": 5}}, "errors": {"hosts": ["scsihost"], "vars"
: {"ansible_ssh_user": "otto"}}, "frontend": {"children": ["web"], "vars": {"ans
ible_ssh_user": "otto"}}, "database": {"hosts": ["backend.example.name"], "vars"
: {"ansible_ssh_user": "database"}}, "failtest": {"hosts": ["failer01", "failer0
2", "failer03", "failer04", "failer05", "failer06", "failer07", "failer08", "fai
ler09", "failer10"], "vars": {"ansible_ssh_user": "otto"}}, "dns": {"hosts": ["b
ackend.example.name"], "vars": {"ansible_ssh_user": "otto"}}, "backend": {"child
ren": ["dns", "database"], "vars": {"ansible_ssh_user": "blotto"}}}
~/src/mastery>
```

And now with the `--host` argument:

```
2. jkeating@serenity: ~/src/mastery (zsh)
~/src/mastery> ./mastery-inventory.py --host web
{"ansible_ssh_host": "192.168.10.25"}
~/src/mastery> ./mastery-inventory.py --host mastery.example.name
{}
~/src/mastery>
```

Now, we're ready to use our inventory file with Ansible. Let's make a new playbook
(`inventory_test.yaml`) to display the hostname and ssh username data:

```
---
- name: test the inventory
  hosts: all
  gather_facts: false

  tasks:
    - name: hello world
      debug:
        msg: "Hello world, I am {{ inventory_hostname }}.
              My username is {{ ansible_ssh_user }}"
```

To use our new inventory plugin with this playbook, we simply refer to the plugin file with the -i argument. Because we are using the all hosts group in our playbook, we'll also limit the run to a few groups to save on screen space:

```
~/src/mastery> ansible-playbook -i mastery-inventory.py inventory_test.yaml --li
mit backend,frontend,errors

PLAY [test the inventory] *************************************************

TASK: [hello world] *******************************************************
ok: [mastery.example.name] => {
    "msg": "Hello world, I am mastery.example.name. My username is otto"
}
ok: [backend.example.name] => {
    "msg": "Hello world, I am backend.example.name. My username is database"
}
ok: [scsihost] => {
    "msg": "Hello world, I am scsihost. My username is jkeating"
}

PLAY RECAP ****************************************************************
backend.example.name       : ok=1    changed=0    unreachable=0    failed=0
mastery.example.name       : ok=1    changed=0    unreachable=0    failed=0
scsihost                   : ok=1    changed=0    unreachable=0    failed=0

~/src/mastery> []
```

As we can see, we get the hosts we expect, and we get the default ssh user for master.example.name. The backend.example.name and scsihost each show their host-specific ssh username.

Optimizing script performance

With this inventory script, when Ansible starts, it will execute the script once with `--list` to gather the group data. Then, Ansible will execute the script again with `--host <hostname>` for each host it discovered in the first call. With our script, this takes very little time as there are very few hosts, and our execution is very fast. However, in an environment with a large number of hosts or a plugin that takes a while to run, gathering the inventory data can be a lengthy process. Fortunately, there is an optimization that can be made in the return data from a `--list` call that will prevent Ansible from rerunning the script for every host. The host-specific data can be returned all at once inside the group data return, inside of a top-level key named _meta that has a subkey named `hostvars` that contains a hash of all the hosts that have host variables and the variable data itself. When Ansible encounters a _meta key in the `--list` return, it'll skip the `--host` calls and assume that all of the host-specific data was already returned, potentially saving a significant amount of time! Let's modify our inventory script to return host variables inside of _meta, and create an error condition inside the `--host` option to show that `--host` is not being called:

1. First, we'll add the _meta key to the inventory dictionary after all of the `hostvars` have been defined, just before parsing arguments:

```
hostvars['scsihost'] = {'ansible_ssh_user': 'jkeating'}

inventory['_meta'] = {'hostvars': hostvars}

parser = argparse.ArgumentParser(description='Simple Inventory')
```
Next we'll change the `--host` handling to raise an exception:
```
elif args.host:
    raise StandardError("You've been a bad boy")
```

2. Now, we'll re-run the `inventory_test.yaml` playbook to ensure that we're still getting the right data:

```
● ● ●                    2. jkeating@serenity-2: ~/src/mastery (zsh)
~/src/mastery> time ansible-playbook -i mastery-inventory.py inventory_test.yaml
 --limit backend,frontend,errors

PLAY [test the inventory] ********************************************************

TASK [hello world] ***************************************************************
ok: [mastery.example.name] => {
    "msg": "Hello world, I am mastery.example.name. My username is otto"
}
ok: [scsihost] => {
    "msg": "Hello world, I am scsihost. My username is jkeating"
}
ok: [backend.example.name] => {
    "msg": "Hello world, I am backend.example.name. My username is database"
}

PLAY RECAP ***********************************************************************
backend.example.name         : ok=1    changed=0    unreachable=0    failed=0
mastery.example.name         : ok=1    changed=0    unreachable=0    failed=0
scsihost                     : ok=1    changed=0    unreachable=0    failed=0


real    0.586
user    0.428
sys     0.246
~/src/mastery> _
```

3. Just to be sure, we'll manually run the inventory plugin with the `--hosts` argument to show the exception:

```
2. jkeating@serenity: ~/src/mastery (zsh)
~/src/mastery> ./mastery-inventory.py --host scsihost
Traceback (most recent call last):
  File "./mastery-inventory.py", line 42, in <module>
    raise StandardError("You've been a bad boy")
StandardError: You've been a bad boy
exit 1
~/src/mastery> []
```

With this optimization, our simple playbook using our inventory module now runs nearly twice as fast, just because of the gained efficiency in inventory parsing.

Contributing to the Ansible project

Not all modifications need to be for local site needs. Ansible users will often identify an enhancement that could be made to the project that others would benefit from. These enhancements can be contributed back to the Ansible project. Contribution could be in the form of updates to an existing module or core Ansible code, updates to documentation, new modules or plugins, or simply testing proposed contributions from other community members.

Contribution submissions

The Ansible project uses GitHub (https://github.com) to manage code repositories, issues, and other project aspects. The Ansible organization (https://github.com/ansible) is where the code repositories can be found. The main repository is the `ansible` repository (https://github.com/ansible/ansible), where the core Ansible code, the modules, and the documentation can be found. This is the repository that should be cloned in order to develop a contribution.

The Ansible project uses a development branch named `devel` instead of the traditional name of `master`. Most contributions will target the `devel` branch, or a stable release branch.

The ansible repository

This repository has a number of files and folders at its root. The files are mostly high level documentation files, code licenses, or continuous integration test platform configurations.

Of the directories, a few are worth noting:

- `bin`: Source for the various ansible core executables
- `contrib`: Source for contributed inventory and vault plugins
- `docs`: Source for API documentation, the `https://docs.ansible.com`website, and the man pages
- `hacking`: Guides and utilities for hacking on the Ansible source
- `lib/ansible`: The core Ansible source code
- `test`: Unit and integration test code

Contributions to Ansible will likely occur in one of those folders.

Executing tests

Before any submission can be accepted by Ansible, the change must pass tests. These tests fall into three categories, Unit tests, Integration tests, and Code Style tests. Unit tests will cover very narrow aspects of the source code functions, while integration tests will take a more holistic approach and ensure the desired functionality happens. Code style tests examine the syntax used as well as whitespace and other style aspects.

Before any tests can be executed, the shell environment must be prepared to work with the Ansible code checkout. A shell environment file exists to set the required variables, which can be activated with the command:

```
$ source ./hacking/env-setup
```

Ensuring tests are passing before modifications are made can save a lot of debugging time later.

Unit tests

All of the unit tests are located within the directory tree starting at `test/units`. These tests should all be self-contained and do not require access to external resources. Running the tests is as simple as executing make tests from the root of the Ansible source checkout. This will test much of the code base, including module code.

 Executing the tests may require installing additional software. When using a Python virtualenv to manage Python software installs, it's best to create a new `venv` to use for testing Ansible, one that does not have Ansible installed in it.

To target a specific set of tests to run, the `pytest` utility can be called directly, with a path provided to a directory or a specific file to test. In this example, just the `parsing` unit tests are executed:

```
2. jkeating@serenity-2: ~/src/ansible (zsh)
devel ~/src/ansible> pytest test/units/parsing
=========================== test session starts ================================
platform darwin -- Python 2.7.10, pytest-3.0.6, py-1.4.32, pluggy-0.4.0
rootdir: /Users/jkeating/src/ansible, inifile:
plugins: mock-1.5.0
collected 155 items

test/units/parsing/test_dataloader.py .....
test/units/parsing/test_mod_args.py .........
test/units/parsing/test_splitter.py ...................................
test/units/parsing/test_unquote.py ..............
test/units/parsing/utils/test_addresses.py ..
test/units/parsing/utils/test_jsonify.py ....
test/units/parsing/vault/test_vault.py ..........................s......
test/units/parsing/vault/test_vault_editor.py .....
test/units/parsing/yaml/test_dumper.py .
test/units/parsing/yaml/test_loader.py ...............
test/units/parsing/yaml/test_objects.py .............

===================== 154 passed, 1 skipped in 45.99 seconds ===================
P
devel ~/src/ansible> _
```

Integration tests

The Ansible integration tests are tests designed to validate playbook functionality. The testing is executed by playbooks as well, making things a bit recursive. Tests are broken down into a few main categories:

- Non-destructive
- Destructive
- Cloud
- Windows
- Network

A more detailed explanation of the test categories can be found in the README.md file found at test/integration/README.md.

 Many of the integration tests require ssh to the local host to be functional. Be sure that ssh works, ideally without a password prompt. Remote hosts can be used by altering the inventory file used for tests (test/integration/inventory)

As with unit tests, individual integration tests can be executed, using the ansible-test utility located at test/runner/ansible-test. This is particularly important as many of the integration tests require external resources, such as computer cloud accounts. Each directory in test/integration/targets is a target that can be tested individually. For example, to test ping functionality, use the ping target:

```
● ● ●                2. jkeating@serenity-2: ~/src/ansible (zsh)
devel ~/src/ansible> test/runner/ansible-test integration -v ping
Running ping integration test role
Run command: ansible-playbook ping-6y55vk.yml -i inventory -e @integration_confi
g.yml -v
Using /dev/null as config file

PLAY [testhost] ***************************************************************

TASK [Gathering Facts] ********************************************************
ok: [testhost]

TASK [ping : ping the test] ***************************************************
ok: [testhost] => {"changed": false, "ping": "pong"}

TASK [ping : assert the ping worked] ******************************************
ok: [testhost] => {
    "changed": false,
    "msg": "All assertions passed"
}

TASK [ping : ping with data] **************************************************
ok: [testhost] => {"changed": false, "ping": "testing"}

TASK [ping : assert the ping worked with data] ********************************
ok: [testhost] => {
    "changed": false,
    "msg": "All assertions passed"
}

PLAY RECAP ********************************************************************
testhost                   : ok=5    changed=0    unreachable=0    failed=0

devel ~/src/ansible> 
```

A large set of POSIX compatible non-destructive integration tests run by continuous integration systems on proposed changes to Ansible can be executed with:

```
$ test/runner/ansible-test integration -v posix/ci/
```

 At the time of this writing, a number of the `posix/ci` tests do not pass on Mac OSX. It is recommended to execute these tests in a recent Fedora environment.

Code style tests

A third category of Ansible tests is the code style category. These tests examine the syntax used in the Python files, ensuring a cohesive look across the codebase. The code style enforced is defined by PEP8, a Style Guide for Python. More information is available in `test/sanity/pep8/README.md`. This style is enforced via the `pep8` make target. If there are no errors, this target does not output any text, however the return code can be verified. A return code of 0 means there were no errors:

```
devel ~/src/ansible> make pep8
test/runner/ansible-test sanity --test pep8 --python 2.7
Sanity check using pep8
devel ~/src/ansible> echo $?
0
devel ~/src/ansible>
```

If a Python file does have a `pep8` violation, the output will reflect the violation:

```
!devel ~/src/ansible> make pep8
test/runner/ansible-test sanity --test pep8 --python 2.7
Sanity check using pep8
ERROR: PEP 8: lib/ansible/modules/cloud/openstack/os_zone.py:185:1: W293 blank l
ine contains whitespace (current)
ERROR: PEP 8: lib/ansible/modules/cloud/openstack/os_zone.py:187:1: E101 indenta
tion contains mixed spaces and tabs (current)
ERROR: PEP 8: lib/ansible/modules/cloud/openstack/os_zone.py:187:1: W191 indenta
tion contains tabs (current)
ERROR: PEP 8: lib/ansible/modules/cloud/openstack/os_zone.py:188:9: E901 Indenta
tionError: unindent does not match any outer indentation level (current)
ERROR: PEP 8: There are 4 issues which need to be resolved.
make: *** [pep8] Error 1
exit 2
!devel ~/src/ansible>
```

The `pep8` errors will indicate an error code, which can be looked up for detailed explanations and guidance.

Making a pull request

With passing tests, a submission can be made. The Ansible project uses GitHub pull requests to manage submissions. To create a pull request, your changes must be committed and pushed to GitHub. Developers use a fork of the Ansible repository under their own account to push proposed changes to. Once pushed, a pull request can be opened using the GitHub website. This will create the pull request, which will start continuous integration tests and notify reviewers of a new submission. Further information about GitHub pull requests can be found at `https://help.github.com/categories/collaborating-with-issues-and-pull-requests/`.

Once the pull request is open, reviewers will comment on the pull request, either asking for more information, suggesting changes, or approving of the change. For new module submissions, there is an extensive checklist to follow, which can be found at `http://docs.ansible.com/ansible/dev_guide/developing_modules_checklist.html`.

Submissions which are found acceptable and merged will be made generally available in the next release of Ansible. The latest details about the Ansible release process can be found at `http://docs.ansible.com/ansible/dev_guide/developing_releases.html`.

Summary

Ansible is a great tool, however, sometimes it doesn't offer all the functionality one might desire. Not every bit of functionality is appropriate to support the main project, nor is it possible to integrate with custom proprietary data sources. For these reasons, there exists facilities within Ansible to extend its functionality. Creating and using custom modules is made easy due to shared module base code. Many different types of plugins can be created and used with Ansible to affect operations in a variety of ways. Inventory sources beyond what Ansible supports can still be used with relative ease and efficiency.

In all cases, there exists a mechanism to provide modules, plugins, and inventory sources alongside the playbooks and roles that depend on the enhanced functionality, making it seamless to distribute.

Enhanced functionality that may benefit other consumers of Ansible can be contributed back to the project. Ansible is an open source project, with much of the contribution coming from community members.

In the next chapter, we will explore using Ansible to create the infrastructure to be managed.

9
Infrastructure Provisioning

Automation needs have expanded in recent years to include management of the very infrastructure required to run services. Infrastructure as a Service providers offer APIs for programmatically managing images, servers, networks, and storage components. These resources are often expected to be created just-in-time to reduce costs and increase efficiency.

This chapter will explore the following ways in which Ansible can interact with these services:

- Managing cloud infrastructure
- Interacting with Docker containers
- Previewing of Ansible container

Managing cloud infrastructure

Cloud is a popular, but vague, term to describe resource service. There are many types of resources that can be provided by a Cloud, though the most commonly discussed are compute and storage. Ansible is capable of interacting with numerous cloud providers to discover, create, or otherwise manage resources within them.

One such cloud provider that Ansible can interact with is OpenStack. OpenStack is an open source cloud operating system. A suite of services provides interfaces to manage compute, storage, and networking services, plus many other supportive services. There is not a single provider of OpenStack, instead many public and private cloud providers build their products with OpenStack, and as such they all share common interfaces for tooling such as Ansible to interact with.

Ansible has supported OpenStack services since very early in the project. That initial support has grown to include over forty modules, with support for managing:

- Compute
- Bare metal compute
- Compute images
- Authentication accounts
- Networks
- Object storage
- Block storage

In addition to performing `create`, `read`, `update`, or `delete` actions (CRUD) on the preceding types of resources, Ansible also includes the ability to use OpenStack (and other clouds) as an inventory source. Each execution of `ansible` or `ansible-playbook` that utilizes an OpenStack cloud as an inventory source will get on-demand information about what compute resources exist and various facts about those compute resources. Since the cloud service is already tracking these details, this can reduce overhead by eliminating manual tracking of these resources.

To demonstrate Ansible's ability to manage and interact with cloud resources, we'll walk through two scenarios; a scenario to create and then interact with new compute resources, and the other scenario will demonstrate using OpenStack as an inventory source.

Creating servers

The OpenStack Compute service provides an API for creation, reading, updating, or deleting of virtual machine servers. Through this API, we'll be able to create the server for our demonstration. After accessing and modifying the server through SSH, we'll also use the API to delete the server. This self-service ability is a key feature of cloud computing.

Ansible can be used to manage these servers using the various `os_server` modules:

- `os_server`: This module is use to create and delete virtual servers
- `os_server_facts`: This module is use to gather facts about a server
- `os_server_actions`: This module is use to perform various actions on a server
- `os_server_group`: This module is use to create and delete server groups
- `os_server_volume`: This module is use to attach or detach block storage volumes from a server

Booting virtual servers

For our demonstration, we will use `os_server`. We'll need to provide authentication details about our cloud, such as the `auth` URL and our login credentials. For the server creation, we'll need a flavor, an image, a network, and a name. These details may be different for each OpenStack cloud.

I'll name our playbook `boot-server.yaml`. Our play starts with a name and uses `localhost` as the host pattern. As we do not rely on any local facts, I'll turn fact gathering off as well:

```
---
- name: boot server
  hosts: localhost
  gather_facts: false
```

To create the server, I'll use the `os_server` module, and provide `auth` details relevant to an OpenStack cloud I have access to, as well as a flavor, image, network, and name. I'll also provide a `key_name`, which will indicate which SSH public key to plumb into the server so that I can SSH into it. Of course, I've obfuscated some private details in this example, such as my password:

```
tasks:
  - name: boot the server
    os_server:
      auth:
        auth_url: "CLOUDURL"
        username: "jlk"
        password: "PASSWORD"
        project_name: "jlk"
      flavor: "1"
      image: "Fedora 25"
      key_name: "jlk"
      network: "internal"
      name: "mastery1"
```

 Authentication details can be written to an external file, which will be read by the underlying module code. This module code uses `os-client-config`, a standard library for managing OpenStack credentials.

Running this play as-is will simply create the server and nothing more. I can use the previously created `mastery-hosts` as an inventory source, as I'm only using `localhost` from it:

```
2. jkeating@serenity-2: ~/src/mastery (zsh)
~/src/mastery> ansible-playbook -i mastery-hosts boot-server.yaml -vv
Using /Users/jkeating/src/mastery/ansible.cfg as config file

PLAYBOOK: boot-server.yaml ************************************************
1 plays in boot-server.yaml

PLAY [boot server] *******************************************************

TASK [boot the server] ***************************************************
task path: /Users/jkeating/src/mastery/boot-server.yaml:7
changed: [localhost] => {"changed": true, "id": "d88095dd-5223-45d2-af15-968dc43
7f677", "openstack": {"OS-DCF:diskConfig": "MANUAL", "OS-EXT-AZ:availability_zon
e": "nova", "OS-EXT-STS:power_state": 1, "OS-EXT-STS:task_state": null, "OS-EXT-
STS:vm_state": "active", "OS-SRV-USG:launched_at": "2017-03-02T06:19:52.000000",
 "OS-SRV-USG:terminated_at": null, "accessIPv4": "169.45.80.10", "accessIPv6": "
", "addresses": {"internal": [{"OS-EXT-IPS-MAC:mac_addr": "fa:16:3e:86:be:ae", "
OS-EXT-IPS:type": "fixed", "addr": "10.168.4.54", "version": 4}, {"OS-EXT-IPS-MA
C:mac_addr": "fa:16:3e:86:be:ae", "OS-EXT-IPS:type": "floating", "addr": "169.45
.80.10", "version": 4}]}, "adminPass": "zahV4C9BDj4s", "az": "nova", "cloud": ""
, "config_drive": "", "created": "2017-03-02T06:19:47Z", "disk_config": "MANUAL"
, "flavor": {"id": "1", "name": "m1.tiny"}, "has_config_drive": false, "hostId":
 "8d434a2b07568a6e7d044f7be85626eaf8f7f24c8fba141c640c0033", "host_id": "8d434a2
b07568a6e7d044f7be85626eaf8f7f24c8fba141c640c0033", "id": "d88095dd-5223-45d2-af
15-968dc437f677", "image": {"id": "01f59def-06f4-4979-b0ee-97cea844d18d", "name"
: "Fedora 25"}, "interface_ip": "169.45.80.10", "key_name": "VALUE_SPECIFIED_IN_
NO_LOG_PARAMETER", "launched_at": "2017-03-02T06:19:52.000000", "location": {"cl
oud": "", "project": {"domain_id": null, "domain_name": null, "id": "44b67672c37
34cac8865538eda20b357", "name": "VALUE_SPECIFIED_IN_NO_LOG_PARAMETER"}, "region_
```

I've truncated the output as there is a lot of data returned from the module. Most importantly, we get data regarding IP addresses of the host. This particular cloud uses a floating IP to provide public access to the server instance, which we can see the value of by registering the output and then debug printing the value of `openstack.accessIPv4`:

```
    tasks:
      - name: boot the server
        os_server:
          auth:
            auth_url: "CLOUDURL"
            username: "jlk"
            password: "PASSWORD"
```

```
          project_name: "jlk"
        flavor: "1"
        image: "Fedora 25"
        key_name: "jlk"
        network: "internal"
        name: "mastery1"
      register: newserver

    - name: show floating ip
      debug:
        var: newserver.openstack.accessIPv4
```

This time when executing, the first task does not result in a change, as the server we want already exists:

```
● ● ●                    2. jkeating@serenity-2: ~/src/mastery (zsh)

"region_name": "", "zone": null}, "port_range_max": null, "port_range_min": null
, "project_id": "", "properties": {"group": {"name": "default", "tenant_id": "44
b67672c3734cac8865538eda20b357"}}, "protocol": null, "remote_group_id": null, "r
emote_ip_prefix": null, "security_group_id": "de0a75ad-585f-498c-8ab5-5072e385af
ff", "tenant_id": ""}, {"direction": "ingress", "ethertype": "IPv4", "group": {"
name": "default", "tenant_id": "44b67672c3734cac8865538eda20b357"}, "id": "f59b3
a5c-27fe-460c-a8af-a9236143332b", "location": {"cloud": "", "project": {"domain_
id": null, "domain_name": null, "id": "44b67672c3734cac8865538eda20b357", "name"
: "VALUE_SPECIFIED_IN_NO_LOG_PARAMETER"}, "region_name": "", "zone": null}, "por
t_range_max": null, "port_range_min": null, "project_id": "", "properties": {"gr
oup": {"name": "default", "tenant_id": "44b67672c3734cac8865538eda20b357"}}, "pr
otocol": null, "remote_group_id": null, "remote_ip_prefix": null, "security_grou
p_id": "de0a75ad-585f-498c-8ab5-5072e385afff", "tenant_id": ""}], "tenant_id": "
44b67672c3734cac8865538eda20b357"}], "status": "ACTIVE", "task_state": null, "te
nant_id": "44b67672c3734cac8865538eda20b357", "terminated_at": null, "updated":
"2017-03-02T06:19:53Z", "user_id": "db35760f08a14b1391d479800769bdfa", "vm_state
": "active", "volumes": []}}

TASK [show floating ip] ***********************************************
task path: /Users/jkeating/src/mastery/boot-server.yaml:21
ok: [localhost] => {
    "newserver.openstack.accessIPv4": "169.45.80.10"
}

PLAY RECAP ************************************************************
localhost                  : ok=2    changed=0    unreachable=0    failed=0

~/src/mastery>
```

The output shows an IP address of 169.45.80.10. I can use that information to connect to my newly created cloud server.

Adding to runtime inventory

Booting a server isn't all that useful by itself. The server exists to be used, and will likely need some configuration to become useful. While it's possible to have one playbook to create resources and a completely different playbook to manage configuration, we can also do it all from the same playbook. Ansible provides a facility to add hosts to the inventory as part of a play, which will allow use of those hosts in subsequent plays.

Working from the previous example, we have enough information to add the new host to the runtime inventory, by way of the add_host module:

```
- name: add new server
  add_host:
    name: "mastery1"
    ansible_ssh_host: "{{ newserver.openstack.accessIPv4 }}"
    ansible_ssh_user: "fedora"
```

I know that this image has a default user of fedora so I set a host variable accordingly, along with setting the IP address as the connection address.

 This example is also glossing over any needed security group configuration in OpenStack, and any accepting of the SSH host key. Additional tasks can be added to manage these things.

With the server added to our inventory, we can do something with it. Let's imagine a scenario in which we want to use this cloud resource to convert an image file, using ImageMagick software. To accomplish this, we'll need a new place making use of the new host. I know that this particular fedora image does not contain python, so we need to add python, and the python bindings for dnf (so we can use the dnf module) as our first task using the raw module:

```
- name: configure server
  hosts: mastery1
  gather_facts: false

  tasks:
    - name: install python
      raw: "sudo dnf install -y python python2-dnf"
```

Next, we'll need the `ImageMagick` software, which we can install using the `dnf` module:

```
- name: install imagemagick
  dnf:
    name: "ImageMagick"
  become: "yes"
```

Running the playbook at this point will show changed tasks for our new host:

```
2. jkeating@serenity-2: ~/src/mastery (zsh)
  "volumes": []}}

TASK [show floating ip] ******************************************************
task path: /Users/jkeating/src/mastery/boot-server.yaml:21
ok: [localhost] => {
    "newserver.openstack.accessIPv4": "169.45.80.10"
}

TASK [add new server] ********************************************************
task path: /Users/jkeating/src/mastery/boot-server.yaml:25
creating host via 'add_host': hostname=mastery1
changed: [localhost] => {"add_host": {"groups": [], "host_name": "mastery1", "ho
st_vars": {"ansible_ssh_host": "169.45.80.10", "ansible_ssh_user": "fedora"}}, "
changed": true}

PLAY [configure server] ******************************************************

TASK [install python] ********************************************************
task path: /Users/jkeating/src/mastery/boot-server.yaml:36
changed: [mastery1] => {"changed": true, "rc": 0, "stderr": "", "stdout": "Last
metadata expiration check: 0:43:12 ago on Sun Mar  5 22:10:56 2017.\r\nDependenc
ies resolved.\r\n==============================================================
=================\r\n Package                    Arch          Version
  Repository    Size\r\n==========================================================
=======================\r\nInstalling:\r\n pyliblzma                 x86_64     0.
5.3-16.fc25               fedora       54 k\r\n python                  x86_64
 2.7.13-1.fc25             updates      96 k\r\n python-libs             x86_64
   2.7.13-1.fc25           updates     5.8 M\r\n python-pip               noar
```

The preceding screenshot is truncated as the output from using the `raw` module is quite extensive. The following screenshot is the final bit of output from the last task of the play, as that output was extensive as well:

```
alled: libdrm-2.4.75-1.fc25.x86_64", "Installed: libtiff-4.0.7-2.fc25.x86_64", "
Installed: libtool-ltdl-2.4.6-13.fc25.x86_64", "Installed: pango-1.40.4-1.fc25.x
86_64", "Installed: libICE-1.0.9-8.fc25.x86_64", "Installed: avahi-libs-0.6.32-4
.fc25.x86_64", "Installed: lcms2-2.8-2.fc25.x86_64", "Installed: xorg-x11-font-u
tils-1:7.5-32.fc25.x86_64", "Installed: gdk-pixbuf2-2.36.5-1.fc25.x86_64", "Inst
alled: libX11-1.6.4-4.fc25.x86_64", "Installed: libX11-common-1.6.4-4.fc25.noarc
h", "Installed: libXdamage-1.1.4-8.fc24.x86_64", "Installed: libXext-1.3.3-4.fc2
4.x86_64", "Installed: libXfixes-5.0.3-1.fc25.x86_64", "Installed: libXfont-1.5.
2-1.fc25.x86_64", "Installed: libxshmfence-1.2-3.fc24.x86_64", "Installed: cairo
-1.14.8-1.fc25.x86_64", "Installed: libXt-1.1.5-3.fc24.x86_64", "Installed: jbig
kit-libs-2.1-5.fc24.x86_64", "Installed: libglvnd-1:0.2.999-10.gitdc16f8c.fc25.x
86_64", "Installed: aajohan-comfortaa-fonts-2.004-6.fc24.noarch", "Installed: op
enjpeg2-2.1.2-3.fc25.x86_64", "Installed: libglvnd-egl-1:0.2.999-10.gitdc16f8c.f
c25.x86_64", "Installed: libfontenc-1.1.3-3.fc24.x86_64", "Installed: libglvnd-g
lx-1:0.2.999-10.gitdc16f8c.fc25.x86_64", "Installed: libXft-2.3.2-4.fc24.x86_64"
, "Installed: hwdata-0.297-1.fc25.noarch", "Installed: librsvg2-2.40.16-2.fc25.x
86_64", "Installed: harfbuzz-1.3.2-1.fc25.x86_64", "Installed: graphite2-1.3.6-1
.fc25.x86_64"]}

PLAY RECAP ***********************************************************************
localhost                  : ok=3    changed=1    unreachable=0    failed=0
mastery1                   : ok=2    changed=2    unreachable=0    failed=0

~/src/mastery>
```

We can see Ansible reporting two changed tasks on the host `mastery1`, which we just created in the first play. This host does not exist in the `mastery-hosts` inventory file.

From this point, we could long our second play to upload a source image file using `copy`, then perform a command using `ImageMagick` on the host to convert the image. Another task can be added to fetch the converted file back down using the `slurp` module, or the modified file could be uploaded to a cloud based object store. Finally, a last play could be added to delete the server itself.

The entire lifespan of the server, from creation to configuration to use and finally to removal, can be managed all with a single playbook. The playbook can be made dynamic by reading runtime variable data to define what file should be uploaded/modified and where it should be stored, turning the playbook into essentially into a reusable program.

Using OpenStack inventory source

Our previous example imagined a single-use short-lived cloud server. But what if instead we want to create and use long-lived cloud servers? Walking through the tasks of creating them and adding them to temporary inventory each time we want to touch them seems inefficient. Manually recording the server details into a static inventory also seems inefficient, and error prone. Thankfully there is a better way, using the cloud itself as a dynamic inventory source.

Ansible ships with a number of dynamic inventory scripts for cloud providers. We'll continue our examples with OpenStack. The Ansible source repository holds these contributed scripts in `contrib/inventory/` and the OpenStack script is `contrib/inventory/openstack.py`, with an associated configuration file at `contrib/inventory/openstack.yml`. To make use of this script, simply copy the `.py` file to the playbook directory that expects to use it, or to a path accessible to all users/playbooks on the system that will be executing Ansible. For our example, I'll copy it to the playbook directory.

The configuration file needs a bit more consideration. This file holds authentication details for the OpenStack cloud(s) to connect to. That makes this file sensitive and should only be made visible to the users who require access to this information. In addition, the inventory script will attempt to load configuration from standard paths used by `os-client-config` (`https://docs.openstack.org/developer/os-client-config/`), the underlying authentication code. That means configuration for this inventory source can live in:

- `clouds.yaml` in the current working directory when executing the inventory script
- `~/.config/openstack/clouds.yaml`
- `/etc/openstack/clouds.yaml`
- `/etc/openstack/openstack.yaml`
- `/etc/openstack/openstack.yml`

The first file found will be used. For our example, I'll use a `clouds.yaml` file in the playbook directory alongside the script itself, in order to isolate configuration from any other paths.

The help output for the script shows a few possible arguments, however the ones that Ansible will use are `--list` and `--host`:

```
● ● ●                    2. jkeating@serenity-2: ~/src/mastery (zsh)
~/src/mastery> ./openstack.py --help
usage: openstack.py [-h] [--private] [--refresh] [--debug]
                    (--list | --host HOST)

OpenStack Inventory Module

optional arguments:
  -h, --help   show this help message and exit
  --private    Use private address for ansible host
  --refresh    Refresh cached information
  --debug      Enable debug output
  --list       List active servers
  --host HOST  List details about the specific host
~/src/mastery> _
```

The first is used to get a list of all the servers visible to the account used, and the second would be used to get host variable data from each, except that this inventory script returns all the host variables with the `--list` call. Returning the data with the host list is a performance enhancement, eliminating the need to call the OpenStack APIs for each and every host returned.

The output from `--list` is quite long, however here is the first few lines:

```
~/src/mastery> ./openstack.py --list
{
  "RegionOne": [
    "bd47daf7-6ab9-4c97-a3e4-cc97418fbe49"
  ],
  "RegionOne_compute_standard": [
    "bd47daf7-6ab9-4c97-a3e4-cc97418fbe49"
  ],
  "_meta": {
    "hostvars": {
      "bd47daf7-6ab9-4c97-a3e4-cc97418fbe49": {
        "ansible_ssh_host": "169.44.171.87",
        "openstack": {
          "OS-DCF:diskConfig": "MANUAL",
          "OS-EXT-AZ:availability_zone": "compute_standard",
          "OS-EXT-STS:power_state": 1,
          "OS-EXT-STS:task_state": null,
          "OS-EXT-STS:vm_state": "active",
          "OS-SRV-USG:launched_at": "2017-03-10T05:18:45.000000",
          "OS-SRV-USG:terminated_at": null,
          "accessIPv4": "169.44.171.87",
          "accessIPv6": "",
          "addresses": {
            "internal": [
              {
                "OS-EXT-IPS-MAC:mac_addr": "fa:16:3e:8f:13:81",
                "OS-EXT-IPS:type": "fixed",
                "addr": "192.168.0.227",
                "version": 4
              },
              {
```

The configured account has only one visible server which has a UUID of
bd47daf7-6ab9-4c97-a3e4-cc97418fbe49, the instance we booted in a previous
example. We see this instance listed in groups RegionOne and
RegionOne_compute_standard. The first group is for all the servers found in the
RegionOne region. The second group is for all the servers found in RegionOne that are in
the availability zone of compute_standard. These groupings happen automatically within
the inventory plugin. The tail end of the output will show the other groups provided by the
plugin:

```
           "volumes": []
        }
      }
    }
  },
  "compute_standard": [
    "bd47daf7-6ab9-4c97-a3e4-cc97418fbe49"
  ],
  "flavor-m1.tiny": [
    "bd47daf7-6ab9-4c97-a3e4-cc97418fbe49"
  ],
  "image-Fedora 25": [
    "bd47daf7-6ab9-4c97-a3e4-cc97418fbe49"
  ],
  "instance-bd47daf7-6ab9-4c97-a3e4-cc97418fbe49": [
    "bd47daf7-6ab9-4c97-a3e4-cc97418fbe49"
  ],
  "mastery1": [
    "bd47daf7-6ab9-4c97-a3e4-cc97418fbe49"
  ],
  "open": [
    "bd47daf7-6ab9-4c97-a3e4-cc97418fbe49"
  ],
  "open_RegionOne": [
    "bd47daf7-6ab9-4c97-a3e4-cc97418fbe49"
  ],
  "open_RegionOne_compute_standard": [
    "bd47daf7-6ab9-4c97-a3e4-cc97418fbe49"
  ]
}
~/src/mastery> _
```

Additional groups are as follows:

- `compute_standard`: All servers in the `compute_standard` availability zone
- `flavor-m1.tiny`: All servers that use the `m1.tiny` flavor
- `image-Fedora 25`: All servers that use the `Fedora 25` image
- `instance-bd47daf7-6ab9-4c97-a3e4-cc97418fbe49`: A group named after the instance itself
- `mastery1`: A group named after the server's name
- `open`: All servers found in the cloud named `open`
- `open_RegionOne`: All servers in the `RegionOne` region of the cloud named `open`
- `open_RegionOne_compute_standard`: All servers in the `compute_standard` availability zone on the cloud named `open`

There are many groups provided, each with a potentially different slice of the servers found by the inventory script. These groups make it easy to target just the right instances with plays. The hosts are defined as the UUIDs of the servers. As these are by nature unique, and quite long, they are unwieldy as a target within a play. This makes groups all the more important.

To demonstrate using this script as an inventory source, we'll re-create the previous example, skipping over the creation of the server and instead just writing the second play using an appropriate group target. We'll name this playbook `configure-server.yaml`:

```
---
- name: configure server
  hosts: mastery1
  gather_facts: false
  remote_user: fedora

  tasks:
    - name: install python
      raw: "sudo dnf install -y python python2-dnf"

    - name: install imagemagick
      dnf:
        name: "ImageMagick"
      become: "yes"
```

The default user on this image is `fedora`, however that information isn't readily available via the OpenStack APIs, and thus it is not reflected in the data our inventory script provides. We can simply define the user to use at the play level.

The hosts pattern we used before of `mastery1` is actually appropriate for use with the inventory plugin. This is the `name` we gave our server in an earlier example, and our inventory script has exposed this as a group.

The rest of the play is unchanged, and the output should look similar to previous executions:

This output differs from the last time the `boot-server.yaml` playbook was executed in only a few ways. First, the `master1` server is not booted. We're assuming that the servers we want to interact with have already been booted. Second, the target host displayed in the output is the UUID of the server rather than the name `master1`. Otherwise the output is the same.

As servers get added or removed over time, each execution of the inventory plugin will discover what servers are there at the moment of playbook execution. This can save a significant amount of time over attempting to maintain an accurate list of servers in static inventory files.

Interacting with Docker containers

Linux containers in general, and Docker specifically, have grown in popularity recently. Containers provide a fast path to resource isolation. Containers can be launched quickly as there is very little overhead. Utilities like Docker provide a lot of useful tooling around container management, such as a registry of images to use as the filesystem, tooling to build the images themselves, clustering orchestration, and so on. Docker has become one of the most popular ways to manage containers.

Ansible can interact with Docker in numerous ways as well. Notably, Ansible can be used to build images, to start or stop containers, to compose multiple container services, to connect to and interact with active containers, or even to discover inventory from. Modules, a connection plugin, and an inventory script are all provided by Ansible.

To demonstrate working with Docker, we'll explore a few use cases. The first use case is building a new image to use with Docker. The second use case is launching a container from the new image and interacting with it. The last use case is using the inventory plugin to interact with an active container.

 Creating a functional Docker install is beyond the scope of this book. The Docker website provides detailed installation and use instructions: `https://docs.docker.com`. Ansible works best with Docker on a Linux host, so the remaining examples will be from a Fedora twenty-five virtual machine.

Building images

Docker images are a filesystem bundled with parameters to use at runtime. The filesystem is usually a small part of a Linux userland, with enough files to start the desired process. Docker provides tooling to build these images, generally based on very small base images. The tooling uses a `Dockerfile` as the input, which is a plain text file with directives. This file is parsed by the `docker build` command, and we can parse it via the `docker_image` module. The remaining examples will be from a Fedora 25 virtual machine using Docker version 1.12.6., with the `cowsay` package and `nginx` added, so that running the container will provide a web server that will display something from `cowsay`.

First we'll need a `Dockerfile`. This file needs to live in a path that Ansible can read, and I'm going to put it in the same directory as my playbooks. The `Dockerfile` content will be very simple. I'll need to define a base image, a command to run to install necessary software, some minimal configuration of software, a port to expose, and a default action for running a container with this image:

```
FROM docker.io/fedora:25

RUN dnf install -y cowsay nginx
RUN "daemon off;" >> /etc/nginx/nginx.conf
RUN cowsay boop > /usr/share/nginx/html/index.html

EXPOSE 80

CMD /usr/sbin/nginx
```

I'm using the Fedora 25 image from the `fedora` repository on the `Docker Hub` image registry. To install the necessary `cowsay` and `nginx` packages, I'm using `dnf`. To run `nginx` directly in the container I need to turn `daemon` mode off in `nginx config`. I use `cowsay` to generate content for the default web page. I'm instructing Docker to expose port 80 in the container, where `nginx` will listen for connections. The default action of this container will be to run `nginx`.

The playbook to build and use the image can live in the same directory. I'll name it
`docker-interact.yaml`. This playbook will operate on `localhost` and have two tasks.
One to build the image using `docker_image`, and another to launch the container using
`docker_container`:

```
---
- name: build an image
  hosts: localhost
  gather_facts: false

  tasks:
    - name: build that image
      docker_image:
        path: .
        state: present
        name: fedora-moo

    - name: start the container
      docker_container:
        name: playbook-container
        image: fedora-moo
        ports: 8080:80
        state: started
```

Before we execute this playbook, let's look at the Docker system to see if there are any
running containers or any created images:

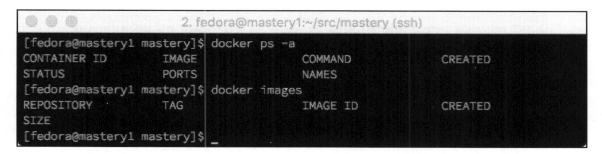

Now let's run the playbook to build the image and start a container using that image:

```
● ● ●                    2. fedora@mastery1:~/src/mastery (ssh)
[fedora@mastery1 mastery]$ ansible-playbook -i derp, docker-interact.yaml

PLAY [build an image] ************************************************************

TASK [build that image] *********************************************************
changed: [localhost]

TASK [start the container] ******************************************************
changed: [localhost]

PLAY RECAP **********************************************************************
localhost                  : ok=2    changed=2    unreachable=0    failed=0

[fedora@mastery1 mastery]$
```

The verbosity of this playbook execution was reduced, to save screen space. Our output simply shows that the task to build the image resulted in a change, as did the task to start the container. A quick check of running containers and available images should reflect our work:

```
● ● ●                    2. fedora@mastery1:~/src/mastery (ssh)
[fedora@mastery1 mastery]$ docker ps
CONTAINER ID    IMAGE          COMMAND              CREATED
   STATUS          PORTS             NAMES
c728ef9abe36    fedora-moo       "/bin/sh -c /usr/sbin"   13 minutes ago
    Up 13 minutes    0.0.0.0:8080->80/tcp   playbook-container
[fedora@mastery1 mastery]$ docker images
REPOSITORY       TAG        IMAGE ID        CREATED
SIZE
fedora-moo       latest     b82819052899    13 minutes ago
461.6 MB
docker.io/fedora 25         1f8ec1108a3f    3 weeks ago
230.3 MB
[fedora@mastery1 mastery]$
```

We can test the functionality of our container by using `curl` to access the web server, which should show us a cow saying `boop`:

```
[fedora@mastery1 mastery]$ curl http://localhost:8080
 _____
< boop >
 -------
        \   ^__^
         \  (oo)_____
            (__)\       )\/\
                ||----w |
                ||     ||
[fedora@mastery1 mastery]$
```

Building containers without a Dockerfile

Dockerfiles are useful, but many of the things done inside Dockerfiles could be done with Ansible instead. Ansible can be used to launch a container using a base image, then interact with that container using the `docker` connection method to complete the configuration. Let's demonstrate this by repeating the previous example, entirely in a new playbook named `docker-all.yaml`:

```
---
- name: build an image
  hosts: localhost
  gather_facts: false

  tasks:
    - name: start the container
      docker_container:
        name: playbook-container
        image: docker.io/fedora:25
        ports: 8080:80
        state: started
        command: sleep 500

    - name: make a host
      add_host:
        name: playbook-container
        ansible_connection: docker

- name: do things
```

```
    hosts: playbook-container
    gather_facts: false

    tasks:
      - name: install things
        raw: dnf install -y python-dnf

      - name: install things
        dnf:
          name: "{{ item }}"
        with_items:
          - nginx
          - cowsay

      - name: configure nginx
        lineinfile:
          line: "daemon off;"
          dest: /etc/nginx/nginx.conf

      - name: boop
        shell: cowsay boop > /usr/share/nginx/html/index.html

      - name: run nginx
        shell: nginx &
```

The playbook consists of two plays. The first play creates the container from the base fedora 25 image. The command given is a `sleep` command to keep the container running for a period of time, as the `docker` connection plugin only works with active containers. The second task of the first play creates a runtime inventory entry for the container. The inventory host name must match the container name. The connection method is set to `docker` as well.

The second play targets the newly created host, and the first task uses the `raw` module to get the `python-dnf` package in place (which will bring the rest of `python` in) so that we can use the `dnf` module. The next task uses the `dnf` module to install the packages we want, namely `nginx` and `cowsay`. Then the `lineinfile` module is used to add a new line to the `nginx` configuration. A shell task uses `cowsay` to create content for `nginx` to serve. Finally, `nginx` itself is started as a background process.

Before running the playbook, let's remove any running containers from the previous example:

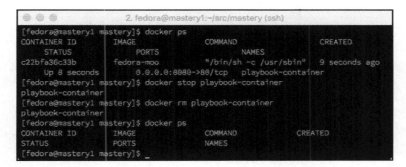

With the running container removed, we can now run our new playbook to recreate the container, bypassing the image build step:

Again, the playbook has been run with minimal verbosity to save screen space. We see tasks execute on the localhost, and then the second play executes on `playbook-container`. Once complete, we can test the web service and list the running containers to verify our work:

```
●  ●  ●                    2. fedora@mastery1:~/src/mastery (ssh)
PLAY RECAP ***********************************************************************
localhost                    : ok=2    changed=2    unreachable=0    failed=0
playbook-container           : ok=5    changed=5    unreachable=0    failed=0

[fedora@mastery1 mastery]$ curl http://localhost:8080
 _____
< boop >
 -----------
        \   ^__^
         \  (oo)_____
            (__)\       )\/\
                ||----w |
                ||     ||
[fedora@mastery1 mastery]$ docker ps
CONTAINER ID        IMAGE                COMMAND             CREATED
  STATUS              PORTS                NAMES
e9fb97915fdc        docker.io/fedora:25  "sleep 500"         2 minutes ago
  Up 2 minutes        0.0.0.0:8080->80/tcp  playbook-container
[fedora@mastery1 mastery]$ _
```

This method of using Ansible to configure the running container has some advantages. One can re-use existing roles to set up an application, easily switching from cloud VM targets to containers to bare metal resources. One can easily review all configuration that goes into an application simply by reviewing playbook content.

Another use case for this method of interaction is to use `docker` containers to simulate multiple hosts in order to verify playbook execution across multiple hosts. A container could be started with an init system as the running process, allowing additional services to be started as if they were on a full operating system. This use case is valuable within a continuous integration environment to validate changes to playbook content quickly and cheaply.

Docker inventory

Similar to the OpenStack inventory plugin detailed earlier in this chapter, a Docker inventory script is also available. The Docker script is located at `contrib/inventory/docker.py` within the Ansible source repository, with an associated configuration file at `contrib/inventory/docker.yml`. To make use of this script, simply copy the `.py` file to the playbook directory that expects to use it, or to a path accessible to all users/playbooks on the system that will be executing Ansible. For our example, I'll copy it to the playbook directory. The configuration file, which can be used to define how to connect to one or more Docker daemons, does not need to be used for this example, as we'll simply be connecting to the local Docker daemon.

The help output for the script shows many possible arguments, however the ones that Ansible will use are `--list` and `--host`:

```
● ● ●                    2. fedora@mastery1:~/src/mastery (ssh)
[fedora@mastery1 mastery]$ ./docker.py --help
usage: docker.py [-h] [--list] [--debug] [--host HOST] [--pretty]
                 [--config-file CONFIG_FILE] [--docker-host DOCKER_HOST]
                 [--tls-hostname TLS_HOSTNAME] [--api-version API_VERSION]
                 [--timeout TIMEOUT] [--cacert-path CACERT_PATH]
                 [--cert-path CERT_PATH] [--key-path KEY_PATH]
                 [--ssl-version SSL_VERSION] [--tls] [--tls-verify]
                 [--private-ssh-port PRIVATE_SSH_PORT]
                 [--default-ip-address DEFAULT_IP_ADDRESS]

Return Ansible inventory for one or more Docker hosts.

optional arguments:
  -h, --help            show this help message and exit
  --list                List all containers (default: True)
  --debug               Send debug messages to STDOUT
  --host HOST           Only get information for a specific container.
  --pretty              Pretty print JSON output(default: False)
  --config-file CONFIG_FILE
                        Name of the config file to use. Default is docker.yml
  --docker-host DOCKER_HOST
                        The base url or Unix sock path to connect to the
                        docker daemon. Defaults to unix://var/run/docker.sock
  --tls-hostname TLS_HOSTNAME
                        Host name to expect in TLS certs. Defaults to
                        'localhost'
  --api-version API_VERSION
                        Docker daemon API version. Defaults to 1.24
  --timeout TIMEOUT    Docker connection timeout in seconds. Defaults to 60
  --cacert-path CACERT_PATH
                        Path to the TLS certificate authority pem file.
  --cert-path CERT_PATH
                        Path to the TLS certificate pem file.
  --key-path KEY_PATH   Path to the TLS encryption key pem file.
  --ssl-version SSL_VERSION
                        TLS version number
  --tls                 Use TLS. Defaults to False
  --tls-verify          Verify TLS certificates. Defaults to False
  --private-ssh-port PRIVATE_SSH_PORT
                        Default private container SSH Port. Defaults to 22
  --default-ip-address DEFAULT_IP_ADDRESS
                        Default container SSH IP address. Defaults to
                        127.0.0.1
[fedora@mastery1 mastery]$
```

If the previously built container is still running when this script is executed to list hosts, it should appear in the output:

```
● ● ●                     2. fedora@mastery1:~/src/mastery (ssh)
[fedora@mastery1 mastery]$ ./docker.py --list --pretty
{
    "7f22ffd044768": [
        "playbook-container"
    ],
    "7f22ffd044768b2f293ca724af86600cb7d7361b8956fe2f88f8f1538fc2e73d": [
        "playbook-container"
    ],
    "_meta": {
        "hostvars": {
            "playbook-container": {
                "ansible_ssh_host": "",
                "ansible_ssh_port": 0,
                "docker_apparmorprofile": "",
                "docker_args": [
                    "500"
                ],
                "docker_config": {
                    "AttachStderr": false,
                    "AttachStdin": false,
                    "AttachStdout": false,
                    "Cmd": [
                        "sleep",
```

As earlier, a number of groups are presented, which have the running container as a member. The two groups shown earlier are the short container ID and long container ID. Many variables are also defined as part of the output, which has been truncated in the preceding screenshot. The tail end of the output reveals a few more groups:

```
                    "StartedAt": "2017-03-15T05:20:18.1360653742",
                    "Status": "running"
                }
            }
        }
    },
    "docker_hosts": [
        "unix://var/run/docker.sock"
    ],
    "image_docker.io/fedora:25": [
        "playbook-container"
    ],
    "playbook-container": [
        "playbook-container"
    ],
    "running": [
        "playbook-container"
    ],
    "unix://var/run/docker.sock": [
        "playbook-container"
    ]
}
[fedora@mastery1 mastery]$ _
```

The additional groups are:

- `docker_hosts`: All the hosts communicated with to query for hosts
- `image_name`: A group for each image used by discovered containers
- `container name`: A group that matches the name of the container
- `running`: A group of all the running containers
- `stopped`: A group of all the stopped containers

This inventory plugin, and the groups and data provided by it, can be used by playbooks to target various selections of containers available to interact with.

Previewing of Ansible container

Ansible container is a set of tools that build upon concepts introduced earlier in this chapter to provide a comprehensive workflow for container development, testing, and deployment. It is currently a tech preview, under active development. As it is a preview, the interfaces provided may change quickly.

Ansible container does not get installed with Ansible at the time of writing, and must be installed separately. It can be installed from `pypi` as the package name `ansible-container`, or installed from the source repository (`https://github.com/ansible/ansible-container.git`).

With Ansible container, one can define one or more services to containerize. These are defined in a YAML file that closely follows the Docker compose version 1 schema (support version 2 schema will be in the next release of Ansible container). Each service defined becomes a container, and is exposed as an Ansible host. These hosts are used by a playbook file to perform all the necessary configuration to prep the container to run the service. Additional files can be used to define any python library requirements for modules used by the playbook, Ansible Galaxy role dependencies of the playbook, Ansible Galaxy metadata for sharing the project, and an Ansible configuration file used with the playbook.

The main executable of Ansible container is `ansible-container`, which includes a number of sub-commands:

```
2. fedora@mastery1:~/src/mastery (ssh)
[fedora@mastery1 mastery]$ ansible-container --help
usage: ansible-container [-h] [--debug] [--engine ENGINE_NAME]
                         [--project BASE_PATH] [--var-file VAR_FILE]
                         {init,version,run,help,install,push,shipit,stop,restart
,build}

                         ...

Build, orchestrate, run, and ship Docker containers with Ansible playbooks

optional arguments:
  -h, --help            show this help message and exit
  --debug               Enable debug output
  --engine ENGINE_NAME  Select your container engine and orchestrator
  --project BASE_PATH, -p BASE_PATH
                        Specify a path to your project. Defaults to current
                        working directory.
  --var-file VAR_FILE   Path to a YAML or JSON formatted file providing
                        variables for Jinja2 templating in container.yml.

subcommand:
  {init,version,run,help,install,push,shipit,stop,restart,build}
    init                Initialize a new Ansible Container project
    version             Display Ansible Container version information
    run                 Run and orchestrate built images based on
                        container.yml
    help                Display this help message
    install             Install a service from Ansible Galaxy
    push                Push your built images to a Docker Hub compatible
                        registry
    shipit              Generate a deployment playbook to your cloud of
                        choice.
    stop                Stop the services defined in container.yml, if
                        deployed
    restart             Restart the services defined in container.yml
    build               Build new images based on ansible/container.yml
[fedora@mastery1 mastery]$ _
```

- `init`: The `init` sub-command will create an `ansible/` directory and the control files described earlier within it. Optionally, it can connect to Ansible Galaxy and use a project template to pre-populate some of the files, otherwise they will be created mostly blank.

- `build`: The `build` sub-command is used to launch containers for each service defined, and one container with Ansible inside of it, which is used to run the playbook against the service containers. Once the playbook is finished, images are created from the configured containers.
- `run`: The `run` sub-command will launch new containers for each service using the images created during the build phase.
- `stop`: The `stop` sub-command will stop containers launched by a `run` sub-command.
- `push`: The `push` sub-command will upload the built images to a target Docker image registry.
- `shipit`: The `shipit` sub-command will generate a Ansible content to deploy containers from built images into container orchestration platforms such as Kubernetes or Red Hat OpenShift.

To demonstrate Ansible container, we'll reproduce our previous Docker service container to display `cowsay` via a web server, and run it locally.

Init

Ansible container relies on a directory tree of content, which is created with the `init` sub-command. This content is what will be made available inside the container used to run Ansible itself:

```
2. fedora@mastery1:~/src/mastery (ssh)
[fedora@mastery1 mastery]$ ansible-container init --help
usage: ansible-container init [-h] [--server SERVER] [project]

positional arguments:
  project                 Use a project template instead of making a blank
                          project from an Ansible Container project from Ansible
                          Galaxy.

optional arguments:
  -h, --help              show this help message and exit
  --server SERVER, -s SERVER
                          Use a different Galaxy server URL
[fedora@mastery1 mastery]$ _
```

For this example, we'll run the `init` sub-command in the same directory we've used for previous examples:

```
2. fedora@mastery1:~/src/mastery (ssh)
[fedora@mastery1 mastery]$ ansible-container init
Ansible Container initialized.
[fedora@mastery1 mastery]$ tree ansible/
ansible/
├── ansible.cfg
├── container.yml
├── main.yml
├── meta.yml
├── requirements.txt
└── requirements.yml

0 directories, 6 files
[fedora@mastery1 mastery]$
```

First, to define our services, we'll need to edit the `container.yml` file within the newly created `ansible/` directory. Our example only has a single service, which we'll name `cowsay`. We'll want to use the `docker.io/fedora:25` image. This time, we'll expose port `8081`, just to differentiate it from previous examples. We'll set the command for this service to be `nginx`:

```
version: "1"
services:
  cowsay:
    image: docker.io/fedora:25
    ports:
      - "8081:80"
    command: ['nginx']
```

With the service established, we need to write the plays to configure the base image to our needs. This is in the `main.yml` file. The tasks should match the tasks we used in a previous example, this time targeting the inventory host name `cowsay`, which matches the service we just defined:

```
---
- hosts: cowsay
  gather_facts: false

  tasks:
    - name: install things
      raw: dnf install -y python-dnf

    - name: install things
      dnf:
        name: "{{ item }}"
      with_items:
        - nginx
        - cowsay

    - name: configure nginx
      lineinfile:
        line: "daemon off;"
        dest: /etc/nginx/nginx.conf

    - name: boop
      shell: cowsay boop > /usr/share/nginx/html/index.html
```

Unlike the previous example, we do not need to add a task to run `nginx`, that will happen when the container is started.

Build

For this example, no other files need to be modified from their initial state. We're now ready to build the images, which is done with the `build` subcommand of `ansible-container`:

```
2. fedora@mastery1:~/src/mastery (ssh)
[fedora@mastery1 mastery]$ ansible-container build
No DOCKER_HOST environment variable found. Assuming UNIX socket at /var/run/dock
er.sock
Starting Docker Compose engine to build your images...
Trying to pull repository docker.io/ansible/ansible-container-builder ...
sha256:ecbf2feee8cfa0b4167ca1bb74bfff62f61c3e7009b048f239da13db3806bc6b: Pulling
 from docker.io/ansible/ansible-container-builder
8d30e94188e7: Pulling fs layer
24cbd75f8b32: Pulling fs layer
d6ee161b4be5: Downloading [=>                                                   ]
d6ee161b4be5: Downloading [==>                                                  ]
d6ee161b4be5: Downloading [===>                                                 ]
d6ee161b4be5: Downloading [====>                                                ]
d6ee161b4be5: Downloading [=====>                                               ]
d6ee161b4be5: Downloading [=======>                                             ]
d6ee161b4be5: Downloading [========>                                            ]
8d30e94188e7: Pull complete
24cbd75f8b32: Pull complete
d6ee161b4be5: Pull complete
a4b49951d8df: Pull complete
853ec44630ce: Pull complete
b7e98f774514: Pull complete
d787669f451c: Pull complete
250fdf0b77c5: Pull complete
33400106458e: Pull complete
Digest: sha256:ecbf2feee8cfa0b4167ca1bb74bfff62f61c3e7009b048f239da13db3806bc6b
Status: Downloaded newer image for docker.io/ansible/ansible-container-builder:0
.2
Attaching to ansible_ansible-container_1
Cleaning up Ansible Container builder...
No image found for tag mastery-cowsay:latest, so building from scratch
Attaching to ansible_ansible-container_1, ansible_cowsay_1
```

The build process will download a container image to run Ansible within. It'll launch a container using that image and map in the contents from the `ansible/` directory. Then it will launch the service container and execute the playbook against it. After the playbook finishes, the configured service container will be exported as an image and saved to the local system:

```
● ● ●                     2. fedora@mastery1:~/src/mastery (ssh)
Attaching to ansible_cowsay_1, ansible_ansible-container_1
ansible-container_1  | Host cowsay running
ansible-container_1  |
ansible-container_1  | PLAY [cowsay] ***********************************************
**********************
ansible-container_1  |
ansible-container_1  | TASK [install things] ***************************************
**********************
ansible-container_1  | ok: [cowsay]
ansible-container_1  |
ansible-container_1  | TASK [install things] ***************************************
**********************
ansible-container_1  | changed: [cowsay] => (item=[u'nginx', u'cowsay'])
ansible-container_1  |
ansible-container_1  | TASK [configure nginx] **************************************
**********************
ansible-container_1  | changed: [cowsay]
ansible-container_1  |
ansible-container_1  | TASK [boop] *************************************************
**********************
ansible-container_1  | changed: [cowsay]
ansible-container_1  |
ansible-container_1  | PLAY RECAP **************************************************
**********************
ansible-container_1  | cowsay                     : ok=4    changed=3    unreach
able=0    failed=0
ansible-container_1  |
ansible_ansible-container_1 exited with code 0
Aborting on container exit...
Stopping ansible_cowsay_1 ... done
Exporting built containers as images...
Committing image...
Exported mastery-cowsay with image ID sha256:0b6121417e3bf12c9f6db341349d778e5d6
202d368751c161dc4d924cfbd1292
Cleaning up cowsay build container...
Cleaning up Ansible Container builder...
[fedora@mastery1 mastery]$ _
```

The image will be named partly for the base directory (mastery in this case) and partly for the service (cowsay), as we can see with docker images:

```
                        2. fedora@mastery1:~/src/mastery (ssh)
[fedora@mastery1 mastery]$ docker images
REPOSITORY                                    TAG               IMAGE ID
      CREATED           SIZE
mastery-cowsay                                20170316055613    0b6121417e3b
      51 seconds ago    524.4 MB
mastery-cowsay                                latest            0b6121417e3b
      51 seconds ago    524.4 MB
docker.io/fedora                              25                1f8ec1108a3f
      3 weeks ago       230.3 MB
docker.io/ansible/ansible-container-builder   0.2               6a0481cdff24
      5 months ago      710.6 MB
[fedora@mastery1 mastery]$ _
```

Run

With the image created, we can now run the service. We could launch the container manually with docker, or write a playbook for it to launch with Ansible. Both of those approaches takes more thought than necessary, since we've already defined how this container should be launched in our container.yml file. We can utilize this configuration and simply use the run sub-command of ansible-container:

```
● ● ●                    2. fedora@mastery1:~/src/mastery (ssh)
[fedora@mastery1 mastery]$ ansible-container run --help
usage: ansible-container run [-h] [--production] [-d] [-o]
                             [--with-volumes WITH_VOLUMES [WITH_VOLUMES ...]]
                             [--with-variables WITH_VARIABLES [WITH_VARIABLES ..
.]]
                             [--roles-path ROLES_PATH]
                             [service [service ...]]

positional arguments:
  service               The specific services you want to run

optional arguments:
  -h, --help            show this help message and exit
  --production          Run the production configuration locally
  -d, --detached        Run the application in detached mode
  -o, --remove-orphans  Remove containers for services not defined in
                        container.yml
  --with-volumes WITH_VOLUMES [WITH_VOLUMES ...], -v WITH_VOLUMES [WITH_VOLUMES
...]
                        Mount one or more volumes to the Ansible Builder
                        Container. Specify volumes as strings using the Docker
                        volume format.
  --with-variables WITH_VARIABLES [WITH_VARIABLES ...], -e WITH_VARIABLES [WITH_
VARIABLES ...]
                        Define one or more environment variables in the
                        Ansible Builder Container. Format each variable as a
                        key=value string.
  --roles-path ROLES_PATH
                        Specify a local path containing roles you want to use
                        in the builder container.
[fedora@mastery1 mastery]$ _
```

There are a few optional arguments to the `run` sub-command, where one can pick a specific service to start, attach volumes, define variables, toggle production configuration, and so on. The argument that we're interested in is the `--detached` argument, as it will run the application in the background, giving control back to the terminal:

```
2. fedora@mastery1:~/src/mastery (ssh)
[fedora@mastery1 mastery]$ ansible-container run --detached
No DOCKER_HOST environment variable found. Assuming UNIX socket at /var/run/dock
er.sock
Attaching to ansible_ansible-container_1
Cleaning up Ansible Container builder...
Deploying application in detached mode
[fedora@mastery1 mastery]$
```

The `run` sub-command will use the Ansible container to bring up the service container(s). At this point, we should be able to see the container running in `docker ps`, and communicate with the container to see what our cow has to say:

```
2. fedora@mastery1:~/src/mastery (ssh)
[fedora@mastery1 mastery]$ docker ps
CONTAINER ID        IMAGE                   COMMAND            CREATED
    STATUS              PORTS                   NAMES
a81ccaac9c59        mastery-cowsay:latest   "nginx"            4 seconds ago
    Up 4 seconds        0.0.0.0:8081->80/tcp    ansible_cowsay_1
[fedora@mastery1 mastery]$ curl http://localhost:8081

< boop >

        \   ^__^
         \  (oo)_____
            (__)\       )\/\
                ||----w |
                ||     ||
[fedora@mastery1 mastery]$
```

This example barely scratches the surface of what's possible with Ansible container. The control files support templating values to make quite dynamic service arrangements, which can easily be tested locally and then pushed into a production deployment system such as Kubernetes. More features are being added, and the functionality may change, so be sure to check the documentation before getting started with Ansible container: `http://docs.ansible.com/ansible-container/`.

Summary

DevOps has pushed automation in many new directions, including the creation of infrastructure itself. Cloud computing services enable self-service management of fleets of servers to run services. Ansible can easily interact with these services to provide the automation and orchestration engine.

Ansible can start nothing but the host it is running on, and with proper credentials it can create the infrastructure it wants to manage, for one-off actions or to deploy a new version of an application into a production container management system.

Index

A

action plugins 235
Ansible container
  build sub-command 284
  init sub-command 281
  previewing 279
  reference link 279
  run sub-command 286
  sub-commands 281
Ansible Galaxy
  about 154
  role, installing from 154, 156, 157, 158
  URL 154
Ansible project
  contributing to 245
  contribution submissions 245
Ansible
  about 7
  configuration 8
  extending 215
  files, including 118
  handlers, including 133
  task, including with loops 129
  tasks, including 118, 119
  troubleshooting 185
  variables, including 135
  version 8
arguments variable 71

B

build sub-command
  about 284
  running 285
built-in filters, Jinja2
  about 79
  count 80
  default 80
  random 80
  round 81

C

callback plugins 232, 233
caller variable 75, 77
catch_kwargs variable 73
catch_varargs variable 74
cloud infrastructure
  about 253
  managing 253
  OpenStack inventory source, using 261
  servers, creating 254
CMBD 14
code execution
  debugging 195
  local code, debugging 198
  playbook debugging 195, 197
  remote code, debugging 209, 212, 213
comparisons, Jinja2
  expressions 92
complex variable 190
conditionals, Jinja2 control structures
  about 58, 60
  inline conditionals 60
connection type plugins 229
contract strategy 164
contribution submissions, Ansible project
  about 245
  ansible repository 246
  pull request, making 251
  tests, executing 246
control machine 37
control structures, Jinja2
  about 57
  conditionals 58

loops 62
macros 68
custom filters, Jinja2
   about 81
   Base64 encoding 86
   filters, dealing with path names 83
   filters, related to task status 81
   searching content 88
   shuffle 82

D

data encryption, at rest
   Ansible-playbook, executing with encrypted files 52
   encrypted files, decrypting 50
   encrypted files, editing 48
   existing files, encrypting 46
   new encrypted files, creating 43
   password rotation, on encrypted files 49
   performing 41
   Vault, using 42
data manipulation, Jinja2
   about 78
   built-in filters 79
   custom filters 81
   Python object methods 90
   syntax 78
   undefined arguments, omitting 89
default filter 80
defaults variable 72
disruptions
   delaying 175, 179, 180
   destructive tasks, running only once 180
   minimizing 175
Docker containers, interacting with
   about 267
   containers, building without Dockerfile 271, 274, 275
   Docker inventory 275
   images, building 268, 270
Docker inventory 277, 279
dot notation 193
DRY (Don't Repeat Yourself) 118
dynamic inventories 14
dynamic inventory plugins

   developing 236
   host variables, listing 237
   hosts, listing 237
   simple inventory plugin, developing 238

E

encrypted files
   creating 44
   password file 45
   password prompt 44
   password script 46
error recovery, tasks
   always section 112
   performing 109
   rescue section 110, 111
expand strategy 164, 167
extra variables 36

F

fact caching plugins 230
fact modules 36
failing fast
   about 167
   any_errors_fatal option 168
   handlers, forcing 172, 174
   max_fail_percentage option 169, 171
filter plugins 230
filters 78
filters, dealing with path names
   basename 84
   dirname 85
   expanduser 85

G

GitHub pull requests
   URL 251

H

handlers inclusion
   about 133
   performing 135
HAProxy behavior 12

I

in-place upgrades
    about 161
    performing 162, 164
infrastructure provisioning
    Ansible container, previewing 279
    cloud infrastructure, managing 253
    Docker containers, interacting with 267
init sub-command
    about 281
    running 282
inventory variables 35
inventory
    behavior inventory variables 12
    data sources 9
    dynamic inventories 14
    inventory variable data 11, 12
    limiting 16, 18, 19
    parsing 9
    runtime inventory additions 16
    static inventory 9, 10

J

Jinja2
    about 57
    comparisons 92
    control structures 57
    data manipulation 78
    values, comparing 92

L

LDAP 14
local code, debugging
    about 198
    executor code, debugging 205, 206, 207, 208
    inventory code, debugging 199, 200, 202, 203
    playbook code, debugging 204
logging 186
logic, Jinja2 93
lookup plugin 37, 229
loops, Jinja2 control structures
    about 62
    loop indexing 65
    loop items, filtering 64

M

macro variables, Jinja2 control structures
    about 69
    arguments 71
    caller 75, 76, 77
    catch_kwargs 73
    catch_varargs 74
    defaults 72
    name 70
macros, Jinja2 control structures
    about 68
    macro variables 69
module transport and execution
    about 31, 33
    module arguments 32
    module reference 31
    task performance 34
modules, developing
    about 215
    basic module construct 216
    custom modules 216
    simple module 217

N

name variable 70
nginx configuration file 12

O

omit variable 89
OpenStack 253
OpenStack inventory source
    using 261, 262, 264, 265, 267
os-client-config
    reference link 261

P

play behavior directives
    any_errors_fatal 25
    become 26
    connection 25
    gather_facts 25
    max_fail_percentage 25
    no_log 25
    port 25

remote_user 25
serial 25
play variables 36
playbook parsing
  about 20
  host selection, for plays and tasks 27
  order of operations 20, 22
  play and task names 28
  play behavior directives 25
  relative path assumptions 22, 24
playbooks inclusion 142
plugins
  action plugins 235
  callback plugins 232, 234
  connection type plugins 229
  developing 229
  distributing 235
  fact caching plugins 230
  filter plugins 230, 231
  lookup plugins 229
  shell plugins 229
  vars plugins 230
Python object methods
  about 90
  float methods 92
  int methods 92
  list methods 91
  string methods 90

R

remote code, debugging
  about 209, 211, 213
  action plugins, debugging 213
Remote Python Debugger 209
role application
  about 148
  implementing 151
  role inclusion 154
  roles, mixing with tasks 151, 154
role default 36
role dependencies
  about 146
  conditionals 148
  tags 147
  variables 146

role sharing
  about 154
  Ansible Galaxy 154
role structure
  about 143
  dependencies 144
  files 145
  handlers 143
  implementing 145
  module 144
  plugins 144
  tasks 143
  templates 145
  variables 143
role variables 36
roles
  about 142
  application 148
  dependencies 146
  sharing 154
  structure 142
run sub-command
  about 286
  running 288

S

secrets, protecting while operating
  about 53
  secrets, logged to remote or local files 54
  secrets, transmitted to remote hosts 54
servers
  adding, to runtime inventory 258, 260
  creating 254
  virtual servers, booting 255, 256, 258
shell plugins
  about 229
simple inventory plugin
  developing 238, 241, 242
  script performance, optimizing 243, 245
simple module
  check mode 227
  check mode, handling 227
  check mode, supporting 227
  creating 217, 219
  documentation 220, 221, 222, 224

fact data, providing 225, 226
single tasks
  serializing 181
string methods
  about 90
  capitalize 90
  endswith 90
  lower 90
  rsplit 90
  split 90
  splitlines 90
  startswith 90
  upper 90
subelement
  versus, Python object method 193, 194

T

task failure, defining
  about 95
  error condition, defining 97, 99, 100, 102
  errors, ignoring 95, 97
task result change, defining
  about 103, 104
  change, suppressing 108
  command family, special handling 105, 107
task status, determining
  about 95
  change, defining 103
  error recovery 109
  failure, defining 95
task variables 36
tasks inclusion
  about 118
  complex data, passing to included tasks 123
  conditional task 125, 126
  included tasks, tagging 127, 129
  performing 118, 119
  variable values, passing to included tasks 121
  with loops 129, 132
tests, Jinja2 93
tests

code style tests 250
  executing 246
  integration tests 248
  unit tests 247
troubleshooting, Ansible
  code execution, debugging 195
  performing 185
  playbook logging and verbosity 185
  variable introspection 187, 188, 190

V

values comparing, Jinja2
  comparisons 92
  logic 93
  tests 93
variable introspection
  about 187, 188, 190
  variable sub elements 190, 192
variable precedence
  about 37
  hashes, merging 38
  precedence order, defining 37
variable types
  about 35
  extra variables 36
  inventory variables 35
  play variables 36
  role variables 36
  task variables 36
variables inclusion
  about 135
  dynamic vars_files inclusion 137
  extra-vars 141
  include_vars 138, 140
  vars_files 136
variables
  about 35
  external data, accessing 37
vars plugins
  about 230
verbosity 186

Made in the USA
Lexington, KY
02 June 2017